EMPOWERING YOUR PUBLIC SPEAKING

The Epic Book on Public Speaking

'Jagged' Matt Parker

Dedicated to Sharon Chaldecott

Who helped me find my inner rock star

Contents

Introduction

I Am Jagged 11
Unlock the Power of This Book 13
Your Empowerment Starts Now 16
Why Is Public Speaking Important? 17
How Can Public Speaking Empower You? 21

Reconsider Your Beliefs About Public Speaking

Your New Approach to Public Speaking 29
Let Yourself Grow 34
"Help, I'm a Beginner!" 36
What Makes You Interesting? 51
Forget About Nerves 55

Empower Your Public Speaking

Collecting Autographs 65
Give Your Audience a Star 67
Two Things You Must Have 74
If You Talk-Down — Your Audience Can't Look-Up 79
Stop Tearing Your Hair Out 82

Your Public Speaking Identity

Make Worlds Collide 89
Do You Play a Character in Speeches? 92
How to Be Different 96
Are You an Impersonator? 104
Finding a Walk 108
Are You Authentic on Stage? 110

Crafting Your Speech

Inside My Creative Process 117
Your Speech Is Like an Essay 126
Keep Your Speech Fresh 135

The Blueprint of a Great Main Message 142
Message First — Fun Stuff Later 147
Are You Teasing Your Audience? 153
Be a Tortoise Tour Guide 156
Start Being Taken Seriously 164
Look Like a Pro 170
Is Public Speaking an Art? 174
An Emotional Journey 178

Preparations
"How on Earth Am I Meant to Practise?" 186
Divorce Your Notes 192
Learn a Speech — Fast 197
Always Do This Before You Speak 200
The Breath of a Mighty Speaker 206
Channelling Your Energy 208
Flatten Your Emotions 212
The Million Dollar Question 214
One Rule When Choosing Props 218
There's Always a Better Way 221
Never Lose Sight of Reality 224

Express Yourself
Feel Expressive While Speaking 237
It's Time to Show Us Who You Are 242
Orthopterophobia 247
Speak on the Spot — Straightaway 253
How to Share Your Inner World 261
Going Back in Time 266
"Where Should I Look?" 270
Singing 275
Speak Up! 276
Deactivate Your Robot Voice 280
Motivate Your Movements 284

Gestures: The Untold Story   287
Is It a Performance or a Speech?   295

Befriend and Understand Your Audience
Everyone Is a Friend   303
Feel Great Before You Speak   304
Uplift Everyone   307
Are They Even Listening?   309
Compensate for Their Lack of Energy   314
Public Speaking Is About Waves   318

Why Do You Speak?
What Fuels You?   327
Why They Quit   331
The Ultimate Escape Plan   334

An Introduction to Feedback in Public Speaking
Positive Feedback Is Paramount   341
Distance Yourself   346
How to Critique and Evaluate   349

Beyond Your Speech
My Rock Star Image   373
Personal Branding for Speakers   375
How Writing Can Help Your Public Speaking   386
Does Every Speaker Need a Book?   391
What's Your Advice?   396

Final Thought
Why There Are No Standards for Public Speaking   401

Questions and Answers
With Questions From: Rachel Nagy, Paula Coutts,   407
David Lark,

Tim Patmore, Henry Bowles, Don O'Neal, Paul
Ovington,
and Nick Dewey

Glossary   424
Acknowledgements   425
About Matt   426

Introduction

I Am Jagged

An unwritten rule when it comes to names is that you're not allowed to give yourself a nickname. It must be given to you by someone else. So why is 'Jagged' Matt branded on the front cover?

My full name is far from unique. Both Matt and Parker are both commonly held names. In this internet age, I can't use my name for most things because there is an online panoply of Matt Parkers who also give speeches. For those of you who are blessed with long and obscure names, you will have to trust me on this — having a common name is frustrating: "Oh, I was thinking of the other Matt Parker. Not you with the scarf and the hair, the one with the hat and the pet duck."

I needed a name for my website, speaking, and coaching that would set me apart from speakers who share my name. I wanted to blaze my own path. The problem was, I could never settle on a nickname that I liked and this delayed me a lot. And names have to be given to you...

When I was in secondary school there was a musical production being put on featuring Dracula. I didn't know much about it to be honest. Everyone else in my drama class was raving about it and how much they were enjoying the rehearsals. I felt like I had made a mistake by not auditioning.

It wasn't long until the school production. One lunchtime I was surprised because my former music teacher Mrs. Chaldecott wanted to speak with me. I no longer took music at school because I couldn't play any instruments, so I had no idea what she might want to talk to me about. Apparently one of the main cast had dropped out. Mrs. Chaldecott and Mrs.Clarke were desperate for someone to take up the abandoned role and they wanted me. I felt touched that they had thought of me, but I knew absolutely nothing about the person they wanted me to play.

The name Mick Jagger sounded familiar to me, but I had no idea who he was. Mrs. Chaldecott gave an excellent introduction to Mick, and I loved the sound of the role. I was playing an older version of Mick — and so he was called Jagged! I found it so exciting getting to have one-on-one singing lessons (the first I'd ever had) and playing such a fun character. I even created my own version of his strut.

I loved the role of Jagged. I wore a sensational rock-and-roll outfit which included leather trousers. I got to experience my first few times going on stage, feeling like a rock star. That's what I've felt like throughout my public speaking journey.

I wanted to dedicate this book to Mrs. Chaldecott because she helped me to believe in myself at such a pivotal point in my life. Without her, there would be no Jagged Matt.

Unlock the Power of This Book

This book is focused on my view and my approach to public speaking. It's for people who have ideas to share and who want to look behind the curtain of public speaking to examine more than just the nuts-and-bolts: "Do this gesture. Speak louder. Smile at people. Use a prop." There's enough of that robotic advice floating around; I want to engage your brain!

I was irked by the public speaking resources that teach speakers a few specific 'tips' on what to say, what gestures to use, and what they 'must do' with their voice to give a speech. In my opinion, this is a flawed solution because teaching lines, some interesting gestures, and vocal techniques only cover up the root of the problem. The majority of people are looking at public speaking in the wrong way. Using a cool gesture will do a poor job at disguising the fundamental problem — that you are not enjoying public speaking.

I believe that public speaking can be genuinely fun and empowering. To express my love for public speaking, I will show you my perspective on some of the main issues. My goal is to get you to think for yourself and to develop your own approach towards public speaking which isn't straight out the bottle.

I sincerely want to challenge your view of public speaking and to make you think. It's not until you start to find your own unique perspective that you will be able to decide where, how, and why you want to improve. I naturally give you permission to get your highlighters out, but also to cross out lines and rip out pages! I actively encourage you to disagree with me throughout the book. If you disagree with me it means that you have formed your own opinion on the matter (which I count as a success). I want you to find your own point of view.

This book is compiled of over sixty of my essays on public speaking. You can read any essay you like and in any order. I have ensured that there are some shorter essays alongside the longer reads. I'm a 'completionist' when it comes to books, and it doesn't feel like I have 'read a book' unless I read from inside the front cover to the acknowledgements at the back. You don't need to do this. When you find yourself wanting to ponder and reflect on public speaking: choose a relevant essay and dip in.

You might be wondering why I have referred to the sections as essays and not 'chapters'. Referring to them as chapters would evoke a sense of completeness. I didn't want to give the false impression that if you read this book from start to finish, you would have heard all of my views on public speaking. If I were to do this, the book would not only be humongous (you would need to rent a moving van to transport it), but it would also be unlikely to ever be released. I feel that it's much better to share my ideas more regularly so that you can benefit from them and so that I can accompany you on your public speaking journey. I have worked hard to ensure that you have a resource that you will find valuable on your quest to becoming an empowered public speaker.

When I read a book, part of my brain is in a rush to get to the next chapter. I can't help but count how many pages are left. However it shouldn't matter how many pages are left, we should be enjoying the book and thinking about what we're reading. Yet as soon as I see 'chapter one' I think: "I've got to get to at least chapter four by the end of the day."

I wanted to present essays instead to remove that competitive element and to reintroduce a time for thinking and reflection. I want you to think about each subject that I discuss. That way you will grow from reading an essay even if you disagree with me — because you would have started looking for your own answers.

This book contains some anecdotes about my life. I personally like to learn a bit about the author as I read through. However, if you want to skip the anecdotes, the rest of the book will still make sense.

The end of the book features a questions and answers session. I asked some of my public speaking friends to ask me some questions. I have incredible friends and one of the many things I love about them is that they ask unexpected and fascinating questions.

I understand that the convention at the moment is to email readers some bonus content once they 'hand over' their contact details. I'll be honest — I put the bonus content straight into the book. I wanted to give you a full product that you can use straight away.

If you find this book useful, please do consider leaving a review for me on Amazon — it will further support me, and it's interesting to hear what you found helpful. And if you want to get in contact with me or to find out about my future releases and events, you can visit me at *jaggedmatt.com*

Your Empowerment Starts Now

To become an empowered public speaker, you need somewhere to speak. There is no getting around this. As you are reading this, it's fair to assume that you have an urge (if not a strong desire) to speak. If you're not doing any public speaking, you're not going to be able to improve.

Do yourself a massive favour: put this book down, go online, and find a local public speaking club. I personally love Toastmaster clubs because the members are welcoming and the evenings are well-structured. Find a club that's right for you.

After finding a club I want you to send an email: "Dear local speaking club, I'm (your name here). I've just picked up a book on public speaking by Jagged Matt Parker and he's told me to join a speaking club. Can I visit your next meeting and what time should I arrive? Best wishes (your lovely name here)." By emailing the club straight away, you will take real action and make a commitment.

If you haven't already, go and do this now. It could be the most life changing action of your year (if not your life).

Why Is Public Speaking Important?

Public speaking is compelling because it's something that is both revered and feared. But why do people think that public speaking is important? If public speaking did not carry a grand sense of importance, people would have no reason to shy away from it. In fact, I think a lot of people would find public speaking a lot easier if they didn't feel like they had to take it so seriously.

People are quick to say: "Oh, public speaking can help with that," or: "You need to be good at public speaking." But these suggestions often come from people who don't know the real value of speaking to an audience. Public speaking is important but not for the reasons you've been led to believe.

Public speaking is important because it's an honest form of communication. It's a way for you to communicate openly and sincerely to an entire room through a shared experience.

Public speaking is a medium for honesty. In a video you can use a script, pause when you make a mistake, and edit the footage so the final product is blemish-free. Even if you went on a live video stream you could quite easily read from notes that were off-camera. When someone sees you speak live, and, in person, there's no cheating. You are there, standing proudly on stage sharing what you know and why it's important.

When we see someone in the flesh, we can start to trust them. They're not hiding or being sneaky and editing what they said in post-production. They're connecting with us; human to human. This is a reason why I always tell people not to read from notes or off of slides when they're on stage. In public speaking, you're being honest and expressing how genuinely passionate you are about your message. To use a cliché: public speaking is about speaking from the heart.

The feeling of honesty that public speaking creates can also extend into authenticity and integrity. This occurs when the speaker engages with her audience in her own unique way, and she delivers ideas that are valuable to everyone present. People will leave thinking: "Wow — she's the real deal. When she's on camera she's not faking it. She's just as energetic and charismatic in person. And she answered my question. She really knows her stuff."

When public speaking is done correctly, an audience will feel close to the speaker. The audience should want the speaker to succeed and look upon her ideas with an open mind. This connection is built when the speaker is honest about who she is (which is authenticity) and about her message and what value it holds (this is integrity).

Public speaking is also important to the speaker for her own self-development and growth.

Public speaking is a skill. Like all skills it can be continually honed, practised, and studied over your lifetime. Each skill is rewarding in its own way but I have found public speaking to be the most rewarding.

Giving speeches to an audience teaches you not just about structure and speaking skills but also about people. It showed me that this world contains many patient and supportive individuals who genuinely want to listen and learn.

We can all feel isolated at times and think that no one will be interested in hearing about our 'mundane thoughts'. Some people doubt themselves so much that they edit everything they say and end up saying very little. They do this despite having a headful of ideas bottled up inside!

An inherent factor in public speaking is you can't do it by yourself: you need an audience. And you have to share who you are — otherwise it's acting. By speaking as openly and honestly as possible to audiences, you will discover that many people want to learn from you. Finding this support will help you to trust in your ideas. All of these fantastic ideas that were locked up inside can not only be let out, but you can stop locking them away in the first place. This means that through public speaking you will learn to trust in your ideas and to learn more about other people. Public speaking will help you to grow as a person.

By speaking to an audience, you'll learn that no one's perfect. You will see eyes wander and learn that people have limited attention spans that need to be catered to. And you will see yawns and phones being checked and discover that other people are susceptible to tiredness and distraction — just like you. No matter how esteemed and revered you might become in life, this won't change.

By frequently witnessing that audience members aren't perfect robots, you will learn not to take other people's apathetic reactions personally. Instead, you will learn to observe, feel, and judge how long people's attention will last and will become much better at delivering messages in a way that is easy, intriguing, and exciting to follow.

And let's not forget, public speaking is important to audiences. When a speech is delivered well, an audience will leave the room feeling better than when they walked in. People will leave feeling empowered. Their heads will have exciting new ideas to think about and to implement into their lives. Your audience might even leave with some funny stories and interesting facts to talk to their family about when they get home. We think so much about public speaking from the perspective of the speaker and nowhere near enough time thinking from an audience's perspective. Put your audience first.

Speaking is not all about the speaker's empowerment, every member of the audience deserves to feel empowered. Public speaking has the ability to not only deliver messages but also to send emotions to an audience. In our 'cold digital world' it's a warm and delightful holiday to learn from someone you admire, and you will leave feeling uplifted. Public speaking is a real experience and it can help people so much. For this reason, public speaking is important for everyone.

You might have your own reasons why public speaking is important. I can almost guarantee that if you stick with public speaking, it will teach you things that you never expected to learn. But please, don't get into public speaking because someone else told you to. Do it for you and for your own growth. Between you and I, it's perfectly fine to be curious and to do it purely to see what happens. I say this because ultimately it's your perspective on public speaking that will make it important or not. Have an open mind and learn the importance for yourself.

How Can Public Speaking Empower You?

My focus as a speaker, coach, and as a writer is to empower your public speaking. I like to specifically discuss public speaking because there are so many people who specialise in helping others with the day-to-day issues surrounding empowerment. I love public speaking and I will forever be obsessed with it, which is why I prefer to focus on helping people grow as speakers. When I hear that I have helped them grow as people too, of course, I'm flattered and very happy for them but it's not my specialism (at least — not at this stage of my life).

The question on your lips for me is most likely, "How can public speaking empower me?" This question can be answered by asking two more questions. Firstly: "How can giving a speech make you feel empowered?" This is a question that fits nicely into my field of focus. However, the second, implied question is: "How can the act of public speaking make you feel empowered in your day-to-day life?" This second question falls out of my 'jurisdiction' but I will give you my answer, based on my own experience.

"How can giving a speech, make you feel empowered?"

When you give a speech you have complete freedom over what you say and how you choose to express yourself. You decide what to talk about. You can be as loud and as expressive as you like. You don't need to stifle yourself or conceal who you are. This is an incredibly liberating feeling. And having a room full of people listening to your message makes you feel that you and your ideas matter. This in itself is empowering.

When aspiring speakers come up to me and say that they're nervous about public speaking, I explain things logically to them: "With public speaking, you are so incredibly fortunate because you get to express who you are to the whole room. It's your time to shine and speak without limits. You get to share your ideas while feeling like a rock star. And everyone will listen to you. No one will interrupt. And no one can just walk away and ignore you. You get to have a one-way conversation where you can just share. It's like playing tennis with no opponent — you've got the court. Alternatively, if you don't want to do public speaking you are going to have to run around and share your message to each person individually. Can you imagine how exhausting all of the back-and-forth exchanges and running around will be? Or what if you had to cold call each and every person to share your idea. Trust me — it would be grim. Why make things hard for yourself? Public speaking is fun, it's just a new experience for you. Go and enjoy it!"

For me, being given a room's attention and having the chance to share my message in my own style with no interruptions, is priceless. I am always so grateful to have people who want to listen to me. Yet so many people take this for granted and squander public speaking opportunities.

Like it or not, we are living in a digital age. Companies are fighting for our attention on all sides and we have a phenomenal amount of choice over where to spend our attention. We can take our phone out and find practically anything we want to see or hear. Having the concentration of every person in the room is both an incredible opportunity and an empowering experience. I am constantly shocked by how ungrateful people can be for a chance to speak and how they don't let themselves enjoy it. This lets both themselves, and their audiences down.

If you approach a speech acknowledging how valuable the opportunity is and let yourself make the most of it — you will feel on top of the world. I feel happiest and most empowered when I'm doing public speaking.

"How can the act of public speaking, make you feel empowered in your day to day life?"

Forget what you might think about how public speaking will change your everyday life. Forget what your family, friends, teachers, and colleagues might have said to you. Public speaking will not make you a 'confident person'. But it will empower you in other ways that you might not have considered yet.

Firstly, I want to debunk the 'confidence' myth (based on my own experience). Public speaking does not magically give you a superpower called 'confidence' that makes you feel at ease and assertive in any possible situation. Public speaking helps you get better at presenting to an audience and allows you to challenge yourself on stage. But it doesn't miraculously transform you into a 'confident person'.

I now block out any discussions or ideas related to the word 'confidence'. As a teenager, I was desperate to get better at interacting with people. My body was growing, I was tripping over my own legs, and I didn't know how to coordinate myself. And suddenly, conversation and interacting with others became a giant chess game: where I didn't know the opening moves, let alone how to win. I felt overwhelmed by all of the new things I needed to learn about and adjust to.

I turned to books for help. They had catchy titles, colourful front covers, and always promised an easy and simple solution. The self-improvement industry's diagnosis was that I needed to be more confident. But what does 'more confident' even mean?

Think of the most 'confident' person you know. If I were to ask that person to knit me a scale model of the Houses of Parliament, in the dark — would they be confident? If you're thinking, "Yes they would be," should they be? They're going to fail. If you were in this situation — regardless of the impending outcome — you could have enjoyed the experience of knitting in the dark, been happy and given it your best shot even though you knew you wouldn't complete the challenge. But thinking and giving off the air of "Oh yeah, I can do that no problem," is lying to yourself.

You don't need to lie to yourself to get better at talking and interacting with people. Instead speaking practice, trial-and-error, and learning make us more competent — which in turn will allow us to be more optimistic. We could make your 'confident' person more competent at knitting the Houses of Parliament in the dark. If I found a blind knitting teacher who specialised in knitting English landmarks (thank you internet) and they practised together in the dark every week for three years, your chosen person would become more competent. And as a result, if set the challenge of knitting the Houses of Parliament in the dark, they could be honestly optimistic: "I'm pretty good at this. I stand a good chance of pulling it off."

Although public speaking can't make you magically 'confident', it can give you experiences and new perspectives that can aid you in your day-to-day life.

Public speaking is good practice for you to express yourself. If you struggle to talk to other people because you're not very good at sharing your thoughts or telling your story — public speaking experience can help. Public speaking can feel like therapy because you get to express how you feel while everyone else listens without interrupting or objecting. For someone who is not used to opening up and sharing their thoughts and feelings: this can be both cathartic and incredibly empowering.

After a speaker feels comfortable with opening up, she will hopefully realise that not only can she feel better by speaking — she can uplift others too. Uplifting others requires a shift in focus from: "How can I feel better?" to: "How can I make other people around me feel better?" This change makes interactions fun for everyone, improves a speaker's presence on stage, and general attitude towards public speaking.

What ultimately helped me with interacting with people, and 'approaching people' was giving myself permission to be a happy and fun person. I got to express my happiness and sense of fun in my speeches and eventually thought: "Why can't I live my whole life spreading happiness?" As soon as I let myself be a happy and fun person, interacting with others started to be uplifting both for the people I spoke to and for me.

I won't lie, public speaking did help to adjust people's perception of me. People who saw me speak on stage got to see me differently to how I would have come across in a one-on-one situation. Because they saw me being energetic, creative, funny, and dramatic on stage, they were excited to talk to me off-stage. Having people approach you with warmth and kind compliments makes it incredibly easy to talk to people and make new friends.

Although public speaking might not give you unshakable 'confidence' — it will empower you in profound ways.

Reconsider Your Beliefs About Public Speaking

Your New Approach to Public Speaking

I have loved public speaking since my teenage years. This is a fact that I always took for granted. I always assumed that everyone else must feel the same excitement from it that I did. It didn't occur to me to read books on public speaking because I didn't need any motivation to speak or help to 'overcome' a fear. It's always been fun for me. However, the majority of people I have met since then have approached public speaking differently.

At the beginning of other speakers' journeys, public speaking wasn't a fun and enjoyable activity that they wanted to do, it was something that they felt like they had to do. Public speaking was a bully towering over them until they improved at giving speeches.

Understanding this perspective took me a while to get my head around. I was seeing speakers go into meltdown and become stressed out over speeches. They would constantly say to me, "I'm not ready to give a speech," or, "maybe in a few months, or next year."

For me public speaking was a fun and exciting game — the more I did it, the more my understanding and abilities grew. Yet no one else saw it the same way. I was desperate to strike up some friendly competition with other new speakers to see who could improve the fastest. It would have been fun, but the reality was: most speakers I met didn't stay at the speaking clubs long — the vast majority quit. For me, public speaking was an exciting roller-coaster, the ride of my life. I imagine to other people it was more like a slow and disconcerting ghost train.

I soon grew to realise something. Everyone else thought I was the odd one out. I was apparently the strange one for loving public speaking!

I have written three books, the first two I decided not to publish. The first was a fictional story (featuring oodles of anthropomorphism and whimsical names and a protagonist called Avocado Leonardo Jumping-Boots Cherry Tree Roots...the second) and my previous book was on public speaking. Before I had finished writing my last book, I had actively refrained from reading/watching public speaking books or pieces of advice. I wanted the book to be from my own experience and to record what I had learnt from giving speeches and watching live ones.

All of this growth had been supported and guided by my numerous public speaking friends and mentors. Reading through my last book, I couldn't believe how many interesting and helpful questions and theories I had written and later forgotten (N.B. I tend to forget things that I've physically done, which is why I sometimes play practical jokes on myself. You read that right – I play jokes, on myself. I set up something harmless but surprising like hiding something funny inside a box, and leave it somewhere I'm not going to look. After a few years, I would have forgotten about it and then, "Woahhh!" I've played a trick on myself). However, at the time I didn't think the book contained enough ground-breaking ideas to share it. My major self-criticism was that the book was focused on the nuts-and-bolts of public speaking. I didn't think it would make a reader ponder and reflect enough on the subjects, let alone have an epiphany.

I later gave myself permission to see what public speaking theories and 'advice' were available. I was disappointed with what I found. The main disappointment for me was not necessarily the focus on the nuts and bolts, but the obsession with overly specific 'tips'.

The advice I was finding wasn't teaching new speakers how to think for themselves, it was a cut-and-dry: "In this specific situation say this old line. And in this situation, gesture with your fingers like you're counting." There was no focus on self-reflection or personal growth, I saw a constant display of 'tips'. Some of the 'tips' were actually good pieces of advice, but they had been simplified to the point where a reader wouldn't understand why the tip worked or how she could incorporate it into her own speaking style and develop it further. I completely disagreed with the, "Have a tip," method of teaching public speaking (if you want to offend me, write on Amazon, "This book had good tips!").

I also disagreed with the advice I found on how to approach public speaking. I saw two clear schools of thought for a new public speaker to choose between, and I disliked them both.

The first way I found was an 'overcome your terror' approach to public speaking. This approach was focused on a speaker slowly and painfully overcoming their fear of speaking in public. This could mean taking small steps towards starting public speaking and improving at it. Or spending a fortune on books, DVDs, and hypnosis so new speakers could practise at home until they were ready. It was throwing money at the problem for glacial progress.

The second approach to public speaking that I saw was: 'keep falling on your face until you get it right'. This was the philosophy of: "Just speak. The more you speak, the more you will improve." Although this approach sounds logical, doesn't it also sound painful? How many new speakers would have the willpower to continually fail until they start to show signs of improvement? Very few.

Both approaches were supplemented with the 'have a tip' method: "Want to look less terrified when you eventually give a speech? Have a tip! Don't put your hands in your pockets!"
"Don't want to make as big a mess of your next speech? Have a tip! Don't forget to smile. That's right, even though you hate every moment of the experience — just smile. It's so easy to forget to smile,

right?" While you continuously smash your face into the pavement, you're pinched by an overly specific tip.

My observations of the ubiquity of 'have a tip' and the negative approaches towards public speaking were what led me to my latest book and the perspective on public speaking that I want to share.

If I had the power to automatically change every 'have a tip' article, chapter, and video, I would make them more open. An expert should not give you the right answers, he should give you the right questions so you can find your own path and your own approach.

"Today we are going to be contemplating how to be more powerful on stage. This is what 'power' means to me... What does 'power' mean to you? What would you do to be more powerful on stage? Think about it. Here are some methods that I have tried in the past... They worked because... What could you try that will fit you and your performance style? Or how can you adapt a method to suit you?"

The above is sadly never going to be popular with writers or readers because it's not a simple answer. For a planet of diverse people with different origins, experiences, ways of thinking, and talents — we often like to imagine that everyone thinks and acts exactly the same way. I had my wake-up call at the beginning of my public speaking journey, other people must have slept through it. Everyone is different!

Each of us has different experiences with public speaking and a unique collection of knowledge and perspectives. We need our own personal answers, not over-simplified and generalised patch-ups. This is why the 'create your own approach' method where coaches help speakers to find their own solutions, is much more likely to work than merely handing out a general tip.

My approach to public speaking is incredibly personal to me. I want to help speakers like you to find your own perspective on public speaking that is equally personal to you. There are however vital parts of my approach that are worth contemplating.

Even if you don't want your path to be 'inspired' by mine, by thinking about some of the key points, you can discover why you agree or disagree with them. My approach to public speaking is extraordinarily positive. I think it's safe to assume one thing: most people would prefer to enjoy public speaking than to fear or hate it. By learning my perspectives on issues, I want you to have seen the brighter side of public speaking. Then at least you will have a choice on each issue instead of having a fixed destination.

Let Yourself Grow

Here is the point that I want everyone to take away from reading this book: your perspective and approach towards public speaking are what you must focus on first.

If you approach public speaking as a horrible, daunting and terrifying ordeal, then it will be a long uphill struggle for you. It doesn't matter how many motivational videos you watch or how many products you buy; if you go into public speaking, seeing it as something scary or as 'work' — you're going to struggle unnecessarily.

When you see public speaking as fun, exciting, and a fascinating form of communication you will improve at an incredible rate and enjoy the journey. It's up to you to nurture this perspective, reading or watching a tutorial (no matter how expensive) will not grow it for you. You need to let yourself grow.

If I taught you five ways to look like a master speaker on stage; you would have five ways to present. However, by showing you how to enjoy presenting; you will uncover many new methods and approaches to speaking all by yourself. That way you will *become* a master speaker instead of always imitating one.

You probably know that changing your outlook on public speaking isn't as easy as 'the experts' say. There is more to public speaking than learning a bunch of new gestures or a memory technique to memorise a speech. But I know those other things require a smaller commitment and sound more appealing than growing and taking a different approach. That's why everyone else is focusing on learning those things, and then re-teaching them.

Please take a different path, as I did. Change your perspective on public speaking first, make it your friend. Then you will have so much passion for speaking that you will become a public speaking spaceship, instead of a mumbling unicycle. A unicycle won't take you to new territory and unexplored worlds of thinking. Don't cheat yourself out of self-growth by going in for cheap gimmicks. Change your perspective and approach towards public speaking. Your messages can change the world.

"Help, I'm a Beginner!"

When you start a new hobby or form of training, you will have many preconceived notions about what it will be like. At age 7 when I went to my first karate lesson, I was expecting to be taught how to chop wood in half. Needless to say, I was disappointed (but fear not — magic taught me to cut bananas in half by throwing playing cards — so I got the last laugh).

On the other side of the coin: sometimes things are more amazing than we might expect them to be. When I went to a parkour gathering last year, I thought I would meet a bunch of video game-loving fantasists who enjoyed jogging around the city centre and hopping over bicycle racks. Instead, I met a pack of fearless daredevils who ran on top of railings and filmed each other doing backflips (I slid down a railing and they said I was cool and that they had never seen *that* move before).

No matter our age, our expectations of something new can often be far different from what we will experience.

Now, you are 'starting' public speaking. The reason why I have written air quotes around 'starting' public speaking is because we have all done it before. At school and further education we had to present our ideas. And we have had many opportunities to say a few words at a birthday party or a celebration. You might have even given a presentation at work or for a club you are a part of. We have all 'started' public speaking already. As a result of this we have ingrained beliefs about what public speaking is about and how it makes us feel. These beliefs about public speaking can either hold you back or give you a running start.

In my opinion, so many people have negative beliefs about public speaking because they had negative, early experiences with it, and that's their most-used frame of reference. Here's a scenario that might be familiar to you:

At school, you were suddenly asked to plan an assembly. Everyone around you instantly became sheepish and nervous. Your teacher set you a topic but was not passionate about public speaking or performance and didn't offer much help. You had little time to prepare, next to no experience, and no guidance to tell you how to use the time effectively.

You wrote down some ideas to speak about, but were daunted by this new challenge and having to do it without help. Not knowing how to rehearse; you talked amongst yourselves and at the last minute wrote a dry and robotic script. You learnt the script, focusing more on remembering every word (like in a vocabulary test) than thinking about what your message was, how you were saying it, or how your audience would react.

You woke up the morning of your presentation with a feeling of dread. You walked to the front of the assembly hall, met by cold stares and the occasional cough. You did not feel at all ready to present, but you were forced to stand up in a row and speak. You felt like you were standing in front of a firing squad. You didn't want to look at the audience, and so you blocked them out by looking at the floor and thought only about the sentences you had to blurt out.

You heard each of your classmates deliver their lines like mechanical parrots. It would be your turn soon. You felt yourself shake and just wanted the experience to be over.

It was your turn now. You rattled off your lines as quickly as possible — the second you finished you were free. Your other classmates continued to speak along the row. But then it hit you. What you had just said wasn't interesting. You're listening to your peers and they're boring to listen to and making no sense! How could you have delivered something so terrible to the entire school? You look at the teachers watching; their faces are turned up and looking unimpressed and disappointed.

It's over. You're given a cold, "Well done everyone," and have to experience a walk of shame as you silently march off the stage. "Public speaking is the worst. I hate it," you think.

What a horrible experience for someone so young to go through. Unfortunately, that's a typical experience for children because few students are given an opportunity to have a positive and uplifting public speaking experience.

If you were one of the many who didn't get to present a speech that you felt proud of and you didn't receive a round of applause and lots of praise, I'm sorry. I'm sorry, is all anyone can say because we can't change the past. What we can do, is consider how things would have been different if you had a different experience. By seeing how things might have been, you can discover a new way of thinking about public speaking that you could have developed.

This is what I would want you to have experienced:

You fell in love with a topic at school, carrier pigeons. You found the subject entertaining but also fascinating. Your teacher then said that no one else in school knew anything about carrier pigeons. He asked your class if you would like to show the rest of the school how amazing and important carrier pigeons were: "Yes!" was your immediate answer.

Your teacher guided you through how to construct a presentation so that it made sense to you and for your audience. You got to include all of your favourite details about carrier pigeons: some were so wacky, they made you laugh. You got to be creative and had special costumes and props, and even a comedy sketch.

Your class was taught how to rehearse your presentation and how to be expressive and show how passionate you were about the subject. And most importantly for a school child, you were taught how to be funny. To you: your presentation felt like the coolest and most entertaining thing you had ever performed. You couldn't stop talking to your friends and family about how excited you were to put on your 'show'.

The day arrived, you knew exactly what to say and you couldn't wait to start. You were greeted with a massive round of applause and beaming smiles, "They love it already!"

You couldn't help but grin as your friends gave their sections. Now it was your turn. You saw how happy your audience looked and you thought: "I want my section to be the best!" So you gave it your all and expressed yourself as much as you possibly could.

The audience loved it! Once the presentation came to an end, you all received the most gigantic tidal wave of applause that you had ever experienced.

Your headteacher got up, smiling. "That was an outstanding presentation. And you have taught us such an incredible lesson about carrier pigeons and how they were important." Your headteacher came up to you, shook your hand, said your name and looked you in the eye while saying: "You were absolutely fantastic. We're never going to forget your presentation. I am so proud of you."

You all walked out of the assembly hearing the other children enthusiastically repeat their favourite parts of the presentation. Even at lunchtime, other children came up to you and said how much they liked it and asked you more questions about carrier pigeons. You ended the day thinking: "I love public speaking. That was the best school day I've ever had."

That's what I want every child to experience. It breaks my heart that most children don't get to. We can't change our early experiences of public speaking. What we can do is re-examine our beliefs about it that we have clung onto since that early age. Have they helped our life at all? If not, why have we held onto them? Isn't it time to update your public speaking frame of reference?

For me, a belief is a tool. I used to think that a belief was an idea that you followed because it was the most rational conclusion you had discovered about how the world works. Maybe that's what you have thought up to now. But ponder this: is being optimistic rational? Probably not. There are problems everywhere and many things for us to worry about; it can feel crazy that people can be so positive. Although being optimistic might not be 'rational' from a scientific perspective of how the world is doing, positivity is incredibly helpful to us. Being optimistic helps us to go for new challenges, make friends and to have (in my opinion) a better quality of life. Positivity is something that I believe in despite it being irrational because it works for me.

It's time, to be honest about the beliefs you hold about public speaking. Are they working for you? Are they making the process of public speaking easier or harder for you?

My advice to you is to re-evaluate what beliefs you hold about public speaking. If you begin practising public speaking with the right attitude and by utilising helpful beliefs, you will not only update your frame of reference but will also get more out of your speeches and enjoy improving.

I am going to vanquish five unhelpful beliefs you might hold about public speaking. And I am going to suggest new beliefs to replace them with which will function as useful tools for you to use. Let's revamp your brain!

Unhelpful belief #1
"Public speaking is scary!"

If you have had bad experiences with public speaking, it's understandable that you might see it as something scary. What doesn't help is how some speakers with more experience of public speaking tell newer speakers that: "It's natural to be scared of public speaking. But it's a fear that you can get over." Of course, most speakers have good intentions and want to provide reassurance by saying that public speaking gets easier and 'less scary' the more you do it. What these speakers aren't noticing is that by doing this they are reinforcing the idea that public speaking is naturally scary.

In reality, public speaking is not naturally scary. Playing badminton isn't scary by default. But badminton can be made to be scary: "If you lose this game of badminton, you will lose your job, your house and your stamp collection! And you will be playing against a ghost." But most games of badminton aren't like that, they're fun. Public speaking is the same, it doesn't have to be scary in the first place. You don't have to approach it as a fear you need to overcome. Public speaking can be a fun activity that makes you feel happy and excited.

"What's so special about public speaking, why shouldn't we quit and play badminton instead?"
Public speaking allows you to share your beliefs and ideas with others. Can you see how incredible that is? Everyone has a unique experience of life. This means that we each have a lot to share. Public speaking gives us the forum to share.

"Oh, but I can do that on social media.."

Public speaking shines because it gives you the gift of a room full of people who will pay attention to you. Online, we have no attention span. If something bores us: we can open up another five tabs, play a game, watch a video, look at memes, send messages and do some shopping. But when you speak in person — you have their attention. You don't need to fight for it.

During your speech, you have an incredible opportunity to share with a more patient audience. Can you imagine how much money advertisers would spend for a large audience to sit and watch their videos all the way through? You don't have to pay your audience to watch you, they want to hear what you have to say.

If you're entering public speaking, thinking that it's scary or a fear to overcome, think for a moment. You have a choice. If you want to approach public speaking as a fun activity instead of a scary one — you can. You don't have to act like it's scary because 'everyone else says it is'. Those people just can't see the incredible gift that public speaking presents you with, the opportunity to share your ideas and beliefs — and to have fun while doing it. Be grateful for the opportunity and treasure it.

Positive belief: "Public speaking is fun, and an incredible opportunity to share my ideas and beliefs with others."

Unhelpful belief #2
"I am so awkward when talking to people!"
New speakers have often told me that they feel 'awkward' while talking to other people. They feel overly self-conscious and just out of place.

Let me ask you this — do you feel awkward while you're watching TV? Or do you feel awkward while you're watching a video? While you're watching things — you probably don't notice how you're feeling because you're so absorbed in what's happening in front of your eyes. In my experience, a lot of awkwardness comes from over-analysing yourself to the extent where you stop paying attention to other people. It's like sitting in front of a TV but not paying any attention to the show because you're too busy thinking about how your reflection looks.

Some new speakers get on stage and think: "Oh I look so awkward. Everyone can tell that I don't know what to say. I must look so bad..." They only think about themselves! If you want to stop feeling awkward the first step is to turn your attention outwards. When you're speaking, think about your audience: how are they feeling? Do they understand what you've said? Do they need clarification? Do they need some help? By turning your attention outwards, speaking will be a lot easier for you. Focusing more on other people will also improve the chances that they will love hearing you speak and will seek chances to interact with you.

People feel for a person who notices them and compliments them on their new haircut and shoes. They feel more for an observant and complimentary person than for someone who just says, "Hello," and then over-analyses and punishes herself for not saying it right. Turn your attention outwards.

When you turn your attention outwards and notice people and comment on the positive things you see, you will start to spread positivity. If you notice that they're not feeling too happy or could be happier and you put in an effort to cheer them up — you will uplift them.

Focusing your attention on other people, either an audience or individuals in conversation will allow you to uplift them. And sooner or later after you have uplifted enough people — they will start to uplift you too. The more positivity you give out, the more you get back.

If people aren't usually positive towards you, ask yourself: "How much positivity am I giving out?" Instead of tormenting yourself for 'being awkward', learn to love uplifting people.

Positive belief: "I love uplifting people."

Unhelpful belief #3
"I'm not interesting enough to do public speaking!"
In my opinion, what usually makes something interesting is how it's presented. A speaker could have the most cutting-edge ideas, but then deliver them in such a dry, nonchalant manner that her audience will almost fall asleep. Whereas another speaker could describe her last trip to the post office in such a compelling way that her audience won't be able to take their eyes off of her.

No matter what you have to talk about: you can be interesting. So don't think that you have to be a prize-winning scientist, an explorer, or a famous actor to do public speaking. No matter what life experience you have, you are qualified to start.

The heart of the unhelpful belief is not actually about how interesting you are. It's the fear that an audience will not gain anything from listening to you. You don't want to waste other people's time. In business we have value for money; with public speaking it's value for time.

The value of what you share can often be in the eye of the receiver and not the giver. Sometimes you can say things without even noticing and it will help someone. People remember and draw meaning from different things. This means that when you speak, there is an increased chance of other people benefiting from you and your unique view on life. It's an opportunity for an audience to directly gain from you and to enrich their lives in some shape or form.

The gains that an audience receives from you can take different forms. You can share with your audience an emotion, knowledge, or inspiration.

- There is entertainment value in public speaking — can you make an audience smile, laugh, cry, feel surprised, or excited?
- There's also educational value in a speech — can you share something about yourself, the world around us, facts, and ideas that they might not have heard before, or discuss the past, present, or future?
- Inspiration is one of the greatest gifts you can give through public speaking — can you encourage someone to try something new, go somewhere, set a new goal, challenge himself not to give up, or to look at life (or anything else) in a new way?

These are just some of the ways that we can benefit an audience in our speeches. There are many more.

Others stand to gain from what you share with them. Even if you tell someone where the bathroom is you have given them some useful information. If you told someone a joke that made them smile, gave them some encouragement, or introduced them to a new fact you read about — you have empowered them by ensuring they gained something.

What you say doesn't have to be ground-breaking for it to be useful for an audience. The things you say without even thinking about it can help someone. If people listen to you, they will gain from you.

Positive belief: "People who listen to me will gain from me."

Unhelpful belief #4
"I have nothing to talk about!"

This unhelpful belief is closely linked to the previous one because the subtext is: "I have nothing to talk about that people would want to hear."

I first want to hammer home that you matter. Your experience in this world matters and it's your right to be able to share it. No one else can see inside your mind: and we really want to know what's happening in there! So tell us. We can only get an insight into what's going on inside your mind, by you expressing yourself.

The reality is that every person on Earth has a lot to talk about. We are experts on ourselves, we all have things we like and dislike, everyone has had experiences (good, bad, and funny), and we all have plans for our future (even if it's just to eat a sandwich and go to bed). Not to mention our own beliefs and ideas, associations, idiosyncrasies, and views on life. We are living, thinking, feeling human beings, and public speaking empowers us to express what we have hidden inside our minds.

People who are peering into the shop window of public speaking struggle to open up and share what's inside their mind. Some people like to sit there and think, "Yup, my mind's empty," and don't even try to get some thoughts buzzing.

You can always come up with ideas by giving yourself prompts and asking yourself questions. If I presented you with one hundred items from a supermarket, you would be able to tell me your opinion, or a personal story about a fair number of them. Similarly, imagine if I leapt out of the book and started interviewing you. If I were to ask you one hundred questions, you would have some kind of answer, if not an opinion or example for most of them.

If you are tired of having a 'blank' mind: take action. Give yourself prompts and ask yourself questions and you will start to generate ideas.

Try it now:
Find five items near you...
- What can you tell me about them?
- What's their story?
- What do they mean to you?
- How do they make you feel?
- And what are your plans for the items?

And now imagine having a mini interview with me:
- What have you been thinking about recently?
- What's been on your mind?
- Where did you go for your last holiday, and what did you do?
- What are you looking forward to?
- What did you have for dinner yesterday?
- Do you think that everyone deserves a birthday party?

You might not have felt like you had a lot to say, but what matters is that you had *something* to say. With practice you will improve at expanding your answers, taking your time, and learning to present them in an organised and structured fashion. You always have something to say. It doesn't matter how much. Only that you have something.

Positive belief: "I always have something to say!"

Unhelpful belief #5
"If I make a mistake, everyone will laugh at me!"

First of all, in the majority of scenarios, after making a mistake if you just carry on, no one will notice or care. That's the truth.

When people do notice your mistake, what matters is not that you slipped up; it's how you react to your error and how you compose yourself. Don't flap around and panic or repeat like a broken record, "I'm so sorry," a dozen times. Why? You don't need to apologise! By being overly apologetic and not taking a clear step to move on from a mistake, it only highlights that you are not used to speaking in an uncontrolled environment.

To move on from a mistake that your audience has noticed, address the mistake, but do not give it too much attention:

- Play it down: "Not to worry, that sometimes happens."
- Make a joke of it: "I didn't think this evening was exciting enough. I hope you enjoyed that surprise."
- Or just be honest: "I got a bit ahead of myself there, I was so excited that I missed out a crucial point."

Carrying on or briefly addressing a mistake is a lot better than stressing out, and turning one into a bigger deal than it needs to be.

You're going to make mistakes. The more you speak, the more things you will encounter that will go wrong, and many of which will be outside of your control. But after you've experienced a particular mistake, you will leave knowing what to do next time. If that mistake ever happens again — you will know exactly what to do. That's a reason for doing a lot of public speaking — to gain experience keeping your composure when things go wrong and to practise responding to mistakes.

When you're new to public speaking, I highly recommend finding yourself a safe environment to make mistakes. Go to your local public speaking club and maybe even find some small improv-comedy and drama groups. And then speak regularly. Just because you're going to make mistakes does not mean that you have to make them in high-pressure situations. By practising your speaking in safe, supportive environments you can make the mistakes we all have to experience, but without fearing or regretting them.

If you're still worried that the entire room might laugh at you, I have two questions for you:

My first question is: "Do you teach comedy classes?" Because hundreds of amateur comedians fail to make a room laugh. You've got a free laugh that you didn't need to rehearse or work for! If you are cynical about this idea, look up videos of comedians bombing on stage. Notice how cringeworthy it is to watch because they can't make the audience laugh or have a positive emotional reaction. Some top comedians spend months, if not years crafting the perfect joke — but you got a laugh without even thinking about it!

My second question is: "If people do laugh, does it really matter?" They'll laugh for a few seconds and then it's over. You can even act like what you did was a joke — that way they will think you're funny. As a teenager I did this all the time: I would make a comment, and someone would laugh and point out to the others that it was a clever play on words (even though it was accidental). Then the others would laugh. I would then go with it by intentionally saying something funny as a follow-up. I was seen as a comedic genius. Why not roll with it?

Laughter will help an audience to warm to you, why do you think speakers tell jokes? After laughing, an audience will like you more, not less. If they're laughing at you for the wrong reasons, you can address your mistake as we discussed and move on. People will respect you for being honest and managing an audience professionally — they'll be on your side.

Positive belief: "No one will notice most mistakes, I can briefly address the other few mistakes."

When you take the next step of your public speaking journey with positive beliefs and expectations, you will be able to enjoy yourself. When you enjoy what you do: you will want to do more of it. And when you devote more time to an activity you will progress faster. Therefore the more you allow yourself to enjoy public speaking and to treat it like a friend and not an enemy the more you will feel energised and ready to speak, and the faster you will improve.

I don't see public speaking as a battle. It's all about friendship. You get to make public speaking your friend and enjoy speaking, share positivity with an audience, and befriend them, and allow your positivity to travel. By having a fantastic time when you speak and by communicating your ideas: you will inspire others to share their thoughts too.

What Makes You Interesting?

"Matt, I'm not a very interesting person," is a phrase I hear all the time. And it's just not right.

What I find is that people have such high standards over what is or isn't interesting. It truly baffles me. Some people filter their lives so much that when I ask them about their interests, they're scared to tell me about a single thing that they like. If you can identify with this — please be kinder to yourself.

You don't have to have lived like an action hero to be interesting. When describing your journey to work, it's not a boring story if it didn't include you jumping across rooftops or speeding down a staircase on a motorbike. You don't have to be a successful businesswoman. It must be nice to have hundreds of employees or millions of followers on social media — but they're not a requirement to be interesting. You don't even have to be particularly daring. All you have to do is tell your story — whatever it is — in a way that does it justice.

To do your life story justice, you need to share with people what's unique about you in a way that only you can. When you do this, people will find your story original and interesting to listen to.

Often when people talk about themselves, they skip over the parts that people will find the most interesting. Instead, they talk about the parts of their lives which they think people will want to hear.

A female speaker from Cornwall might tell you that she ate lunch while on her way to London and then spend the majority of her speaking time describing London. In England — most people have been to London. Granted, it's famous and full of history, but when it's talked about generally, it's not that interesting. If we were to find out more about the speaker herself, we might discover that she packs quirky lunches. She might have an interesting way of slicing cucumber for her salad or indulge in a juggling routine with her apple before she packs it away. It's these small details that help an audience to get a sense of your character, and why you're unique. Yet it's these particular details that we often gloss over: "No one will want to hear about my lunch. Why did I even mention it? I better remember as many facts as I can about London!"

Everyone has quirks, idiosyncrasies, first impressions, and their own way of approaching situations. Tell us about them and include them in your storytelling.

My recommendation is to ask for help. Ask your friends and family what kinds of things you do, that no one else does. Or find out what things you've said in the past that they found hilarious, shocking or even life-changing. Getting feedback from your close circle is vital if you want to stop selling yourself as a bland and boring person. The next step is to get feedback from new acquaintances. In my own experience, a new acquaintance can often point out something about me that other people (myself included) take for granted because it's "Just who I am."

Never forget the value of sharing your thoughts. I'm talking about the ideas you are consciously aware of: your inner monologue. Your inner-monologue can be a commentary, an internal debate, or even a full-blown melodrama. If you practise telling people about your thought processes or try re-enacting how you think, people will become interested. Humans can't read minds. You can't walk up to a cashier at a fast-food restaurant double tap on her forehead and project her thoughts onto the counter! Our inability to mind-read makes any insight into how other people think, instantly intriguing. We long to find people who think like us but also to discover different ways of perceiving the world.

Sharing your story in a way that only you can is essential if you want your audience to give you their full attention. Your story is just that: your story. So tell it in your own way. Think about who you are as a person, what's important to you, what your beliefs are and what you're interested in. How would you; a person with all of these wonderful facets — share your story?

Consider how different people would tell this simple story: "I was bored so I had lunch in the park."

- A trendy businessman might describe how he dresses to go to the park and then offer a fashion tip. He could explain how he makes the most of his lunch hour before he has to go back to his work.
- A creative and energetic person could tell us how fast he got to the park. He might go into fine detail about how he designed his own lunch box. He would richly describe what in the park inspires him and how he plans to use his newfound inspiration.
- An on-site architect might talk to us about what it's like working on a building site and why the park is a relaxing break. She might share how in her experience, some quiet time is essential to her and why it's vital to her work. She could even describe how she measures her sandwiches to make them even in length and square!

The story and its setting do not have to be inherently interesting. The best stories are character driven. Think about it: If you were in an empty room with grey walls and grey tiles with no windows, it might seem like the dullest place on Earth. But if one of your heroes was in there with you, making the best of the situation, and sharing a rare insight into his perspective on the world: you would be mesmerised. We can get so distracted trying to impress people with fancy places and amazing coincidences that we forget it's us and our interactions that are the most interesting.

If you are one of the many who thinks that you're not interesting, consider changing how you tell your story. Pay attention to your inner-monologue during an average day: what kind of things are you saying? And what things do you do that make you think: "I must be the only person in the world who would do this." Listen to the feedback you're given about yourself: there will be absolute gold hidden amongst the stuff you already know.

Then you can start looking at how you tell your stories. Tell them in your own unique style. And if you don't know what your own unique style is yet — experiment. See what uplifts you, what gets reactions, and what comes naturally to you.

Not a single person who has told me that they are, "Not an interesting person," has been what they have claimed to be. They just didn't know how to find the special and personal elements of their lives that truly engage others. Now you have some advice to get started with: give yourself some self-love and stop calling yourself 'not interesting' because you are interesting. I promise you.

It's now time for you to go and start discovering what makes you interesting!

Forget About Nerves

If someone tells you that nerves can help you: don't believe them. It's a myth. Feeling nervous makes speaking harder.

My opinion on nerves is that to begin with you just have to work through them, but you also need to be logical and kinder to yourself.

Formal public speaking might be a new experience for you. This will mean you won't know what to expect. Your body has no idea how you will react or what you should do in this situation. Your brain has no reliable frame of reference. And it's before approaching an unknown situation that nerves can take hold.

I have been nervous about going on stage twice. The first time was before a school talent show doing stand-up comedy; which was my first time creating and organising a performance by myself. My voice dried up, and I honestly thought I was sick.

But what did I do? I went and had a chat with the other performers. They looked terrified. I reassured them and built them up, forgetting about my own throat problem. After making everyone else feel better, I became excited about going on stage and I loved the experience.

Before any performance or contest: I am the one who's relaxed and reassuring everyone else through comedy or kindness. Learning early on that other people needed me to be this person made me think more of others than myself before a performance or speech.

The second time I felt nervous was the only time I've ever been nervous about a speech. I wasn't even nervous about the speech itself. It was my birthday, it was a contest, I had until the end of the week to finish my coursework for my degree...and I wanted to play a game of

Russian roulette that had a chance of impaling my hand on a sharp 6-inch nail!

My hand would come crashing down on a cup selected by an audience member (one had the nail underneath, pointy side up). In my head, I thought that if I messed it up: I would stab my hand, be unable to perform magic ever again, lose the contest, be unable to hold a pen again let alone complete my coursework, never graduate, and scar every future birthday for the rest of my life. No wonder my stomach was in knots!

I got through the experience by being logical and by being thorough with my checks. Then I said to myself that the only thing that would mess it up was nerves. I forbid myself from indulging in nervousness — doubt was too dangerous. I did this, and it all went smoothly. I won the contest and celebrated my birthday afterwards with a nice pint of tap water.

I shared my experiences with you because it's easy to think that no one else gets nervous, only you. This is just not true. When I speak to new speakers: the same 'symptoms' are described to me time and time again.

You might be worried about your voice or your hands shaking when you speak. Your vision might be blurry, and it might feel impossible to make eye contact with others. And you might find yourself speaking at an accelerated rate or being simply unable to think of anything. Allow me to reassure you, these initial difficulties will go away. After giving a few speeches: you will start to feel everything begin to relax.

When I started performing magic for people I was shocked to find that my hands would shake. Card manipulation is hard enough — let alone with spontaneous jazz hands! I have asked other magicians about it, and it's incredibly common for beginners. I got over 'the shakes' by practising in public. I would do tricks at bus stops, while walking along the street, and in shops. The shakiness went away very quickly because I got used to the new situation (doing sleight of hand in public) and so my body started to relax.

When you start public speaking it's like staring into a car's full beams — it's dazzling. After a few speeches, the intensity changes to looking into the headlights. A few more and it changes to side lights. With experience it becomes like looking at small, warm candles. The 'dazzle factor' decreases with exposure and through your boldness and desire to challenge yourself.

New speakers tell me how hard it is to make eye contact with an audience. A new situation is overwhelming for the mind and senses. This is because there's a lot to take in. Of course, you're going to find it difficult to calmly make eye contact. Your mind will be preoccupied with your speaking and what you have to say. But it doesn't take as long as you think for you to calibrate yourself and to clear more mental space for connecting with your audience.

Nerves can be off-putting, but they do go away once you've had enough exposure to the new situation. Starve them of your attention and acknowledge that they will pass. Nerves are unhelpful and should be viewed as a temporary hindrance. They're similar to jet lag in that you get them when you try something new. You might feel put off thinking: "I'm going to hate my holiday if I feel this bad the entire time," but it goes away, and you will have many amazing adventures. This is also what will happen with nerves when you speak more regularly.

After you have had some exposure to public speaking, your nerves should no longer be present when you are in that speaking situation. For instance: speaking to the same ten people in a village hall every week. However, public speaking situations can be very different and so it's natural to feel a bit out of place when you find yourself in a new one.

I believe in challenging myself, and so I love plunging into new public speaking situations. Different audience sizes and compositions, venues, restrictions, and reasons for speaking will help you to become more dynamic as a speaker and more relaxed in new situations. If you feel wobbly: challenge your wobbles away until you are like a mighty tiger.

Every speech you give is a speech in your mental 'public speaking portfolio'. Your mind can flip through it and remember all of your successes. The more you challenge yourself and try new things, the more useful your mental speaking portfolio will be for you. You might feel daunted if yours feels empty but don't. Just start filling it. It will fill up a lot faster than you think! And the more speeches you add to it, the more mental references you will have to reassure yourself in the future. A varied, populated speaking portfolio will crush nerves. (N.B. If you are a fan of scrapbooking and journaling: creating a real life public speaking portfolio can facilitate this process and motivate you to challenge yourself).

When you have built up enough experience, you will have a much higher 'self-worth' on stage. You will learn to slow down and to take your time. You will breathe more and allow yourself to indulge your creativity. Audiences will mirror how you feel, and so they will be far more relaxed once you are surer of yourself. What I'm trying to say is, speaking gets a lot easier as your mental public speaking portfolio fills up.

I have covered the part of nerves that you need to work through. The nerves that appear when you are trying something new and have a lot to think about. However, some nerves arise from a speaker's doubt. To remove these, I sincerely believe that you need to be logical and kinder to yourself.

I used to think that if I was nervous about something, I would be more likely to succeed. I somehow equated nerves to humbleness. I thought that if I was nervous for an exam, a business meeting, or a dentist appointment, things would be more likely to swing my way. What utterly insane logic! Being nervous doesn't make you lucky or encourage audiences to like you. It just makes things difficult for you and makes an audience feel uncomfortable. Trust in logic and not in nerves.

One of the most powerful uses of logic I recommend is to ask yourself, "What's the worst that can happen?" The answer I give myself and others is: "You'll be so boring and bland that audiences will forget about you and your speech." That's the worst case scenario. You want your performance and your message to be remembered — so never be afraid of being courageous, different, and taking risks. What's the point of giving a talk that no one will remember or be moved by? Logically it makes sense to be braver with your speaking than to become more reserved.

It can be easy for new speakers to be overly harsh on themselves. They can raise the stakes so high for a speech that they make something simple and straightforward seem like a terrifying and impossible task. This is when it's time to be kind to yourself.

What do I mean by 'be kind to yourself'?

Pay close attention to the story within your mind: your self-narrative. Are you the victim of your inner story? Is everything just happening to you, outside of your control? This doesn't have to happen, you can be the hero of your own story. When you speak to loved ones about your speech: focus far more on your successes than your mistakes. Make this a habit. Be your own hero.

Focus on the things that make you feel great. Before you give a speech: play one of your favourite games with someone, exchange funny stories, or listen to comedy. Get yourself into a fun-loving state of mind. And when you leave the stage, allow for self-kindness by letting yourself feel proud of your speech. Enjoy your 'speaker's high' and the positive vibes while you can! Wait for the euphoria to pass before analysing your performance. That way you will associate speaking with feeling great. Then before you know it: public speaking will become a mood-lifter for you.

Whenever you are faced with a speech or an activity that feels daunting: create your own games and challenges. That way you can have more mini-victories. When I had to cold call 100 people, I would get out 100 playing cards. Each time I completed a call, I would permit myself to take one card from the pile. The more calls I made; the more cards I had to build card towers and structures with. It didn't matter what happened on the call because I would always get a new card. I created my own motivation by inventing my own game.

I would also like to mention that to be truly kind to yourself: you must keep going, no matter what happens. If you were swimming in the ocean and swallowed a mouthful of water, it would be unpleasant. But you wouldn't stop swimming and let yourself drown! You would swim through the unpleasantness until the feeling passed. Give yourself the chance to recover from nerves by forging ahead. It's far better than giving up the second you swallow some salt water and sinking down to the ocean-floor.

One thing I would like you to ponder is the nature of an audience. An audience is composed of individuals, but together they can act as one entity. If one person in an audience starts clapping and others follow, the entire audience will clap. Knowing how to manage an audience as one collective being is something that will come to you over time but is helpful to be aware of now. Instead of seeing a room filled with 100 individuals: see a room with one audience. Doesn't that sound nicer?

While seeing an audience as one social entity: seek out positivity and reassurance from individual audience members. When you see someone in the audience smiling at you, you've got someone supporting you. Let yourself find these supporters by looking for them. If you don't look for the people supporting you, you'll be less likely to find them. Look for those who believe in you!

One of the best lessons I have learnt from drama, martial arts, comedy, magic, and rebelliousness in general, is not to do things half-heartedly. Commit to your moments of madness! If you're doing something that makes you feel uncomfortable: put your all into it. It's when we half do something that it feels awkward and weak to us and to our audience. When I took Kung Fu classes, I always lost fights to aggressive fighters because I would half attack and half retreat. It wasn't until I committed to one action that I was able to stand my ground. Similarly, when telling jokes if I only half-thought they were funny, they wouldn't work. But my success with them soared once I started having complete faith in them. Being courageous and putting your all into what you do sends out a strong message: "I believe in what I'm doing." Give 100% commitment to your choices on stage!

Remember that nerves are unhelpful, but they're temporary. Work through your nerves and be logical and kind to yourself. Be courageous and let yourself forget about them.

Empower Your Public Speaking

Collecting Autographs

I like to collect magicians' autographs. Whenever I have seen a magic show: I wait around at the end until everyone else has left (magicians have a lot to pack away) and ask if I can have an autograph. Most people collect autographs for the autograph itself so it can be displayed or sold. Sure the autograph makes a nice memento, but for me, an autograph is mainly a means to an end. By asking for an autograph it buys me the star's undivided attention. I would have spent the entire magic show thinking of a question to ask and while the magician signed their name, I would ask my question.

Every magician has always been happy to answer my questions. I think asking for an autograph made them feel important and also safe knowing that once they had signed they could walk away. My questions were never about magic tricks — and I think this intrigued them (most amateur magicians only ask professionals about tricks and methods). I would ask questions about books, comedy, writing, memory, stagecraft, and even places to visit. With every autograph, I left with an invaluable piece of wisdom or insight.

I used to have playing cards signed and I would frame my favourite ones. If I own a magician's book, I will carry it with me to be signed (they're usually large and heavy hardback books). Recently I have been using a suave looking black scrapbook with questions I have pre-written in a metallic pen. Having the questions pre-written helped a lot when meeting magicians who weren't native English speakers. It's also useful in case you become star struck — this doesn't happen to me now, but whenever I used to see a hero of mine: I could only think of compliments. In the worst case scenario, if the questions are written out, and your excitement has made your brain melt: you can read out the questions or hand them to the star to read.

I wasn't really collecting autographs; I was collecting insights and wisdom.

Give Your Audience a Star

Life is relative. We're the best at everything, that is until we compare ourselves to other people. This is not necessarily a bad thing because other people's successes can motivate us to aim higher. But the trap is chasing other people's achievements and trying to be just like them. It's good to be inspired by others, but we need our own target.

How are you supposed to improve at public speaking without a target? You can't empower your public speaking unless you know what you want to be like as a speaker. It can be tempting to look up to your heroes and celebrities and to use them as the gold standard. But this is a speaker's journey of chasing others instead of creating your own path. I believe that finding your own brand of star quality is the target you need to discover.

I have been lucky enough to meet a number of my heroes. The main reason for this is that I don't look up to many 'A-list celebrities'. Alice Cooper was probably my highest profile hero, all of my other heroes have been performers and creators who are famous in their industry, not the tabloids.

What I came to realise was that many of the people I looked up to had what you would call 'star quality' about them, but others didn't. When I met a 'hero' who didn't have it, I usually stopped looking up to them. This is one reason why people say not to meet your heroes. The cliché tells us that when we have idolised someone, our mental picture of them will be so flawless, it would be impossible to measure up to. But in my experience, this isn't true. For me, the real stars were those who were even better in person.

I want public speakers to be better in person than they are online or in someone's head. Seeing a public speaker and then meeting them should feel like an extraordinary and dare I say, magical experience.

Such an experience can be remembered for a lifetime and can shape a person's life.

It's not melodramatic saying that meeting a speaker can be life-changing; I believe that it literally can be. If you follow a public speaker online and like her ideas, you would be excited to see her speak. If she turns up thirty minutes late, nursing a hangover, and contradicts her own advice for an hour — your mental image of her will be crushed. As you have probably experienced, when this happens you can lose all of the inspiration and drive that her ideas and values used to give you. Instead you are left with resentment for being 'tricked'.

Alternatively, the speaker could elegantly walk on stage looking like a million dollars and rock the venue. But then be rude and selfish when she met you. You will likely think: "She's not a nice person. I'm not a fan anymore, I want nothing to do with her," and then donate all of her products to a charity shop. It might be a fallacy thinking that unfriendly people have no positive ideas, but it's how we react on an emotional level. No matter how great an idea is, we're going to want to reject it if we see the speaker act unkindly.

As a public speaker yourself, you might be wondering how you will benefit from being a real 'star': someone who is a star on stage and off. Is it worth the effort? The benefit is that people who like your work will like it even more after meeting you. And they will likely want to consume more of your ideas and content. Alternatively, if you don't present yourself as a star — or at least as a kind human being — you will lose their interest (likely forever) and will start to develop a bad reputation. The ramifications of not being a star are a big deal: can you afford not to be a star?

The road to developing star quality is straightforward because it's once again about your approach, not overly specific tips and tricks. To find your version of star quality, follow this exercise with me:

Imagine that you are going to see one of your heroes give a speech — think of one who really inspires you. You've paid a reasonable price for a ticket, and you've sat down in the audience:

- How do you feel?
- What are you hoping to see?
- How should your feelings change when your hero enters?
- How do you want your hero to be dressed and to carry her/himself?
- How do you want your hero to treat you and the rest of the audience?
- What are you looking forward to learning?
- What would make the experience truly memorable?
- How do you want to feel after the speech?

After the speech, you head to the back of the room where your hero is sat signing copies of her/his book. You queue up and after a wait, you are now next in line! Suddenly your heart sinks as you remember: you've left your copy of the book at home. There's no way of fixing the situation because it's now your turn to meet your hero:

- How would you like your hero to look at you?
- How would you want your hero to greet you?
- What would you say to your hero?
- What would you want her/him to say back?
- What question would you ask?
- What kind of answer would you feel happy with?
- How should your hero react when you tell her/him that you've left your copy of the book at home?

- How would you want your hero to react when you ask to take a selfie together?
- How would you like your hero to say goodbye?
- And how do you want to feel afterwards?

By going through the exercise and answering the questions, you will discover your own idea of what star quality is. Generally, when you see a speaker, they're the check-boxes that you want ticked.

To empower your public speaking, you need to know what you're aiming for. No matter how you perform or act: some people will respond positively and others won't. You can't make everyone love what you do. If you try to be liked by everyone you will be bland and forgettable (the worst fate for a speaker). To not be continually blown around by other people's approval or disapproval you need to have your own path and target to aim for. When you have a clear image of your own brand of star quality: you will have a target.

The next thing to do is to find your own specific star target for yourself. Run through the drill and answer the questions again but this time, you are the hero! Imagine that one of your fans is coming to see you give a speech. What do you want her experience of you to be like? Afterwards, you will know what you need to do to have your own brand of 'star quality'. Feel free to type up your answers and print them off.

I understand that a list of unanswered questions can be daunting, so here are my answers. This is my brand of star quality, when someone comes to see me speak, this is what I would like to happen:

A reader of my work (let's call her Stephanie) sits down in the audience to see me give a speech, after buying a ticket. The ticket itself has an attractive design to it, and it makes a nice souvenir.

Stephanie feels excited to see me and is intrigued to see how I will demonstrate my ideas and put them into practice. She is hoping to see the full Jagged Matt experience and to confirm to herself that this approach to speaking is something that is for her and is a style that she can continue to aspire towards.

Stephanie would want the feeling in the room to noticeably change when I enter and for everyone to feel uplifted, energised, kinder, and more thoughtful. She would want me to own the stage like a tiger and to be dressed like a creative, public speaking rock star.

Stephanie would want me to treat her and the rest of the audience with respect, to give them real value for their time, to cater to their attention spans and to entertain, empower, and inspire them. She would be looking forward to learning more about how to empower her speeches by approaching public speaking in a new way and to see live examples of how to do that.

A strong message, entertaining and live action examples, positive audience interaction, and a focus on inspiring and empowering the audience would make the speech memorable. Stephanie would feel empowered and uplifted afterwards and feel inspired to look at public speaking in a new way and to give her next speech with love and power.

After the speech, Stephanie queued up for her book to be signed — but realised she had left it at home. Soon she was next in line...

Stephanie would want me to look her in the eye as she approached, with a warm smile and to call out a friendly greeting before she even got to the table. She would want me to greet her like we were old friends and for me to give her a chance to speak. She would tell me about how much she enjoyed the speech and how excited she was to see me in person. She would want me to be humble, and to thank her for being so supportive.

Stephanie would then ask me a question about a topic from my writing that was less well-known, to prove that she was very familiar with my work. She would want me to instantly understand her question and to give an answer she was expecting and an extra piece of advice or information for her to remember and think about.

Stephanie would not expect it but would be over the moon if I gave her a signed gift on hearing that she had left her book at home. My reader would like me to respond enthusiastically when asked to take a selfie together and to give her a truly unique and memorable photograph.

Stephanie would want me to say goodbye to her by name and to ask her to stay in touch and to ask follow-up questions anytime. She would want to feel special and most importantly, valued highly by me.

Above is my idea of what star quality is. It was influenced by all of my heroes that I have met. It might change as I grow as a thinker and as a speaker over my lifetime. But right now, that's how I want to present myself.

One part of star quality that is especially important to me is how a speaker enters and how they leave. When a public speaker comes on stage, I want the tone of the room to change. That to me is the first sign of star quality. Even if no one knows who the speaker is, if she can change the way people feel and react, very early on — in my eyes she has star quality.

Then there is how a speaker leaves, how they say goodbye. If a speaker treats their audience members like dirt, "I don't have time to speak to fans," I see the speaker like dirt. My heroes who have had star quality always made time for people and were both kind and patient. Even if a speaker has to leave straight after a speech, she can at least give a warm goodbye or offer a way to stay in touch (which incidentally sounds a lot better than a way to 'connect').

You might be wondering where the idea of giving a gift came from. Earlier in the year, I saw a speaker talk for over three hours (it was a glorified sales pitch). Afterwards one of his assistants gave me a copy of his book. I was very grateful and thought that maybe I had misjudged the speaker — I wanted to like him. But five seconds later the speaker snapped at the assistant to only give a book to people who had signed up for the expensive course he was selling, and to take the book back. My 'gift' was taken away from me. My opinion of the speaker now hit the floor. The book probably cost him a few pounds. Not wanting to spend a few pounds to make me a supporter of his, felt stingy, and highlighted to me that he did not have star quality.

A few weeks later I met one of my magic heroes after his lecture. I asked him some intriguing personal questions and asked for an autograph. Without even thinking about it, he gave me one of his DVDs. That to me was serious star quality! For me, generosity is an essential component of star quality.

The goal of this essay was not to get you to memorise what my idea of star quality is. Instead, it's for you to answer the questions and to conclude what star quality means to you, and how your speeches and interactions with audience members will need to change to obtain it. If building a personal brand and making audience members leave feeling inspired and wanting to hear more of your ideas, is what you wish — work on this. Understand your own star quality.

Two Things You Must Have

I believe that in every speech you deliver you need to project love and power. You need both to speak in harmony.

If you only project love in a speech, you can come across as patronising or difficult to trust. Your speech might show a lot of love for your subject, and your audience, but if you appear unsure of yourself then your audience will also feel unsure and might doubt whether she can rely on your content.

In contrast, if you only project power, you will appear cold and unlikable. You might show that you really know your stuff, but if your audience doesn't feel like you care about them or want the best for them, why should they like you and why should they listen to you?

The terms love and power might make you feel a bit uncomfortable. It's important to understand that you can be feminine and still be powerful. And you can be masculine and still be loving. Love and power are not tied to the classical identities of 'female' and 'male.' They are two feelings that you should be able to experience simultaneously while speaking, if not while living.

The easiest way I've found to project love and power is to experience and feel both of them:

Projecting love comes naturally to me. I feel incredibly grateful being able to speak to audiences because I care about people. To spout a superhero cliché: caring is my weakness! One of my life values is to be positive and to uplift others. Public speaking makes me feel great, and I genuinely love helping other people to grow and improve at it. I want my audiences to do well. I want every single audience member to leave the room feeling better than when they walked in. And I am so grateful to have the opportunity to share my opinions on a subject I love, with others.

When projecting love, you cannot allow yourself to see a room full of strangers. You need to care about the people in front of you as if they were close friends or even your family. When you sincerely care about the people you are speaking to: you will become more receptive to them. You will notice their expressions and the feelings they are broadcasting to you. This will allow you to build a mighty rapport with them.

What I also find is that when you have a real love for your audience you will want to be more of a giver and less of a taker: you will genuinely want to help the people in front of you. When you want to help your audience, and you strive to put them first, you will win their hearts.

I also feel and project a lot of power when I speak. I get to enter the speaking area like a rock star and fill the room with energy. While speaking, I know that I have the power to change lives and so I believe in myself and what I'm saying. I know that what I'm saying is important and deserves to be heard and remembered.

My power can be seen by how I: lead my audience through my speech, while trusting in myself enough to allow them to interact with me. I also project power by having complete faith in what I am about to say, I give myself time to breathe, I communicate clearly and loudly so that people can hear my message, and use I the space and different methods of self-expression to hold people's attention. I stand with a feeling of strength because I know that I am there to help everyone and to support them in changing their perspectives on their fears and problems.

I feel powerful on stage, which helps everyone in the room, not just me. My audience needs me to project a sense of control over my speech and the entire room. It's up to me to be in control so that everyone else can relax and listen to what I have to say. I am the designated driver!

It's easy to obsess over the 'negative' feelings that we might experience before and during a speech. We neglect the fact that our audiences can experience these feelings on our behalf. Concern, worry, and fear can be felt by your audience. Projecting a sense of control is a vital antidote for these feelings. Feeling powerful benefits your audiences even more than yourself.

It's easy to describe a list of ways that you can look powerful, or speak in a loving way: that's why most people struggle with these feelings — they want the easy way! The way I would recommend isn't hard, it just requires some self-discovery and patience.

To project love to an audience, you need to spend time learning to feel love. You need to feel love for yourself, your audience, your ideas, and your subject. Over time it will become easier to express these things, and audiences will warm to you.

When I see a speaker who is talking at me and not to me, and who isn't making me feel uplifted or inspired, my advice is to project more love. I would ask the speaker to think about her passion for the subject, and how what she's saying is going to help her audience and why she wants to help the people in front of her. I ask her to fill her entire body with these feelings. I usually notice that her voice will develop a sense of warmth and her eyes will look kinder. It creates a huge difference. When you speak, if you feel robotic or insincere: try projecting more love.

Having power when speaking is fantastic. But what no one seems to want to talk about is — why do you need power and what should you do with it? For me, power represents control. You need control to share your message effectively. Otherwise, it's like having an egg and spoon race in space against hyperactive monkeys. You're going to float weightlessly around while your competition makes a racket while causing mayhem. As I explained before, watching such a scenario would be stressful for an audience to watch.

When you have authority over a room, I suggest being respectful towards your audience and using your power to benefit them. Being powerful is another state that's achieved by looking outwards. Your audience needs you to step up and take control, so they can take a step back and listen. There are different ways to control a room, you need to find out how you will control it. Find what makes you feel powerful on stage and in control of not only your speech but of the entire room. When you are powerful on stage: audiences will start to sit-up and take notice of you and what you're saying.

When I'm watching a speaker who is floating around the speaking area like a leaf in a breeze, not projecting her voice, and in general not looking in control of her speech (let alone the room): I would urge her to be more powerful.

I have taken many kinds of martial arts classes over the years. The most imposing martial artists I have met were rooted to the ground like a tree. They didn't float around, they took control of their space. I believe you need to do the same with your speaking area. To demonstrate that you are in control of your space, you need to be able to root yourself and be unshakeable.

To help root yourself on stage, I use the 'rugby tackle test' with clients. At any point in your speech think: "Could an audience member run up and rugby tackle me right now?" If the answer is yes, adjust how you're standing because you're floating around. Sometimes, all you need to do is widen your stance a little and open up your body. Experiment with it and see how you feel you should be standing to fend off a listener from the front row who starts charging at you!

By taking responsibility for your speech and the learning experience of everyone in the room, you can become entirely in control. It's a balance of knowing that whatever happens you can handle it and also proactively fixing or catering to problems as they arise. Taking control is a service you're providing. You have been asked to give a speech. That means being in control of your speech:

- Knowing what you want to say, how you want to say it, and being confident that from your perspective what you're saying is the truth and helpful to your audience.

- You need to take control of the room, to own your space, hold people's attention and to lead your audience.

- You also need to be in control of people's learning, ensuring that your audience understands you, can see and hear you, feels noticed, engaged, and energised, and that they know you are looking after them. When you take on this kind of responsibility and find ways of doing so in your own unique way, you will feel powerful.

My plea to you is to remember not to focus on projecting love, or power alone. You need to focus on both and to balance them. How you balance them will depend on you. However, by utilising both love and power, you will help your audiences to like you, respect you, trust you and to relax and enjoy learning from you. Project love and power.

If You Talk-Down — Your Audience Can't Look-Up

You might be afraid of your audiences feeling like you're patronising them. After all, you want to benefit and inspire them — not to talk down to them.

When someone talks down to a child, a stranger or even a work colleague they oversimplify their content, and relinquish their power. By not oversimplifying or giving up your power: you can feel assured that you are not patronising your audience. Then by putting in some effort to make your audience feel clever or empowered you will build up your audience instead of talking down to them.

A speaker is being patronising when they explain something in such a simplified way that it becomes too vague or inaccurate to serve as a good foundation for practical use or self-learning. I'm a great believer that if you can't explain a complicated idea simply; you don't understand it well enough. What people often forget about this idea is that when you describe a big idea simply, it must retain enough weight and substance so that it's still useful.

I like simplicity in speeches, but there comes a point where if you make it any simpler, what you say will no longer be useful to your audience. For example, if you give your audience a basic overview of black holes and how they're being researched, your audience will be able to read up on the topic later. They'll think: "Now I understand the basics of what a black hole is and how they're being researched, I'm not as daunted to learn more about them. I know what style of research I want to learn more about..." You've not transformed your audience into black hole experts, but you have given them the tools they need to embrace the topic and to learn more.

If you give your audience an overly simplified version: "Black holes are things in space. They're being researched by men and women in white coats, called scientists. They run tests called 'experiments'..." no one will experience a smooth transition into self-learning. You would have given them no foundations to build on and to set them off on the right track. Keep your speeches simple, but always ensure that you give your audience members a sturdy launch pad to take-off from.

If a speaker removes her power during a speech in a bid to connect with her audience, she will come across as patronising. Relinquishing her power was likely done with good intentions, to show herself as 'an ordinary person' and not an expert. However, I don't think this works.

Presenting yourself with no power does not empower your audience. If anything your powerlessness makes people feel uncomfortable; that's why being 'patronising' is not a good quality! Would you feel comfortable if you were being examined by a doctor who looked amazed by your basic knowledge of human anatomy and acted like you knew more about the human body than he did? No! Of course not. In your moment of vulnerability, you would have wanted to feel safe and to have been examined by an expert. If you deliver your speech with power, your audience can relax and feel like they are in safe hands. When you are in this position of trust, you can start empowering others.

Now you know how not to be patronising, it's time to make your audience members feel clever and to build them up.

I enjoy watching a comedy that's easy to follow, that anyone can enjoy. However I love it when there are occasionally some 'clever jokes' that I understand, and feel somewhat smug/proud that I understood them. These 'clever' jokes feel like a special nod to me: "Hey there smart guy, this is flying over everyone's head except yours. Because you're smart." but it doesn't ruin the experience for anyone else in the audience who doesn't quite catch them.

I am not suggesting to conceal hidden jokes and messages into your speeches. What I'm saying is to empower your audiences and to stroke the egos of audience members with more knowledge and experience, and to make them feel like the 'smart guy' who understood something clever. Everyone in your audience should benefit in some way from your talk; including the more experienced.

When you are aware of your audience and are delivering a speech that has been tailored to them, you are likely to empower them. Imagine you are giving a speech on information technology to a room of senior citizens. If you create a positive atmosphere and discuss the information technology topics that senior citizens are most interested in, you will empower them.

When you have a connection to your audience and are delivering a speech that is focused on providing value specifically for them, two things can happen: There might be some audience members who think: "Aha! I know this! I like this speech because it's confirming stuff I know. Oh, but I didn't know that, I better listen," and there will be other audience members who will be thinking,
"This is so helpful!" By connecting with your audience and tailoring your speech to them, they will either be more familiar with what you have to say or will find your speech insightful and useful for them as an individual.

To build up your audience instead of talking down to them: ensure you provide a good set of foundations on your subject for your audience while maintaining your sense of power. To then truly empower your audience, connect with them and deliver a speech that has been tailored to them so it can best help them.

Stop Tearing Your Hair Out

When you're new to performing, you are bound to make mistakes. As I discussed in *"Help, I'm a Beginner,"* responding calmly and positively to a mistake can raise your audience's opinion of you. However, speakers who are less-experienced when it comes to speaking to an audience will follow their emotions after a mistake and not their head. They could get upset or feel embarrassed, but the worst reaction they can act on is anger. Especially when a speaker's anger at making a mistake or receiving an unexpected reaction, is taken out on their audience.

Anger can be self-directed when you make a mistake, or even when you receive an unplanned reaction from your audience. You might feel angry at yourself for making such a simple mistake or for making a large one and for 'ruining' your speech and all of your hard work. You might not have even made a mistake — something else could have triggered your anger. It's of no consequence what caused the rage or who it was intended for — when you feel angry you will project those aggressive feeling to the entire audience.

"This is all your fault for distracting me!"
"You are so horrible to me!"
"When I performed this speech at home, my family loved it — you just have no taste!"
"How dare you laugh at me when I've worked so hard on this!"

These are the kind of anger fuelled reactions that a speaker can project to their audience. They might not say them out loud — but somewhere in their mind, they'll be thinking them. These thoughts will become the vicious director for the next part of the speech (if not for their entire time on stage).

An enraged speaker will stop smiling, be impatient with volunteers and vocal audience members, engage in spiteful humour, and generally be unpleasant to watch. Nothing turns an audience off faster than anger.

When you have given a number of speeches to live audiences, you will soon realise that mistakes happen. And it doesn't matter that mistakes happen. You will have experienced so many mistakes that you will stop attaching blame to yourself or other people. If you're anything like me, your reaction will either become, "Whoops. Never mind," or you won't even give the mistake a second thought. You will be in the habit of moving on or fixing the error without needing to think too much.

If you are at a stage in your public speaking journey where you are experiencing emotional reactions to unplanned events and mistakes in speeches — don't worry, it's natural. Awareness is the first step to stopping emotional reactions and outbursts. When I started performing magic to audiences or spoke to slightly more hostile crowds, I would feel a wave of heat, or my mind going into 'defense mode' when I was under fire. It lasted less than thirty seconds, but I regretted it instantly every time. I felt like a complete amateur.

It's important to note that not all emotional reactions are undesirable. Feeling happiness or gratitude are desirable reactions for a speaker. When something happens while giving a speech that makes you feel better or more energised, it's a good thing! For instance, if you see an audience member smiling at you, hearing loud laughs to your jokes, or receiving a massive round of applause (if not a standing ovation) will make you feel fantastic. Positive reactions will improve how you present to an audience. I wanted to mention this because emotional reactions aren't always negative — but you need to be in control of yourself, so you learn not to feed or even experience negative emotional reactions while presenting.

What follows is my method for preventing the undesirable emotional reactions:

1. Make it clear in your mind that feeling angry while speaking is unacceptable and an amateurish mistake. By doing this, you will expand your awareness of your emotions while speaking and know what to avoid.

2. Be more daring during speeches. Get into the habit of introducing an element of risk by trying things that might not work. For instance, use some electronics (they fail all the time). By actively welcoming mistakes and for things to go wrong, you will learn through repeated exposure, not to worry about mistakes. Of course, you will still address them after the speech, but during the speech, you will learn not to concern yourself with them. If you're using a microphone that suddenly stops working — is it the end of the world if you have to wait half a minute for a replacement or need to go without one? No!

3. If you experience a hot flush of anger while on stage: be aware that you are under its influence. Refrain from improvisation until you feel it pass. If you happen to be improvising your speech — stick to your message and avoid telling jokes or commenting on your audience until you feel anger's influence leave you.

4. While experiencing an emotional reaction: focus on feeling a positive emotion instead. You can remind yourself how lucky you are to be there and to have an audience. Or you can look for smiling audience members. Failing that, think about the people you care about, and how loved they make you feel. If you were speaking to them right now, what energy would you want to project to them?

Now that you know to look out for anger (it might not have occurred to you — it certainly didn't occur to me when I was new to performing) you can feel more in control during your speeches. Not only that but you will ensure that you spread positivity each time you speak.

Your Public Speaking Identity

Make Worlds Collide

I used to feel like a walking contradiction. My mum is an artist, right brained, and values creativity. But my dad is an accountant, left-brained, and puts the most stock in logic. This meant that sometimes I would feel logical and other times I would feel creative. I didn't know who I was. Should I be fired up and express myself? Or should I stay calm and play things smart? I used to feel like a strange blend of both as if I was experiencing a constant live debate where an accountant and an artist were furiously arguing about who I should listen to.

I have always wanted to be funny, but at the same time I wanted to share wisdom and to inspire others. At age nine my dream job was either to be a comedian or to be able to help others with their problems through talking.

Growing up: I would always find myself leaning too far one way or the other. If I focused only on entertaining others, I felt pained by the lack of meaning in what I was doing. Whereas if I concentrated purely on sharing my calm and collected thoughts, I felt like I was missing life's warmth.

At age 11 teachers referred to me as 'Doctor Jekyll' because I would be so quiet in the classroom and then be the loudest and most exuberant on stage. This idea led me down the wrong path for quite some time. I became obsessed with duality and the idea of having two sides that express themselves in different ways. Dual identities are a popular topic for films and television, and so my mind ran wild.

I used to think that who I was while performing was an entirely different person to who I was in 'real life'. For that reason, I exaggerated myself more on stage, took more risks, and presented my mind like an open book. Except the book was stuck on one page:

entertaining others. And often at my own expense.

I have to admit, it was liberating feeling like another person. I loved giving a history presentation on Germany and spontaneously composing a song for it on the piano. I can't play the piano. At all. I also got a kick out of being overly animated and dramatic on live video streams: I once acted out the experience of a rollercoaster — including the upside down parts. I never mastered the handstand — but I sure went for it on that live stream...on the back of a sofa.

I would always support the least popular opinion in a debate, often for no other reason than to get a laugh. I could be as honest as I wanted and share anything about myself. When I performed anything could happen. This was exciting for people watching but also a little scary for me. Would I ever go too far?

I spent a long time struggling with duality. When I went on to give speeches and presentations, there would be times when I struggled to balance my abundance of humour with my love of wisdom. I had a lot of conversations with my friend and fellow Oxford Speaker, Nick Dewey. He always gave me a lot to think about. Each time we spoke I had a few more ideas to help me with my problem. They were a time I could work on balancing my logic and expression.

I learnt by doing a lot of public speaking that I wasn't a 'different person' when I gave a speech. I was still me. Except I was myself in a public speaking environment, and so of course I acted differently to when I was in a 'library environment' or a 'queuing at the bank environment'. However, it took me longer to find a way to balance my wisdom and my creativity.

My answer was contraposition. I found that it was okay to have interests and influences that were 'opposite' to each other. You didn't have to pick one or the other. I found that by combining two interests that seemed to be opposites, they could fuel each other. The more creative I was on stage, the more wisdom I could share. The more wisdom I shared, the more opportunities I had to be creative.

You can even apply contraposition to a conversation. Talking and listening seem like opposites. You might think that you are only in a listening or a talking mood. However, I find that the more I listen to people, the more I have to say. And the more I have to say, the more replies and ideas from other people I have to listen to.

I had a significant breakthrough when I realised that I didn't have to split my personality in two. I could relax about discovering things about myself that felt 'opposite' because they actually had a complementary relationship.

If ever you can't decide what direction to go in with your public speaking because you feel like you are being pulled in two opposite directions: see if you can use contraposition. Combine the two opposites in a way that they fuel each other and make worlds collide.

Do You Play a Character in Speeches?

Thirteen is meant to be the age where you start to intensely question the world and discover what things you like and believe in. At thirteen, the person who rocked my world was Alice Cooper. I had spent my whole life being taught to look up to the heroes and the rule followers. Seeing Alice burst on stage as the bad guy with a riding crop, make-up, a villainous scowl, and unparalleled stage presence blew my mind. From that moment I wanted to feel powerful on stage and to do things my way.

The second thing to strike me about Alice, was just how chilled out and, I have to say it — nice he was in interviews. His autobiography is as much about golf as it is about his rock-and-roll antics. Who he is on stage is a character.

Some performers like to play a character on stage, and other performers insist that they don't play a role: "I'm being myself." It's funny because you probably think that one way is purer or more desirable than the other. The reality is that different people have different opinions on the debate.

My view on public speaking is that when I speak I'm still myself, but the version of myself that is best suited for speaking on stage. When we present, we should share the more expressive and powerful version of ourselves.

I'm not telling you to dress up like a pirate or an 18th-century aristocrat (although by all means, feel free to do so) — you're still being yourself, but the version that is most appropriate for public speaking. It's what happens when you give yourself the chance to be creatively fearless on stage, to make the most use of your voice and body, and to share your public speaking self with others.

When I first started performing on stage, it felt like free therapy. I got to express all of my repressed feelings and thoughts that I was afraid to share. I could also move and act like I always wanted to. I could let my energy EXPLODE through the room. Over time I grew to realise that expressing myself and feeling free were my most abundant sources of fun and audiences — loved it. Public speaking became a time when I could introduce people to the performer in me.

People who argue that you should 'be yourself' on stage are missing the point of what I do entirely. Some of these speakers seem to think that it's okay to walk up on stage like you're popping off to the corner shop. I'm referring to their bland clothing, how they ignore their audience, look like they're a million miles away, and just going for a little wander. They also think that they can use the same voice and communication style to a larger audience as they would with a small group.

Newsflash: being Mr. Wander-down-to-the-shops is boring, looks weak and forces the audience to strain their hearing. Yet the speakers who embody this bland, moping around the house look, and want to 'be themselves', seem to assume that people will hang off of their every word because they're sharing *who they really are*. In reality, they're disrespecting and boring their audiences. To share who you are you have to express who you are.

If you spent a large sum of money hiring a famous speaker to give a speech: would you be pleased to see them wearing their 'comfies', looking down at the ground, and acting shyly (no relation to the singer) with a quiet and disinterested tone: "Hey everyone...You know who I am...What's up?" Of course, you wouldn't! You would want them to be wearing something elegant or utterly creative. You would expect them to work the crowd and run on stage while high-fiving everyone. You would want a passionate, expressive, and compelling speech that would leave everyone with a humongous:

"Wow!"

I think that people genuinely want to be 'wowed'. They want someone who is going to respect their time and attention levels and who tries hard to interest them. An audience wants to see a speaker with a strong stage presence and a powerful voice. It's also my belief that the speaker has to 'raise the bar' for her audience with her self-expression and power, so people watching feel more freedom to feel and to express their own feelings. To achieve all of these things try believing that you need to be more expressive and powerful while presenting than in your ordinary, off-stage life.

"But can public speaking benefit your off-stage communication skills if you play a different version of yourself when you're on stage?"

I understand that a lot of people get into public speaking because they want to develop their everyday speaking skills. One of the most amazing things that I have found from public speaking and performance is that people start treating you differently. The difference in treatment makes you start to look at yourself in a new way. After an audience member has seen you as the 'all-powerful public speaker', they are more likely to initiate dynamic interactions with you and to give you sincere compliments. These interactions will make you feel incredible and so much better about one on one conversations with strangers.

When you get used to empowering your audiences, it's only natural that you're going to want to uplift people in everyday life too. When you start making people feel great — they're going to love interacting with you.

Do you allow yourself to be expressive on stage? Or are you caught up trying to be your 'normal-talking-to-two-people self' while speaking to a room full of people?

Let yourself be more expressive and powerful!

How to Be (\ /) Different
(^_^)

On the surface, being different is one of the most natural things in the world. To be different: all you need to do is observe what everyone else is doing and either put your own spin on it — or go in a completely different direction.

If everyone in town is wearing black trousers, you can adopt the style but with your own twist and wear white trousers. Or you can wear what no one else in town is wearing: a scuba-diving wetsuit! If you only see speakers give dry and overly severe speeches, you could be the first to give serious speeches with some jokes in. Or if you want to defy the convention: you can become the most entertaining speaker possible.

The difficulty of being different arises because many speakers refuse to make 'being different' a goal. They refuse to take a definitive leap towards being different when they give a speech. I notice these speakers have a priority while speaking on stage to go the safe route and to try to avoid criticism. By this, I mean that instead of fully expressing herself and trying to do something new; she would go the safe route.

The safe route is to talk about an established message that everyone will accept, instead of sharing a brand new idea. The safe route is to be bland and devoid of creative elements and striking visuals. And the safe route also entails not sharing who you are and what you believe in but instead pretending to be a more subdued and 'normal' version of yourself. Speakers go down the safe-route to be accepted and to protect their ego/self-esteem, but they don't realise how much easier speaking would be if they let themselves be different.

When you allow yourself to be different while giving a speech: you will develop your own brand of speaking. Audiences will start feeling intrigued by your ideas and style of presenting and over time will come to expect certain things from you. The best thing an audience can learn to expect from you is a feeling.

Audiences will be excited knowing that when they see you they will be: surprised, shocked, delighted, inspired, energised, or a combination of emotions: "I can't wait to hear Svetlana's speech because her energy always makes me feel so motivated afterwards."
"Jeremy always surprises me, I can't wait to see what happens this time."
"Patti has such a positive outlook on everything, she really inspires me. This is going to help me with everything that's going on right now."

Making your audience feel something based on your own unique speaking style is the goal that we should all be aiming for as speakers. Otherwise, why are you giving a speech? Why not simply type your ideas and email them?

When it comes to self-growth: one of the most overused visualisations is of the caterpillar becoming a butterfly. I am only mentioning it because I see this process in public speaking. There are newcomers to public speaking who creep along, afraid to make mistakes and to be daring, or to share who they are. But after speaking often enough, receiving feedback, learning, reflecting, and experiencing self-discoveries; they learn to express themselves and to fly — not creep. For they will know that no matter what happens, they can handle it.

I'm sorry I had to use a butterfly visualisation: I'm now going to share with you what I literally see. When I look at a new speaker, it's usually quite telling what she's done. She will likely write a speech on her computer, print it out, and practise reading it. She will treat rehearsing a speech as serious business like learning lines for a play. She will spend a long time preparing, and the preparations will not be remotely enjoyable. Her speech will stick to the facts, even in stories and will avoid emotion and unpredictable elements.

The new speaker will take the safe-route all the way and not even consider how to present her speech in a way that no one else could. She will not allocate any room for experimentation or challenges. What she had written on the paper is all that is going to happen. As a result, she will deliver a speech that anyone could have given.

As the new speaker put in so much hard work to give a flawless performance instead of trying to be unique and different, any feedback that is not, "That was amazing!" will crush her. She will then wait and wait until she musters the motivation to write another speech.

What pains me is that there are speakers who never develop past the creeping phase. However, there's always hope — it's never too late to take your speaking to the next stage and to emerge as a unique speaker. Don't ever let anyone tell you otherwise. To move on from 'creeping', there are actions that you can do and things you can contemplate to find your unique identity when you do public speaking. Let's start with what you can do.

What can you do to start showing that you are different to other speakers?

1) Limit your preparation time for speeches.

When you start to limit your preparation time you will learn that you don't need to scrutinise your speech so much. This will help you to relax more about public speaking and not to worry so much about it. If you always treat speech preparation as a 'big deal' and a 'serious exercise' — that's what it will feel like. When you have less time, you will come to realise how your brain works and will start to develop a unique process for generating speeches.

2) Turn your sharing and expressiveness up to 110%.

Share your thoughts, your emotions, your view of the world and your love for your audience, more than you ever have before. Express yourself with your voice, your body, language, props — anything you have that will allow you to communicate beyond your current limit.

100% is the most that you can physically do; I am asking you to aim beyond what you think is possible. I know you'll surprise yourself. If I said to aim for 80%, you would likely give me 60% and say: "It felt like I was sharing too much and being too expressive!" when in reality, your audience would like to see more. Aim for 110%. It's always easy to slightly turn it down if you ever need to, but until you can actually get to 100%, keep aiming for 110%!

3) Strive to do something memorable in every speech that you do. It's up to you to devise memorable moments. Not only will this method make audiences start to remember you but how you choose to be memorable will also reveal a lot about your performance style. Doing something memorable is doing something out of the ordinary. It can mean to subvert from conventions and to do something that feels rebellious or not what you would expect at the venue. It could even mean sharing a story that is told with such feeling that everyone will remember it.

4) Put yourself in as many new public speaking situations as possible. When you have been in a wide variety of public speaking situations: you will come to realise that you 'survived' every time. Eventually, you will recognise that no matter what happens you can handle it. The safe route will dictate to you to do as little public speaking as possible in as controlled an environment as possible. Defy the safe route! Challenge your public speaking skills and you will grow.

5) Devise your own crazy public speaking challenges and experiments and test them out.

This is how I learnt. When I had an idea, I would go and test it out. Unlike while studying for my psychology degree, you don't need to wait for an ethics committee to give you a seal of approval before testing an idea. If you want to know if a new voice you're doing is funny: try it. If you want to add mime into your speech: test it out. If you have an urge to try giving a speech entirely in the third person: go and see if it works. Or maybe you want to challenge yourself to see if you can look at everyone in the room at least twice during your speech: accept your challenge! When you start doing these things you will stand out from the crowd of other speakers in no time.

How do you find what makes you unique?
1) Think about how you see yourself now — are you satisfied? How would you define yourself? What things about you and your life do you feel are special and unique to you? What are your strengths? And now ask yourself — how would you like to see yourself?

Every answer you find will aid you in both expressing yourself while speaking and in knowing what you would like to share about your personality and your life. My philosophy since I started to understand myself has been: "The more you understand yourself, the easier it becomes to connect with others." If you understand yourself and your identity you can be open with your audience and that will encourage them to trust you.

2) Pay attention to the compliments that other people give you. Are the compliments you are given consistent with how you want to see yourself now? If not: make changes.

The compliment that I received growing up was that I was 'quiet' and 'responsible'. I always took these comments as insults because they made me feel boring. I made changes and by the time I started public speaking I was being called: 'confident', 'fearless on stage', and 'hilarious'. This was exactly what I wanted to hear in my teenage years, but when I reached my twenties I wanted to hear another word: 'inspiring'. I had to rethink my approach and develop my speech construction and public speaking style to finally hear: "Your speech really inspired me." Don't rely on other people's compliments, but understanding what you want to be complimented on can guide your focus.

3) Identify who has influenced you.
Which people in your life have influenced you the most? Have there been any positive influences that you have forgotten? And have there been negative influences that you think it's time to move on from?

We are heavily influenced by our parents, families, teachers and peers, the people we work with, our mentors, and of course our friends. Many of the influences would have been positive: "If you want something, work hard and get it," or,
"Never be afraid to wear something different." Remember these influences and think of ways to integrate them into your speaking.

However, other influences hold us back: "Being creative is a waste of time, there's too much real stuff to be getting on with," or:
"You've always been shy, there's nothing you can do about it." You will come across these kinds of influences that you know it's time to move on from. I wouldn't say to delete them from memory. Your negative influences are part of your life story, understanding how you used to be influenced will allow you to share more about your life. Doing this will help you to connect with audience members who are currently hindered by similar negative influences. Move on from your negative influences but understand how they impacted you.

4) Learn from the people who inspire you.
Make a list of answers to these two questions: Who inspires you? And why do they inspire you?

Once you have a list of inspirations and why they inspire you: try taking one detail from each inspiration and applying it to your speaking.

Your mind will be attracted to specific details about an inspiration that others wouldn't have noticed. Of course, you can take a feature that is bang on the nose: a rock star's energy, a dancer's poise or a voice actor's way of slipping into voices. Try to be aware of the details that you notice but other people probably missed. You might see a historian giving a speech and notice that you love what colours he's wearing. Or you might see a fashion designer's lecture and adore how she composes her similes. After completing this exercise: you will have many new details to practise implementing while speaking (refer to step 5 of the list on doing).

Being able to find things you like and trying them on like new clothes will allow you to grow continuously as a speaker. Whenever you feel that you are at a dead end: find new inspirations. Explore subjects that you have never looked into, read new books and magazines, watch films, and talk to people. You are bound to find new inspirations when you feed your brain fresh information and perspectives.

Growing up I was always inspired by fictional characters, and as a teenager I was fixated on performers because they could do what I wanted to do. However, over time I found many new inspirations from other fields that helped me to grow including from the worlds of: marketing, writing, fashion, memory, video making, cooking, arts and crafts, and interior design. The sky's the limit. Equally, if you find that you have a 'problem area' when you speak, look for a subject expert in that area and let the inspiration hit you.

Being different is a simple task on paper, but it's not always the most natural thing to do when you are new to public speaking. What I want you to take from this essay is that you should want to be different while speaking and there are many ways for you to become a unique speaker. No one wants to be replaceable, by being different you will become irreplaceable. No other speaker will be able to give an audience the feelings and the experiences that you can.

Are You an Impersonator?

You might be led to believe that being a speaker — and one who coaches other speakers — that I would have been glued to every viral public speaking video possible since day one of my speaking journey. I wasn't.

At a time when I wasn't sure of my identity, people I met through public speaking would often tell me that they were inspired by a famous public speaker or that they wanted to perform, "...just like them". This comment came up so often that I made an active decision: not to watch any popular public speaking videos until I had spoken on stage for several years and knew what my unique style was. It was the right decision.

When I started to do public speaking regularly I didn't know who I wanted to be on stage, I was still figuring things out. I knew that if I began to try acting like a charismatic speaker that I had watched and studied, it would be far too tempting to start imitating his identity and stage presence, instead of working out my own. Our brains always look for shortcuts and that's why I knew I had to be firm with myself. The world already had all of these other speakers, there wasn't room for another copy.

My belief about how we form 'an identity' is constructive in nature — your identity is not a concrete statue, it keeps growing. I'm not of the Freudian belief that your real-self is all grown by your teens but mainly hidden within the unconscious. Can you imagine having a conversation with your teenage-self? There will be a stark difference in your identities and way of thinking. That's why you need to be careful about who you choose to study and who your influences are.

I also want to mention that I personally reject the labels 'introvert' and 'extrovert'. For me those labels are the same as saying, you either like sweet things or savoury things. I like both, but what I choose depends on the time, place, what mood I'm in, and various other factors. I dislike the prevalence of bifurcation in general (you're either this, or you're that).

I didn't want to fit into a broad category that someone else had made for me: I wanted to be my own category, containing only me. You can make your own category too.

There are 52 playing cards in a deck (once you remove the advertising cards and jokers). Do you know how many different orders you can put them in? Apparently, the number has 67 zeros in it. It's mind-blowing. Imagine if everyone on the planet was given 52 sets of identical clothes and we randomly chose what order to wear them in, people would match us from time to time — but the chances of people having the exact same order every day would be tiny. And in our real lives, we have so much choice — it keeps getting easier to be unique.

So why do we want to copy other people?

My general answer is that if you see human beings as social, tribal creatures with an intense yearning to belong, it makes sense that we copy other people we see. Just like trying to fit in with the cool kids at school, you try to copy them so they will accept you, and so you can be in the 'cool kid club'.

As adults, we still want to fit into other people's groups. If you go through an 'Are you an introvert or an extrovert' questionnaire you will likely ignore all the statements that don't sound like you: "I prefer books more than people," but actively remember the statements that do: "I sometimes feel shy in social situations." That way you can feel like you belong to a group of people who like similar styles of activities and face similar challenges. When in reality you are all likely to be very different.

In the case of people wanting to copy viral or popular public speakers — they're famous. We try to copy famous people all the time. People probably think: "If I perform just like that famous speaker, I can be well-liked and famous too." There are incredible, famous public speakers, but they didn't get to where they are right now just because of their speaking skills. No one gets anywhere because of one talent. Even a competitive short distance runner needs more than an exemplary running technique. She needs the inspiration to start running, self-discipline, the right knowledge (what to eat, what stretches to do, how to train), a good coach, the right circumstances....and the list can go on for a long time. You can't carbon-copy a person. You can imitate them, you can learn from them, but you can't *become them*. Otherwise, we would have Elvis impersonators on the radio.

I took the road of not being able to copy famous speakers, but what happens if you speed down it instead? A few weeks ago I sat in the audience and watched a long speech by someone who was trying to be just like one of the world's most well-known public speakers. He had the same clothes, the same music, identical breathing exercises, and even the same style of storytelling. You might say the speaker was not authentic. What struck me was how he didn't put any of his unique personality into his speech. It was like seeing a bad impersonator. He didn't know who he was as a speaker.

"But, if I can't copy people, what am I supposed to do?"
Instead of copying other people: study from a wide variety of sources and learn and grow from their expressions and experiences. Let people inspire you. Inspiration is a precious gift. When someone has inspired you, use the inspiration to find a new way of doing things. The person you look up to should challenge you and make you think and ask questions in order for you to come up with your own answers. We are all unique, and there is no best-fit solution for everyone.

Which is why we should learn from others, and take their ideas in new, uncharted directions.

Finding a Walk

I can empathise with speakers who are having difficulty learning how to move on stage. I used to have a lot of trouble understanding how to walk, stand or sit 'normally'.

I never used to have a problem with how I moved or held myself until I was approaching my late teens and people started pointing out: "Hey, why don't you move your arms when you walk? Why are you sitting like that? Why are you standing so unconfidently?" For a teenager who wanted to be 'Mr. Cool' the comments I received about my body and how I held myself made me overly aware and conscientious of what I was doing and how I was doing it. I over-analysed everything I did.

I read several books on 'body language' and 'confidence' and none of them were helpful. All they did was offer me 'tips and tricks' without explaining what would make me look 'normal', at ease or like a roguish rock star.

As I couldn't find a step by step guide, I cherry-picked pieces of advice from books and tested all of them. I looked incredibly out of place while stiffly walking with my head tilted up at the sky and my chest puffed painfully out.

I then started imitating what other people did — and by 'other people' I mean film and music stars (it never occurred to me to imitate people I knew). I tried several different ways of walking, at one point I had a different walk every few months. The walk I eventually settled on was that of one of my favourite video game characters. This was the easiest walk to learn because the movements in the game had been made using motion capture, so it was like I could control and then copy the actions of an actual person.

There are three things which I credit for helping me to get over my 'obsession' with how to walk and hold myself:

1) From the stars I imitated, I eventually learnt the 'thinking' behind the movements instead of the tips and tricks. I learnt that if I could move and hold my body, so it was saying: "Hey, I'm powerful, I own my space. And right now I'm relaxed," I wouldn't need to concentrate so much on what my body was doing.

2) I learnt to focus a lot more on other people and less on myself. Finally noticing the uncertainty and 'mistakes' being displayed in other people's 'body language' was an eye-opener for me. I had assumed that it was normal to obsess over body language when other people had no self-awareness of it at all. When my focus changed from: "What do I need to do to look confident right now?" to: "I can't wait to make this person laugh," I got over the problem.

3) When I started public speaking, I was complimented a lot on how I held myself and how I gestured. I seriously thought that people were just being friendly. But the compliments continued, and other speakers even wanted my advice. Then I realised that my struggle wasn't for nothing, it had given me experience that I could share with others.

The problem with how we move and hold ourselves is that there's always room for improvement. Last year when I took dancing lessons I found more things to improve on. It's good to improve. But it's even more important to learn how to switch off your insecurities and to know what you want your body to communicate and then to focus more on other people so your body can guide itself.

Are You Authentic on Stage?

The word 'authentic' is used all the time by speakers and self-development authors. But have you honestly considered what it means? "Of course I have, Matt. It means I have to be true to myself and not try to be someone I'm not, right?" I think that definition of authenticity is incredibly vague and hard to follow. My view of authenticity is much easier to accomplish.

To present with authenticity, you simply deliver a unique experience that only you can provide. Think about it. If only you can provide an experience – you are being authentic when you deliver it. On the other hand, if you're trying to directly copy someone else, you're just providing a watered down version of that person's experience. Give your audience a speech based on your beliefs and interests in a way that only you can.

The easiest way to deliver a unique experience is to play to your strengths. You do this by sharing your own beliefs and interests. Your beliefs and interests open the doors to 'who you are' – improving your connection to your audience. And more specifically:

- Your beliefs give your speech a shape, set the tone and are what will inspire others.
- Your interests give your speech variety and are fantastic for creating memorable moments.

Beliefs are your tightly held views on the world. They can include who you are, how you think the world can be improved, how people should be treated, and how to feel happy. There is no end to what you can have beliefs about (Please note that I will not be talking about religious, spiritual or political beliefs – for obvious reasons).

Beliefs give a speech shape, a way for you to approach the topic. They set a tone, how the room will feel. And beliefs inspire your audience to re-evaluate their own beliefs, to do something, or to be struck by a feeling that will later encourage them to do something. Below are some examples of how beliefs can change the shape and tone of your speech and give an audience inspiration:

- **You believe that you're a funny person**
  Your speech has humour woven into it, your audience is ready to laugh. They are inspired to include more laughter in their lives.
- **You believe that people need to take more risks**
  Your speech is daring, there is a feeling of excitement and anticipation in the room. Your audience is inspired to take more risks (however small).
- **You believe that a stranger is a friend you haven't met yet**
  Your speech includes good natured and fun audience interaction, the room has a warm and loving feeling. Your audience is inspired afterwards to talk to one another and to be friendlier.
- **You believe that the best way to be happy is to be a giver, not a receiver**
  Your speech is focused on giving value to your audience, materials, and gifts. Your audience is excited about the next giveaway. They feel inspired to be more generous and to give to others.

Your interests include: your hobbies, things that bring you happiness, and the different fields and disciplines that you have studied or been a part of.

Your interests are what give your speech variety and are what help craft the memorable moments. Simply put: insert your interests into your speech to keep your audience interested.

It's your interests that make your speech original and creative. They break up your speech with your own brand of excitement to capture your audience's attention. Here are some examples of how your interests give your speech some exciting variety and create memorable moments:

- **You read a lot of history books**
  Your speech includes historical dates and anecdotes to give context and evidence. Such tales can be surprising, tragic, hilarious, and even rather epic — the makings of a memorable and shareable story.

- **You are a huge fan of comic books**
  Your speech includes comic references, jokes, themes, costumes, sound effects — what you choose to utilise is sure to add variety to your speech! Comic books are attention-grabbing by nature and boldly including elements in your presentation is sure to be remembered for a long time.

- **You love knitting**
  You wear clothes you have knitted or use your knitting to illustrate a crucial point in your speech, knit your message or even use the wool in a creative way that includes the audience. If your knitting contains colourful wool and plays big — it's sure to be remembered.

- **You enjoy eating ice-cream**
  You eat an ice-cream on stage, give out ice-creams to the front row, or tell the story of the best ice-cream you ever tasted. People aren't used to seeing food in presentations, let alone ice-cream, it's a memorable addition to a speech.

Take action now by writing two lists: a list of your beliefs and a list of your interests. Spend at least five minutes making sure you have as many written down as you can. Once you've done that it's time to practise using them.

Set a timer for two minutes:

1. Talk for two minutes on a topic of your choosing (if stuck talk about 'Your perfect holiday'). This will serve as your mini-speech to practise with.

2. Select one belief from your list. Think about how it will give your mini-speech a shape (how you will approach the topic), a tone (how the room will feel) and how it will inspire people. Re-time your two-minute speech, and deliver it using your belief.

3. Select an interest from your list. Now think about how you can insert your interest into your speech to keep your audience engaged and to create memorable moments. Speak for two minutes on your topic which now contains a belief and an interest.

4. Repeat as necessary with different topics, different beliefs, and different interests.

You now have all you need to feel 'authentic' in public speaking. I have presented the topic here in a general and straightforward way — so naturally, there is more to be said. Start to use your beliefs and interests to share who you are and what your unique perspective of the world is like.

Crafting Your Speech

Inside My Creative Process

Every speaker and 'creative' has his or her own process for creating. What I do is nothing ground-breaking, but I'm always curious about other people's processes, so I'm happy to give you a sneak-peak into mine.

My view on creativity is that it's not a one-way street. When people talk about creativity: they seem to focus solely on input (inspiration, where to find ideas) or on output (what you make and how consistently you put it out into the world). In my experience: solely focusing on one direction is unsustainable. If you just concentrate on inspiration — you'll feel down because you never make anything. And if you only focus on output, you will also be unhappy because your ideas will be bland and uninspired.

Focusing on both input *and* output will make your creative efforts sustainable. Creativity is yet another example of contraposition and the need for balance.

Input and inspiration feed my mind. Every time I give my mind an idea that is new to me, watch a new film, read a new book, try something new — it gives me creative fuel. After my brain has been exposed to new ideas and concepts, my mind races around looking for new ways to apply them or other ideas that they can combine with. I then have my new idea.

As a speaker, my output can take the form of a speech or the components of a speech. But there are many other things for a speaker to create. As well as planning and delivering your speech, you might make your own props and costumes, create your own music, make slides, and work on new ways of expressing yourself. As we are living in a digital age, our output can take the form of an e-book, a blog post, an audio recording, or a quote stamped onto a photo or a video.

To introduce you to my creative process we need to be clear of our starting point. When you need to be creative: either you have the desired output that you need to balance with your inspirations, or you have an idea that you need to implement.

When people speak of 'creativity' most people dwell on the first starting point: where they have a clear goal, but they worry about not being able to bring it to life with inspired ideas. Or more plainly, they know what they have to do, they just don't know how to do it: "I know that I have to give a speech. I just don't know what to give a speech about or what to include..." I will delve into this dilemma first.

I have never had a problem with finding inspiration and generating ideas. Personally, I always have ideas to share, and I am delighted to have opportunities to express myself. But some people aren't so lucky, or they don't know how to think of their own ideas. My process will hopefully give you some inspiration if you are one of these people.

Step 1: Get the full brief

When someone asks you to give a speech, find out as much as you possibly can about what they want. You can't plan or get creative until you have been fully briefed. Specifically, find out about:

The timings

How long your speech will be. Find out the minimum and maximum duration. Often you will be asked to speak for a particular amount of time, but after being prodded the organiser will say: "But if you could actually speak for 'this' long it will help a lot."

The content

What does the organiser want you to speak about? You're not unprofessional for asking! Find out why they want you specifically to give a talk. They might have read something you had written about happiness in the workplace and seen a small line about how plants can make you happier. You don't know until you ask. If the organiser hadn't thought about it, find out if the event has a theme and see if you can give a talk on that theme (if you can't it helps to be able to say so straight away).

The audience

"How many people will be in attendance?" will likely be your first question, but it shouldn't be your only question about the audience. You also need to find out as much as you can about the demographics of the audience:

- Where are the members of your audience from?
- How old are your audience members?
- What do they do for a living?
- Why are they at the event?
- What do they want to gain?

The more information about your audience that you can find out, the easier it will be to plan your speech.

The venue

Where is the venue? What dimensions will your performance space be, and what will it be like?

Ensure you find out how the audience will be arranged, you want to ensure that everyone will be able to see you and your props and visuals. I learnt this from performing magic where the tricks I performed required me to know the angles that audience members would be looking from. Even pulling a rabbit out of a hat is unimpressive if half the audience can't see it. For non-magicians it's just as important: if you're using a flip chart or signage you will need to work out where it will be visible to everyone.

Resources
What resources will be made available to you?

You might assume that you will be given lights, a microphone, a projector, or even something to drink. Assume nothing! Find out for certain what will be provided for you and ensure that the specifics are sent to you in writing. Otherwise, you could waste hours making the most aesthetically pleasing slides, only to discover on the day that the organiser doesn't believe in using electricity — it's a candles only event. Assume nothing.

The day itself
Find out when you will be performing. I don't just mean what time you need to arrive and the time you need to be ready to speak — but when in the day you are being positioned.

Are you going on first?
If so the task of warming up your audience will often be up to you and you won't be able to just 'plunge in'. Think up ways to welcome your audience and to get them excited for the rest of the day.

Are you going on just before lunch?
Your audience will be getting hungry at this time and won't appreciate being made to wait with roaring stomachs because of a super lengthy speech. Keep your speech to time and anticipate a tailing off of attention. On the positive side, if you deliver a punchy and exciting speech: that's what your audience will discuss over lunch!

Maybe you're to speak after lunch or near the end of the event?
At both of these times, your audience will be sleepier and you need to
factor that into your planning. Endeavour not to give your audience
too much to remember. Do whatever you can to wake-up your
audience and to keep those eyes open!

Anything else

If you have any other questions or concerns — ask the organiser. The
more 'intelligence' you can gather, the easier it will be to create a
speech that will wow the organiser and the audience. Even tell the
organiser this if they're not used to answering so many questions: "I
want to deliver a presentation that you and everyone in attendance will
love. I need to be fully briefed to do that."

Compose your own brief

Now you have all of the answers you need, compose your own brief.
Essentially, put all of the information in one place so that you can
easily check it and remind yourself of the specifics. If you put it in a
document — print it!

Now that you have your brief printed out and sitting next to you: there
will be no need to guess anything. You know what to talk about, how
long to speak for, what your audience and the venue will be like and
what will be available to you.

Step 2: Set yourself a working title and search your mind

Your goal here is to create a suitable title for your speech that is in
keeping with your brief. This title will form the foundations of your
main message.

The first thing to do is to consider your brief. For this example let's
imagine that you are a world-class fashion designer and you have been
asked to talk about women's shoes:

Your initial title will be 'Women's shoes'. As a title, it's to the point — but it's not main message material. To construct a great main message read the essay: '*The Blueprint of a Great Main Message*'. What I think is essential is to fulfil your brief in a way that only you can. This means drawing on your own unique set of experiences and knowledge.

Asking yourself questions about 'women's shoes' will help you to start searching your mind for ideas related to the topic like you're using a search engine. You might be surprised by what you are able to dig up. Here are some questions to contemplate:

What experiences have you had that involved women's shoes?
Have you designed any?
How do 'women's shoes' fit into your life story?
What do you know about shoes for women?
Do you have any opinions on them?
Are you aware of any problems with them?
Can you think of any improvements?
Are you aware of the history?
Have you researched/written about shoes before?
What films/TV shows/videos/books/podcasts have discussed or portrayed women's shoes in a way that you liked or found inspiring?

While you think about the subject you don't need to sit still. I think on my feet, often by walking. Going for a walk with a specific question in mind can be helpful. For me, having a shower while thinking about an issue has often been beneficial (must be my inner Archimedes).

Watching films and reading books is fun — but when you have a specific brief and a burning questions to answer: these experiences become useful. It's up to you to decide what to watch and read. Choose what inspires you or relaxes you — both of these outcomes are desirable. I like comedy shows and films that have an upbeat and positive message, non-fiction books (I soak up ideas from different fields and disciplines), and any show, film, or game that features strategy, excellent character development, and some fantasy.

Always have something to write with when inspiration strikes. Often your brain will digest your inspirations and answer your questions at the most random times. Maybe even when you're trying to sleep (if you don't write those ideas down, don't expect them to be there the next morning).

Most of the time I like just to start writing. It's strange how I decide on a title, write my answer out, and then afterwards think: "Wow that makes a lot of sense. I didn't know my brain had that answer in there, but I've got it on paper now." I think that a certain amount of this comes down to practice. If you regularly ask yourself interesting questions, you will become accustomed to finding new answers.

You might not have an answer to a question straight off the bat, but you will definitely have an opinion about it. From that opinion, you can search for experiences that reinforce it. Then you can shape your thoughts by using your beliefs, and your answer will appear.

"What do you do if you have ideas and inspirations but don't know how to implement them?"

This is the opposite problem to before. This time you have inspirations, but you don't know what to do with them or how to use them.

A problem I used to find with ideas and inspirations is that they are not 'concrete'; sometimes they can just be a feeling you have. The first thing I recommend doing to pin down your ideas and inspirations is to write them down (I go into more detail about this in the essay '*How Writing Can Help Your Public Speaking*'). You should be specific about what your idea is and what exactly about your inspirations inspired you. When in doubt, ask yourself questions.

Once you have clear ideas and inspirations, see if they will fit in with your brief. If they do, look for a main message that would help your audience and structure it into a speech, supported by your other ideas and inspirations.

Organise your speech so that it will interest and benefit your audience. That way you will be talking about your own idea that you believe in, the event organiser will be happy that you have met the brief, and your audience will receive a speech targeted at them.

You might have ideas and inspirations remaining about how to perform your speech. Make a note of these ideas and try them out when you practise and rehearse. Don't spend forever dreaming about an 'epic' moment when you are only half-way through planning. There will be opportunities for you to work on amazing moments to add once your speech is all written.

If you have a problem with outputting your ideas, the problem might simply be that you struggle with perspective or you overthink things. It's fantastic to think and dream, but if it takes up all of your time, so you only have six sentences to present – that's no good. Be strict with yourself, create your speech first, and then play around with your additional creative elements. Otherwise, you could spend days on a fantastic and original prop or moment, construct your speech and then discover that it doesn't fit in anywhere.

Speaking of being strict: give yourself creative limitations. Having 5000 ideas is great, but when it comes to implementing them it's overwhelming. Instead of using fifteen props, it's much more effective to use a single perfectly chosen one. When in doubt: use your main message to rein in your creativity: "Does this idea reinforce or supplement my main message?" If it doesn't, move on and choose one that does. Then add it to your speech.

When you have added an idea to your speech, play with it. It's far better to have your idea in your speech and to work out its position through trial and error than to add it at the last minute. The reason for this is: nine times out of ten, when leaving the implementation of an idea to the last minute — you'll just end up abandoning it. For example if you want to use a tin of beans: get them out of your cupboard and start rehearsing with them. Or if you want to use a quote or statistic: learn it and start using it. With all ideas it's very much a case of use it or lose it!

My advice is to get into the habit of doing. I personally find that by getting my ideas out of my head and into the real world: it becomes easier for me to get started on the next idea. Writing this book is helpful to me because it gives my brain room to create the next one!

If you struggle to act and to implement, you might be too concerned with finding a 'perfect idea' instead of choosing a good idea, working on it and getting the most out of it. There are no perfect ideas! Go with your intuition: choose an idea and run with it. That's why I can speak off the cuff and create so quickly: I resist filtering my ideas and trust in what my mind comes up with. I take action quickly!

That was a sneak-peak into my creative process. Hopefully, by seeing it, you can re-examine how you approach creating speeches or coming up with ideas. If you want to truly benefit from my way of doing things, remember to balance your inputs and outputs.

Good luck creating!

Your Speech Is Like an Essay

Have you listened to a speaker who said a lot while she was presenting, but you left thinking: "Oh my gosh, I can't remember anything she just said!" I'm sure you have. These speakers actually had things to say — but their message just didn't pop out. In fact, nothing popped.

I have often used the simile with speakers that: your speech is like an essay. A good reason for this is that most people first learn about speeches in essay format. At school when a teacher asked you to write a speech — it usually took the form of an essay. An essay has a definite structure to it; just like a speech. And like a speech, an essay has a purpose which is backed up by evidence and supporting ideas.

Some speakers deliver speeches that are more like a collection of bullet points than an essay. It's fine to do a 'brain dump' while planning: where you write a title and throw into the mix every relatable idea that comes to mind while looking for a main message. But when you're actually delivering a speech, I personally feel like a speaker has severely weakened his speech by not having a structure. A speech is like a story, it shouldn't feel like a planning session. Organising your speech like an essay with a main message and an understandable structure will tighten and strengthen what you have to say.

An important detail about the 'essay' is what its purpose is. It's not being given to a teacher or a marker. It's not even an essay you're going to mark. It's your essay — that your audience will study. The purpose of a speech is not to receive praise or a sticker: it's to share your message with an audience. The test, is whether your audience will leave having understood and remembered your message.

Listening to a speech is a form of learning. Your audience is learning about you, and your message, as evidenced by what you used to support your message. While your audience is listening to what you're saying you want them to remember the important details in your speech. You don't want them just to go, "That was great," having learnt nothing about you or what you were talking about. So keep in mind that you want your 'essay' to be easy to revise and learn from.

Now comes the part that will help you if people have a hard time remembering your speeches. Think about how you format and present an essay:

If an essay is one monstrous paragraph it's going to be hard to follow. You need to put in paragraph breaks (the equivalent of pauses) and continuations that make logical sense. The same rules apply to when you speak. If you present a swift message, with no pauses and dot all over the place — audiences won't be able to keep up. Instead use your pauses and logical continuations to make distinctive 'paragraphs' which will help your audience to follow your speech.

Some people assume that a speech should be full of surprises. They seem to think that there's no need for a clear structure (every good story has a structure). The reality is that if you have too many surprises — you're speech will become very confusing: "I walked down the road the other day. Surprise! It was all a dream. So I woke up and went to the bathroom. I brushed my teeth. Surprise! I was actually in the kitchen. So I went to work and opened my emails. Surprise! It was a Saturday....." No one will be able to follow that!

Don't overuse surprises, create suspense and intrigue instead. You can build suspense by asking a question — and giving the answer later. Another suspense builder is to give a spoiler about something shocking that will happen at some point (just please don't make them wait until the end). Using suspense will mean your audience will not only follow along — they will be intrigued and excited.

An essay has a clear structure and your speech should have one too. Here is one way of structuring your speech that works for me:

Introduction

A strong opening line is essential. Say something that will capture the room's attention and set the tone for what you are about to deliver. Create an intriguing or powerful opening sentence. The introduction is where you introduce your main message and describe how your speech will be laid out. I prefer to do this plainly; however, you can even start with a story that embodies your main message. If you want to introduce yourself and what you do, do it in the introduction. The introduction is also where you start connecting with your audience. My advice is — don't make the introduction too long.

Body

You have introduced your audience to your main message, in the body you develop it logically and back it up. It's the place where you present evidence to support your claim. This can be in the form of a story, or you can deliver your points with evidence such as personal experiences, anecdotes, and facts. By the end of this section, your audience should have heard all they need to understand and to adopt your point of view.

Conclusion

The unsung hero and the most undervalued part of a speech. The conclusion gives your audience a recap of your main message and your key points — but that's not all! Do not add any new evidence here, instead focus on your other two jobs: a call to action and a snappy one-liner.

Insert your call to action: You've shared your main message — now what should your audience do? This can be a specific action: "Do twenty press-ups as soon as you get home," or it can be a piece of wisdom for people to actively apply: "Before you make a decision, ask yourself..."

To finish your talk give a snappy and memorable line that sums up your speech. This can be how your audience will benefit, what they should remember most, or the line can be a visual piece of imagery to solidify your idea in their mind.

Recap, call to action, snappy one-liner.

When you have organised your speech like an essay, you need to highlight the key lines to make them stand out. If you had a massive essay to memorise, you would highlight the essential words and lines. You could even use different colours to distinguish the key points. You can do the same thing when you give a speech:

To put it all together, below is a speech in the form of a mini-essay (please don't pay too much attention to the content, it's for demonstration purposes only and is a work of fiction). Notice how it is broken up into paragraphs, has an introduction, body and conclusion, and that the key lines and phrases have been highlighted:

*"**Is there an easier way to start the day?** That's a question we all must ask. **Who here hates the morning rush?** We all do, but we don't have to. I am **Dr. Charlene Yawnyson** and I'm a **sleep scientist.** I'm going to reveal to you the **easiest way to get ready in the morning.** There are **three steps** to this: **Preparation the night before, good sleeping habits, and making the most of your first hour.***

*Two years ago **I was in a bike accident.** My arm was broken and couldn't lift a pencil, let alone an iron. **I just couldn't cope with frantic mornings** anymore. That was when I uncovered the first step to an **easier morning.***

The first step: *is to* **prepare the night before.** *There are many things that you can do the night before, to help you to get ready a lot faster the following morning. Firstly you can* **get all of your clothes out for the next morning.** *I learnt this idea from* **this book on how to be a butler.** *Getting your clothes out for the next morning will save you from having a frantic rush to find something to wear, the following day. You can* **get your bag packed** *and even* **make your lunch.** *Finally,* **showering the night before** *will save you even more time. All that's left then is to* **get some sleep.**

Good sleep habits are essential. *By* **going to bed at a regular time each night,** *you will be* **rested in the morning and ready to start the day.** *On average we need* **seven hours of sleep** *each night but a recent medical survey found that* **80% of us are not getting enough sleep** *(I made up these statistics for this example, obviously use real ones in your speech).*

If you do not get to bed on time, it will be difficult to get ready in the morning. You will be drowsy, irritable, and **you might not wake-up at all! How many times have you overslept when you needed to get up early?** *I know it's happened to me a gazillion times. When you oversleep, your day will have a stressful start because you will be in a rush.* **To get up on time the next morning, you just need enough sleep — that way you won't be as tempted to sleep in. If you go to bed at a consistent time each night, you will find it easier to fall asleep at that time.**

My cousin, Jim complained to me every day for a year on the phone saying, **"Gee Charlene, I just can't seem to get enough sleep."** *It took me a year to find out why this was.* **Do you know why?** *I've already given you a clue. It was because he was* **on his phone until early in the morning every night! Relax for an hour, without technology, before your bedtime.** *When you do these things, it's a lot more likely that* *you will get enough sleep and wake up on time the next morning: feeling rested and ready to go.*

The morning is finally here – this is how to make it as easy as possible. What I recommend is to make the most of the first hour when you wake-up. When you wake-up it can be tempting to waste it by checking your emails, watching videos, or daydreaming. If you do these things, even after all your preparations – you will still be in a rush. Instead, stay focused during your first hour. The best way to do this is to make a morning schedule to follow in the morning, so you know exactly what to do and how long to do it for. If you follow it, you will have a stress free start to the day.

My easy morning routine was followed by 100 people for a year, who I interviewed. Almost all said that their mornings were easier as a result. Forty of them described it as life changing. But what really inspired me was hearing what these people were able to accomplish because of their easier mornings. Look at these achievement pictures.

Those were my three steps that you need to follow to have the most leisurely morning. Prepare the night before, get into good sleep habits and make the most of your first hour. I implore you to follow these steps tonight and tomorrow morning.

Mornings are best when they're easy."

This essay is structured chronologically and in an easy to follow way. Despite how straightforward it is, if we used it as a speech – it would lose a lot of its clarity. This is simply because unlike an online video: when an audience listens to a speech, they can't go at their own pace, rewind or rest a second if they need to think about something else. Think about how many times you have read a line in this book for a second time – you can't do that when listening to a speech! Therefore we need to highlight the essential parts of our speeches.

I have highlighted in bold the important parts of the essay. As you can see, I haven't highlighted everything. This isn't to say that the parts that are not highlighted should be deleted — those parts make the speech flow, but the speech will work in memory without them. It's also important to remember that during a speech if everything is highlighted, nothing is emphasised.

When I speak, I prefer to emphasise the positive directions "Do this. When you do, this good thing happens." This is simply because, when someone recalls your speech they might remember the negative parts you emphasised and act on them: "Don't eat nothing but ice-cream. Ice-cream alone is bad for you. You shouldn't just eat ice-cream."
"That was a cool speech. I think I'm going to go and get some ice-cream." However, this choice is up to you.

Read the above speech out loud. Try to make the highlighted sections stand out. Below are some of my suggestions for how you can make the highlighted parts stand out:

1) Change the energy and tone of your voice
Pay attention to your vocal energy as you read a few lines out loud. If you wish to highlight a word (or an entire line) change the energy. If you are talking in a high and upbeat voice: make a conscious effort to slow down and lower your voice as you deliver a section. Or if you're talking with lower energy: try raising it for a highlighted section.

You can also change the tone of your voice. You can change your tone in any way you like to highlight a section, but one of the most effective ways is to create a contrast. You can go from a playful mood to a serious tone. Or you can go from a sad tone of voice — to bouncy and exuberant.

2) Pause

One of the easiest ways to highlight a section is to pause after saying it. That way everyone in the audience has a few extra seconds to register what was just said instead of having to start concentrating on the next sentence: "The easiest way to peel ginger root is with a teaspoon..." Two-second pause: "...There are other methods, but I find it's the most effective."

You can even pause before the section you want to highlight to create some anticipation: "I discovered an easy way to make a house on the ocean." Four-second pause while looking around at the audience, "I built it on an oil rig!" When you do this, everyone will be listening-out for the next sentence.

3) Use your body

Don't forget that you can communicate with your body as well as your voice:

- A visual gesture or movement can make what you say more memorable.
- A recurring gesture or movement can link ideas together. For instance, you could pretend to play the air guitar each time you deliver a benefit to the audience.
- An attention-grabbing gesture or movement can make people pay attention to a section. If you said that you were going to tell everyone about your favourite story, and mimed getting out a hefty tome and began flipping through the pages — your audience will become curious and start watching. Using your body to communicate physically will help to make the section stand out.

4) Use visuals

Using a prop, an image, or another visual can also make a section of your speech stand out. For example, it's one thing to say that your favourite food is a sandwich — it's another to say it while holding a four-foot square prop sandwich. Using a visual image will help the message visually stick inside your audience's minds.

5) Use audience interaction

I wouldn't recommend using audience interaction every time you want to highlight a section. However, when used sparingly it can be effective. You can survey your audience before a key point: "Please raise your hand if you have ever had a free cup of coffee. I get a free cup of coffee every week!"

You can use an open question if you want to, however when under time pressure it slows down the pace of your speech (as audience members often need a certain amount of time and encouragement to start speaking to you). Whereas a survey is quick to conduct.

If you want to highlight your speech effectively: use a combination of methods. With practice, you will find what works for you and what methods you prefer, but in the meantime try using some of the above in your next speech.

I find it helpful to compare a speech to an essay — and now maybe you will too! An easy to follow and logical structure will always serve to empower your speaking and help people to listen to your speech without having to concentrate too hard. And highlighting the important parts of your speech will help your audience to know which parts they should be paying most attention to. If you are struggling with your speech construction and delivery — see your speech as an essay.

Keep Your Speech Fresh

Have you ever had to watch a presentation that felt lifeless and stagnant? I'm talking about one that's obviously been performed over and over in the exact same way. A presentation that has been repeated verbatim so many times that it is now devoid of pizzazz or zeal. One that made you think: "Well it's clear he knows this presentation, but it's like he's talking to an empty room. It's like he doesn't even know we're here. And he sounds bored." I know I have. I am going to share my way of preventing this, how to keep a speech 'fresh' for you and your audiences.

I've had a life-long love of magic. Whenever I see a magician, I like to see them perform for me before I share just how much I know about magic. This is because I'm very good at switching off my 'magician brain' and just enjoying the performance. I watch magic for the performer more than the tricks.

What I found interesting was spending time with 'magic friends' — friends who love performing magic a lot. We would be talking about something, and then they would ask me an intriguing question, "Do you believe in fate?" After giving my answer, I would be shown something utterly unexpected and just plain impossible.

To me, it was a personal and special moment. It was an intimate interaction. But whenever I saw my magic friends interact with anyone else (often complete strangers) they would ask the exact same questions that they asked me, "Do you believe in fate?" They would then repeat the performance they gave me, line for line. When I witnessed this: I lost my special moment. From then onwards I never wanted to deprive an audience of a special moment that they'd shared with me by carbon copying my speeches and not keeping them fresh.

The way that I approach 'keeping a speech fresh' goes against what a lot of professional performers and speakers' advise. The time-tested wisdom is to learn to deliver the same performance over and over again. However, this wasn't right for me. I love thinking on my feet. When I acted, I would frustrate my fellow actors to high heaven because I would delight in ad-libbing and making changes based on what I thought would work in that moment.

My approach might not be a perfect fit for you. You might prefer to take a few ideas to create a slight draught instead of trying to make your speech completely 'fresh'.

Some speakers discuss the value of 'being present' — being aware of yourself and of what's going on around you. My method allows you to reap the benefits of being present. For me, the real value of presence is being able to capitalise on the things that you notice.

If your speech structure is rigid and inflexible, you can't make sudden changes based on your observations. I know that if I had to continually repeat a speech in the exact same way without being able to adapt based on what I noticed, I would become bored. If I'm bored, my audience will also become bored because the room will be smogged with my lack of enthusiasm. No one wants that outcome.

I believe that a speech should change depending on the audience, the environment, and based on your own intuition. Your speech's main message will stay the same, as will the majority of your speech. However by allowing your speech to adjust it can breathe and stay fresh.

When you let your speeches breathe, an audience member who sees your speech for the second time won't feel bored. This is because there will still be an element of unpredictability. The audience member will expect new things to happen this time that didn't happen last time. And you will not 'fall asleep' giving the same speech because the changes will keep it fresh for you and keep you present and on your toes.

Adjust your speech for your audience

Two ways of adjusting your speech for your audience are to observe how your audience is different from previous audiences and to let your audience have more input.

If you have planned exactly what you're going to say word for word, you could deliver your speech to an audience no problem, and they'll love it. However, you could deliver the same speech to another audience, and they might be baffled by what you're saying. A different audience might stay silent after jokes that brought the house down last time. Each audience is different: by observing what makes your current audience different you will be able to adjust your speech so that it is a better fit for them.

You don't necessarily have to adjust your speech on the spot. If you can find out information about your audience before your speech, you can make alterations in advance. However, if you have a need to make changes in the moment, it's straightforward if you pay attention to your audience:

- Who is in my audience?
- Do they look happy?
- Are they understanding me?
- Is the subject matter too challenging or not challenging enough?
- Are they enjoying the speech?
- If not, why not?

When you have answers to these kinds of questions you can adjust your speech to fit your audience. You can go into more detail on a concept that the audience seems to be struggling with, you can use jokes that capitalise on the audience's shared knowledge and observations, and you can even alter your energy levels. Adjust your speech and your delivery so that it is customised for the audience in front of you.

My dad has always been mad about technology. He has state of the art speakers (that look like coffins), he fixes computers and sells software, and for some reason, he seems to collect cables (yeah, I never got it either). It's easy for me to forget sometimes that not everyone older than me knows about internet culture, social media, and all of the latest electronic devices.

I once planned a presentation on social media to give at a Toastmaster club officer training, but five minutes in I noticed puzzled looks and asked if an idea wasn't making sense. I heard from my audience that they were in the dark about what a hashtag was. I had taken it for granted that everyone would know why we use hashtags online let alone what one was #Whoops.

Other speakers who were sticking to the script would have ploughed on and left their audience behind. Instead, I adjusted my speech so that it was more about hashtags than some of the more advanced social media features — because to them that was more useful. If ever you are unsure if your audience members are keeping up with your speech, the easiest way to find out is by asking.

How could my magic friends have ensured that I kept my special and personal experience? Instead of asking, "Do you believe in fate," a question that will go down one of two paths — yes or no, they could have asked an open question, "What do you think about fate?" They then could have threaded my answer throughout their presentation or at least come back to my answer at the end of the trick. That way: no two performances would ever be the same! My special moment would have remained special, despite how many times my friends repeated the trick in front of me.

If you have ever been to a show that used volunteers, you might have noticed something striking. More often than not it's the volunteers' off the cuff comments and actions that help to get the laughs and big reactions.

My girlfriend Claire and I went to a local comic convention where Tony Robinson was giving a talk. During the Q and A, I asked him about practical jokes. Tony's response and follow up story got a huge reaction (the largest in the talk), but he would have never been prompted to talk about it if no one had asked. One of the easiest ways to adjust your speech for your audience is to let them have some more input. Survey your audience, give them a chance to ask questions, and give members of the audience your attention.

Make changes based on your environment

As well as each audience being different, each environment where you perform will differ from the last. You had a stage last time, but there isn't one this time. The room for your next speech is circular, but you're used to presenting in square or rectangular rooms. The room might be larger or smaller than you're used to. There might be interesting decorations on the walls. Perhaps you will discover that the venue has wooden flooring which makes your movements echo, unlike carpet. Your audience could be five inches away from you or fifteen metres back. It could be hot and stuffy, or it could be cold, with everyone shivering and huddling together for warmth. It might be well lit, or it could be difficult to discern things. These are some of the conditions that will require you to adjust your speech.

It's interesting watching a speaker who is used to presenting in a small room because when she performs in a larger one — she doesn't use most of the space and she forgets to project her voice. When you know that your next speech will be at a different location, adjust your speech for the venue.

Instead of seeing a change of venue as a set of limitations, see it as a list of opportunities. Make sure that you can seize the opportunities that the venue will give you. You can do this by finding out about the venue before your speech and rethinking your choreography and delivery. Or you can do it on the day by being observant. If you arrive early, you might even be able to rehearse in the new environment. Pay attention to what opportunities the venue is affording you, and take them!

Be receptive to your intuition

Each time you deliver your speech you will be building on a unique set of circumstances. You will never experience the same moment again, there will be differences each time you present your speech. You'll be in a different mental space, you'll be more experienced and would have been exposed to new personal events. What you and your audience recently experienced before you walked on stage, will also be different from speech to speech.

The difference in circumstances between speeches will have an impact on you and your audience. In particular the exact timing and delivery of your words will alter, and your audience's reactions will differ.

The feel of each delivery of a speech will be slightly different. Ignoring this fact prevents freshness. Use your intuition to seize the opportunities given by the unique set of circumstances that your speech is built on.

The following are examples of your intuition in action during public speaking:
"I don't know why, but I have a strong feeling that if I said this right now, my audience would love it."

"It might be crazy, but I really think I should climb-up there."
"I just get the feeling that I need to speak slower than normal today."

When you speak, you will have an urge to try something and won't be sure why. Instead of repressing these urges, go with your intuition. Often you would have picked up on something that everyone in the room was collectively feeling. It can be tempting to charge through your speech and to only think about your next point. But if you take the time to observe what's going on around you and act on your intuition, you will stay alert while holding on to your audience's attention.

In my view, a speech cannot be 'one size fits all' because every audience, venue and set of circumstances will be different. Insisting that your speech is inflexible is a clear way of boring yourself and losing your audience.

Learn to adapt and adjust, not only to keep your speech fresh but also to give the speech that is right for your audience. It makes no sense to give a speech that is right for one specific audience and then forcing it to fit every other audience you stand in front of.

The Blueprint of a Great Main Message

I've often referred to a speech's 'main message' and why it's critically important. The main message is essentially your speech's ultimate takeaway refined into one sentence (and in this essay, will now be referred to as a M.M.). The M.M. is the soul of your structure. It's what will help your audience follow your talk, and change their thinking. This is an introduction into what makes a great M.M..

A great M.M. is: personal, adoptable, shareable, and positive. There are of course other factors that can contribute towards a main message, but focusing on these four will serve you well.

Your M.M. has to be personal

Why are you giving this talk in the first place? And why couldn't someone else in your industry, such as a competitor (or someone similar to you) be giving the speech instead?

It's tempting to simply tell speakers to be original. However, it's incredibly difficult to come up with 100% new ideas. Even if you think an idea is new, it probably isn't. It was because of this difficulty that I decided that focusing on creating new ideas was the wrong target for speakers to shoot for.

If you deliver a message that has been shaped by your own beliefs and personal experiences, you acquire an M.M. that is strongest when it's delivered by you.

Telling an audience to: "Turn the lights off when you're not using them," is not a new idea. The originality appears when you go into detail about why turning lights off is important to you and what experiences taught you this lesson.

Your M.M. must be adoptable

Now that you have shaped your M.M. using your own beliefs and experiences you need to ask yourself: "Can other people use this message?" If your message can only ever be used by you, then other people won't be able to adopt the message into their way of thinking. If a message can only help you, why are you sharing it?

If your M.M. is: "Everyone in this room who is a twenty-nine-year-old woman who owns two cats, an orange bicycle, and cuts the crusts off her sandwiches — deserves a pay-rise!" next to no-one in your audience will be able to adopt your message. This is because the message will not apply to the audience or anyone they know.

If your message is only helpful to you: look for the main message hidden inside which is adoptable by others. Depending on the speaker's intention (I don't know what her intention is) her message could become one of the following:
- "Everyone deserves a pay-rise."
- "All women deserve a pay-rise."
- "All young people deserve a pay-rise."
- "All young women deserve a pay-rise."
- "All cat-owners deserve a pay-rise."
- "All cyclists deserve a pay-rise."
- "If you cut the crusts off your sandwiches, you deserve a pay-rise."

All of the above messages can be adopted by everyone in an audience. This is because everyone will either match the description or know someone who matches it. If an audience member at least knows someone who matches the description, they can adopt the message into their perception of the world. If you asked an audience: "Who knows a woman? Who knows a young woman? Who knows a cat owner? Who knows a cyclist?" All hands should go up.

When presenting your main message, you must ensure that it's adoptable. If your M.M. applies to members of your audience or someone they know, it can be adopted:
"I'm a cyclist. I deserve a pay-rise!"
"Oh yeah, Sarah is a young woman I know. She deserves a pay-rise!"

Even if the M.M. does not currently apply to your audience, if it features something that is achievable it will be adoptable. We can't change our age at will, many parts of our identity, or guarantee success with more ambitious changes. But discussing something that is achievable with a simple change that is within everyone's reach will make a message adoptable: "Oh, I don't cut the crusts off my sandwiches. But I can easily do that. Then I'll deserve a pay-rise!"

If an M.M. is adoptable by an audience, regardless of whether the message directly benefits them, their perspective on the issue can be altered.

Your M.M. should be shareable
Ideally, you want your message to not only be adopted by your audience but for them to share your message with others. One way of facilitating this is by checking that your M.M. solves a problem.

When I'm asked for help, I can suggest someone's idea that helped me with the same problem. If a M.M. effectively solves a specific problem — why wouldn't people share it? If a speech helps me with an area of my life, I'll bring it up in conversation and share it with other people.

If I'm able to adopt a helpful, problem-solving message — I want it to be easy to share with other people who are experiencing the same problem. I want other people to get on the 'same page' as me! The easier a message is to share, the easier it will be for adopters to share the message. If your M.M. is easy for people to talk about – it's more likely to be shared.

When your M.M. solves a problem, other people will be inclined to share the solution. People discuss their problems with their friends and family all the time. Friends help each other by asking: "Hey, why don't you try this?"

If your main message is 'Meditate for five minutes before lunch' – you're sharing a solution. When two friends are talking, and one says: "I don't have a minute for myself in the evening. I'm so stressed out." The other friend who saw your speech might chip in with, "Why don't you try meditating for five minutes before lunch?"

In contrast, if your M.M. does not take the form of a solution, 'Meditating is cool', it would be adoptable but difficult to share. Telling people that meditating is cool, will reshape how your audience perceives meditation, but it's a statement, not a solution. Unless the two friends randomly decide to list what things they think are 'cool', the M.M. is unlikely to come up in conversation.

A great M.M. is positive
I am using the word 'positive' with a dual meaning:
1) A great M.M. should be uplifting.
2) A great M.M should tell your audience what to do and never what not to do.

At the core of my public speaking philosophy, I want to fuel happiness. If you do not share this belief, there are logical reasons to adopt it. If your speech uplifted an audience member they will be more likely to contemplate your M.M. and to share it (and probably become a fan of both you and your message). But if your speech made an audience member feel guilty or upset, they're not going to want to look for the merits in the M.M.. Also they will be unlikely to share your **M.M.** (at least not in the way you want them to). So my advice is, ensure your **M.M.** is uplifting.

Telling your audience what to do instead of what not to do is equally important. If you spend your entire speech lecturing: "Don't do this, don't do that," then not only will your audience feel like they're in school — a number of them will want to rebel.
"I'm going to do this, and do that! That'll show her."

Focusing on 'what to do' makes you look like an expert and strengthens your speech. Anyone can point out ideas that don't work: "This will change your life. If you fill a car with washing powder instead of petrol — it won't work," but few speakers can actually lead by offering solutions and alternatives to problems. I urge you to be one of the few.

As we have seen, if you provide solutions, your audience can adopt and share them. The speaker who has answers is the speaker who has authority because she can help fix problems, while others can merely highlight them. Audiences will respect you, see you as an expert and want to learn from you.

As I said at the beginning, these four factors are only a handful that contributes towards a great main message. There are many others out there. I hope that with time you will discover your own. But to get to that point, you have to practise crafting strong main messages. Make them personal, adoptable, shareable, and positive. If you do that, you will share consistently great main messages throughout your public speaking journey.

Message First — Fun Stuff Later

Audiences are often intrigued by my style of delivery because they find it 'more creative' and outgoing than 'conventional public speaking'. When some speakers try to be 'creative' with their public speaking, they can be misinformed by an onlooker that what they presented was too crazy or too out there and that they should rein it in.

I have never seen a speech that was too creative. Instead what I have seen are speakers who put their innovative ideas first and their message second. Your message must always come first.

When I start coaching a speaker with their next speech, the coloured pens come out, and I ask: "What's your main message?" At that moment I don't care about anything else. I know that the speaker might have planned an elaborate speech with well-thought-out twists and turns. But if there's no main message, it's going to be a weak speech, no matter how nicely it's dressed up.

Not making your message your first priority is such an easy mistake to make. But it's where people go wrong from the word, "Go!" Some talented speakers are so excited to show their skills in other disciplines and performance arts that they forget to focus on what they're trying to say.

The fundamental purpose of public speaking is for you to share your message. Not your neighbour's, not your boss's, your favourite celebrity's or your partner's — *your message*. Once you have your message planned out: you can share things about yourself that support it. But your message has to come first.

When I write, the very first thing I do is jot down a title. I then write in: what my message is, what I'll be answering, and what I will be talking about. That's how I stay on topic. If a paragraph does not support my main message it gets deleted.

If you are trying to squeeze a creative idea into your speech, ask yourself if it supports your message. If it doesn't, no matter how brilliant it is — it's not the right time to use it. Make a note of the idea, file it and save it for another speech where it will really make your message shine.

If you're planning a speech and your inspiration is a funny story or a creative idea: find the message. There's always a message to be found. Once you've found the message, you can look for other evidence, stories, and ideas to support that message.

Imagine that inspiration hits you: Wallop! You want to give a speech where you walk on stage in a bird costume. What's the message?
- Do you like birds?
- Are you raising awareness about endangered birds?
- Or are you simply showing that wearing a bird costume is funny?

If you want to do it for the last reason, you could talk about the importance of first impressions, what not to wear to a job interview or even why people can be treated differently because of what they look like.

Once you have a message: make it personal — make it your message. From there you can start building your speech up. That is the difference between walking on stage in a bird costume for a laugh, and creating a striking piece of visual evidence for your argument:
- "Hey guys, look at me — I'm dressed as a bird," = you've lost it.
- "Each and every one of you are prejudiced. No matter what my qualifications are, or what experience I might have — you

are all judging me because of what I look like. There's no denying it. Luckily for me, this is a bird costume, I get to take it off. Everyone else can't simply unzip and change how they appear to others," = you're a clucking genius.

A piece of advice I have for people showing a skill on stage is to know when to put it away. If you've advertised that you have a certain talent — say juggling, your audience is going to want to see you do it. Otherwise, they will be half-listening the whole time and thinking: "When is he going to juggle? He's meant to be a juggler." Therefore, by all means, give a performance in your speech. But then put it away.

In my opinion, one performance can empower a speech, but several performances dilute a speech's power and meaning. When I have advised magicians who wanted to give a talk, I always said: "Perform one trick that brings your message to life," instead they often want to show at least three throughout the speech. Too many showcases of skill not only butchered their structure and flow, but also gorged into their speaking time. If you have ten minutes to speak and you spend seven minutes showcasing your skills — you're left with three minutes to share your message verbally. Very few performers have the restraint to use their special skill once. Be an exception.

One gang of villains who conspire against you putting your message first are tangents. People are often confused about how to prevent going off on a tangent while speaking. The answer to this once again is to put your message first. If you're telling people why reducing sodium in your diet changed your life: you know that what you say must be related to reducing sodium in your diet and the changes that followed. If you suddenly want to talk about the circus, your love of horticulture, or something profound that happened to you last night — stop. Ask yourself: "Is this related to my message? Does it support my view?" if both answers are no, avoid it — it's a tangent.

Some may argue that a tangent is a necessary evil, as a tangent can keep an audience engaged. I couldn't disagree more. If you need to temporarily change your subject to keep people interested — you need to work on how you construct and deliver your message. The problem could even be that you didn't have a clear and personal message to begin with.

If you want to add in moments to keep your audience focused, don't use a tangent — instead consider using engaging repetition, such as a running gag.

In comedy, a running gag is a joke such as a visual moment that continually reoccurs throughout your performance. This keeps an audience alert because they vigilantly wait for the joke to reappear. Then when the audience stops waiting for it, and they relax — the joke happens again, and they laugh and become alert once more. A running gag or repeating something that happened earlier also gives audiences a breather for a few moments. When done well, a running gag can even serve to reinforce your message throughout your speech. Below is the difference between using tangents and a running gag:

1) Tangents galore:
"Today I am going to tell you why eating less salt has changed my life for the better. I used to eat several packets of salt a day. And when I say several packets of salt, I mean at least two dozen. Anyway — I was at the circus the other day, and the funniest thing happened....and then the elephant ate his hat. That night I ate lots of salt as I usually do. The next morning I woke up and thought, I need to cut down on my salt, there should be something else I could do. For instance, I love gardening...and my favourite flower is the Lilly because...and that's why I'm never allowed to go back to the gardening centre. So I stopped eating packets of salt, and soon I was feeling much better. I was feeling more relaxed and serene. So serene in fact that I had a profound thought...my grandfather always said to get a new

doormat...so I got an old toolkit...and that's why I installed a cattle grid. Now as you can see — eating less salt really changed my life for the better!"

What an absolute mess that was. But now contrast that banquet of tangents with:

2) Running gag:
"Today I'm going to tell you why eating less salt has changed my life for the better. I used to eat several packets of salt a day." The performer removes two packets of salt from inside his mouth, "And when I say several packets of salt, I mean at least two dozen." The performer removes many more packets of salt from his mouth. "One morning I woke up and thought, I need to cut down on my salt. And so I decided to stop eating packets of salt." The performer tries to take a packet of salt out of his mouth, but nothing's there. "Soon I was feeling much better. I was feeling more relaxed and serene. I could think clearer and felt less stressed. I haven't given up salt entirely, you need some salt," the performer removes one packet of salt from his mouth, "but having less salt has given me a much calmer and more thoughtful way of living."

As you can see in the above examples: tangents severely weakened the speech, but a well-planned running gag added a unique, visual, and comedic spice. What you say and do must support and reinforce your message and not distract your audience from it.

If you don't want to use a running gag you can use a recurring gesture. This is a gesture that is repeated to create a pattern for your speech and to add a visual element to your message. And if that's also unappealing, you can always rely on repetition — repeat a specific sentence. Find methods to bring more attention to your message instead of going off on a tangent.

The one thing I want you to take from this essay is: your message must come first. If you want to be clever, creative or daring — start with your message. I know that spicing things up is fun and that some ideas feel hard to ignore. But no matter what happens, your message must always be your first priority.

Are You Teasing Your Audience?

Chekhov, the Russian playwright, said: "If in the first act you have hung a pistol on the wall, then in the following one it should be fired." This is known today as Chekhov's Gun. Essentially the principle means that in storytelling: each part of the story should contribute to the overall story. This is very similar to what I discussed in the previous essay — if a story does not fit into your structure and is not reinforcing your main message, it's not helping you and should be removed. By introducing an element that you are not going to expand upon, you will tease your audience.

Are you teasing your audience?

- "I swam with sharks once. But that's a story for another day..."
- "The craziest thing happened last night. I can't go into it now..."
- "You should have seen what happened last time I gave a speech!"

Any line without a follow-up like the ones above is a tease. It's a tease because you're not being explicit about what happened. And because you're never going to go into more detail about the teased story during your speech — you're teasing your audience for no reason.

But be warned: if you go on to give explicit information, the tease will become a tangent. Unless it's an appropriate joke or reference, if a line doesn't fit into your structure or support your main message, just don't say it. Because otherwise, you're adding a tease or a tangent (you can't win).

"But where's the harm in a tease?" The harm is that you are going to distract or disappoint your audience. After hearing that you swam with sharks, some audience members are going to start thinking about sharks. And the others are just going to be thinking: "Why on Earth are you talking to me about your business? You swam with sharks! Why aren't you telling me about the sharks?!"

If you happen to have some outrageously cool stories like you once swam with sharks — use them. But use them in a speech where they fit, support your message, and wow the sunglasses off of everyone. That way the inherent spectacle and intrigue from the stories will serve you instead of working against you. Contrast the following:

1. "Hi everyone. I'm here to talk to you about a brand new type of cable that's just been invented and how internet speeds have come a long way. You might not know, that I once swam with sharks. Yup. So this is how the cable works and how many devices it can be used with..."

   Compared to:

2. "Hi everyone. I'm here to talk to you about internet safety. I know a lot about safety: I once swam with sharks. I swam with them while on holiday last year — here's some photos... What you might not realise is that although there was an element of real danger, by taking precautions, it was a remarkably safe experience. And very fun. And this is how I want you to view internet safety..."

By using your stories in the right speech — so they fit and support your message, you end up with an original and powerful speech. Whereas if you tease your audience, you lose their attention and support. On top of that — you also end up ruining the surprise for when you do decide to tell your incredible story.

The take-home message is that if you're not going to talk about the story in the current speech — don't tease it. Instead, save it for a speech where you can do the story justice, and it can help you.

Reference

Chekhov's gun. (April 13, 2018). In Wikipedia. Retrieved April 27, 2018, from

https://en.wikipedia.org/wiki/Chekhov%27s_gun?nononanette

Be a Tortoise Tour Guide

I used to believe that it was always possible to pick up a book and extract and understand all of the information contained in its pages. I love learning, and so when my burning desire to learn something new arose, my first port of call would be finding a book on the subject and reading it. I believed that if I had an interest in the topic and I wanted to learn, that I could grow my knowledge from that book.

Unfortunately, I found that few authors could help me to learn their subject progressively. There was always one paragraph (if not an entire chapter) that was way too complicated. It was like looking at pictures of animals in a zoo: "Tiger, lion, zebra, monkey," and then suddenly seeing an alien pinecone-lightswitch-penguin with tenure and a Swiss passport, "What's that supposed to be?" It often felt like authors didn't know how to describe a fundamental idea that was more complicated — simply. This meant that progression was impossible without help.

No matter how entertaining or inspiring you are, if your audience can't follow and understand your idea — they will lose interest. Your audience will not always lose interest by choice, many will be dedicated and force themselves to persevere until they realise that it's just not making sense.

When you keep the content of your speech simple and easy to follow, no one will be forcibly barred from listening: Like following a tortoise tour guide, if you want to follow him — you can! Keep your message clear and learn to prefer giving a speech that has less content, so you can further explain your ideas and perform them in an engaging and memorable way.

Creating a speech that's easy to follow

I don't like writing speeches. I really don't. I find that how we write is distinctly different to how we speak. We have a writing voice and a speaking voice. Our writing voice goes into a lot more depth and detail than our speaking voice. If we were to talk out loud and remember what we said: it would be a lot easier to recall than writing something and trying to remember it. A reason for this that I want to expand on, is that when writing a speech: we cram in way too much and struggle to keep it simple. A verbally prepared speech becomes simpler and clearer with repetition. However a written speech becomes different and in particular more complicated each time we go through it.

When writing a speech, most speakers know what they want to discuss. A speaker interested in baking might want to discuss: "How to make the best cake on Earth!" But when the speech is written down it often proves to be a mish-mash of ideas that only sound ground-breaking, in the speaker's own head.

To begin with, when being written down the speaker's initial thoughts come out as a confusing scattering of ideas and concepts: "The best chocolate icing. Why chocolate is better than custard. The flooring in my kitchen. How to whisk faster than anyone else. Why you don't prove cakes. How the brewing of tea works. How to set the table. Oh yeah — how to make the sponge..."

When planning a speech in your head you might see your thoughts as a collection of vivid photographs. With each run through photographs are removed until the speech becomes simple and impactful. In contrast, when a speech is written on paper you will have flicks of colour, finger paint, glued on newspaper clippings, and crayon scribblings. To make things worse, even more distractions are thrown on with each review. When in this position the answer that a speaker usually arrives at is: "I need to make this more presentable, I should structure it."

What happens when the speaker structures their unrefined ideas? She is constantly hit with more ideas and remembers older ideas that she can 'link in'. Instead of tidying up the speech, the paint brushes come out again and swish a whole rainbow of paints all over the speech. Now what she has in front of her is so busy and splattered with ideas that no one will know what to make of it.

The speaker herself can understand her message because they're her ideas: "I'm explaining how to make the best cake on Earth. Why cakes are different from other baked goods. The science of food. My kitchen set-up. And obviously the perfect way to fold napkins and set up the table to eat your cake." The problem is, her audience won't have this knowledge.
"Did she tell us how to make the cake? I'm not sure if she did or not..."

Writing down all of your ideas can be helpful. I'm not telling you not to do that (it's writing out your whole speech that I dislike). What I want to reinforce is that ideas that have been jotted down will make sense to you, and only you. At this early stage, it's essential that you find and decide on your main message that your audience *will* understand. Out of all of your ideas:
1. Choose one.
2. Make it into a title.
3. Explain it.

"From my list of favourite things, I will give a speech on my favourite superhero. I can present it as, 'Why 'the White and Brown Bunny of Justice' is the best superhero'." This is where you might be tempted to try and explain three or more separate ideas: "I can also talk about my favourite film, my favourite day-out, my favourite flower..." Stick to one specific idea for your main message. Keep it simple for your audience.

The idea that you've chosen will be your main message. This is the running theme that will go through your speech like a spine. Every other idea, anecdote, and piece of evidence should support it.

Two possible objections to this method of keeping your speech simple are:

1. "I like to combine ideas together to be original, I would never pick one idea."

My brain is wired to combine ideas — that's how my creativity works. My answer to this objection is: timing. If you want to combine ideas: when you're starting to plan, look at all of the ideas you have written out, and combine two of them, or a selection into a new one. Then make this new idea your main message.

Combining ideas at the onset to make a main message, works. What doesn't work is selecting an idea, making it your main message and then when you've created your structure thinking: "I want to throw this idea in as well now, oh and this one, and this one." Haphazardly chucking in extra ideas will cause your speech to jump around all over the place and make it confusing.

2. "But what if other ideas need to be discussed?"

I think that there is a considerable difference between discussed and mentioned. If you're giving a speech on your idea that eating grass can make you live longer, it's okay to mention other methods that encourage longevity in relation to yours. For instance, why your idea of eating grass has shown more success than using steam. Your audience might think: "Oh I was thinking of trying steam, but look how much more effective consuming grass is." Or to mention that your grass diet is to be used in conjunction with exercise, "Well that makes sense." Mentioning these kinds of details act as evidence and disarm your potential opposition.

Although it's a benefit to mention competing ideas, resist going into too much detail and discussing them at length. If you're speaking about why eating grass makes you live longer: don't talk for ten minutes about the benefits of steam, or your audience will try steam instead! Giving too much positive attention to competing ideas plants the ideas in your audience's minds and allows them to grow.

Similarly, if you say that the grass diet is to be used in conjunction with exercise and you then speak for twenty minutes about the types of exercises you recommend, your audience might start to think: "I bet it's the exercise causing those results, not the grass." By going into discussions that are not concerning your main message, you will weaken your case, and usher your audiences towards your competitors.

"What should I do if I have been told that I must discuss in detail at least three ideas?"

When you have to talk about three ideas, create a unifying heading: a heading that encompasses all three ideas. Don't act like you're giving three separate speeches or a confusing assortment of ideas. Find a clear main message to serve as a heading for all three of these ideas to sit under.

Unifying headings work because they ensure you find a way to connect several ideas at the initial 'finding a main message' stage. If you were told to talk about the past, present, and future of your company, you could use 'time' as a unifying heading and share your opinion on: "How our company has and will continually improve over time." Find what links the three parts, make one main message and plan your structure accordingly.

In contrast, a heading that focuses on one idea when you have three to cover, is just not up to the job: it will confuse your audience. For instance if you use the heading, 'What our company used to be like', you will be forced to make the past your primary focus. This puts you in a difficult position when you want to discuss your other two ideas (the present and future). When you need to discuss several ideas: use a unifying heading.

Once you have a clear main message and have not tried to sneak in a bunch of other ideas that don't support it, there are some more considerations to keep your speech simple and easy to follow:

Would an audience of non-native English speakers and of a much older/younger age than you be able to follow along?

From the education system, I picked up two falsehoods. I had wrongly learnt that 'big' and archaic words impressed people and that referencing popular culture and internet memes was always a big hit.

When I joined Oxford Speakers I was 20 years old and the youngest person in the club. There were also guests and members from other countries — English was a second or third language for them. When I made cultural references that would have delighted a roomful of English teenagers, there was no reaction. None. And when I tried using a big or archaic word, half the audience would be confused by it — and being Oxford, the members who understood it were concerned that I hadn't used it in the right context!

I learnt to develop more universal ways to make people laugh (physical comedy, props, funny voices, wry humour, surprises, using contrast) and also how to communicate.

No matter what you're talking about, it's imperative that everyone in the audience will be able to understand your speech. This includes people who might not be in the same industry as you. Are you explaining what your industry's 'made up words' mean? Are you explaining what the acronyms you're using stand for? You might use a particular acronym or abbreviation every day without thinking about it, but other people won't have heard of it. And are you using real-life examples and situations that everyone can identify with?

You might feel like you're watering down your speech by making your speech understandable to everyone in the audience. But in reality, you're improving it. Why? Because instead of giving a speech that only a few people fully understand, you're giving one that everyone can comprehend and engage with. A speech is not a whitepaper, use words and examples that everyone can understand.

Does your speech tell a clear story?

Just because you have 100 examples doesn't mean you should use all of them. If examples get in the way of the flow of your speech: cut them out. Your speech needs a clear message, with a structure that is effortless to follow, like blooding flowing around the body. When rehearsing your speech if certain parts make you cringe or grimace because they block you and make you 'lose your rhythm' — remove them.

I have seen so many speakers who had an unjustified reluctance to edit their speech. If a part of your speech is doubling the length of your introduction, fix it. Speakers seem to have a fear that if they cut too much out of their speech, they will have nothing to say. That belief is not true, and most times, the speaker hasn't worked out how long their speech will take to deliver.

If you have to speak for 15 minutes, don't insist on using 20 minutes' worth of material. It's better to have twelve minutes' worth of material and to be able to expand on your points and deliver it effectively instead of rushing, stressing and not finishing your speech.

The next time you have finished writing your speech: be honest with yourself. Is there a clear main message? Will the entire audience understand it? Then, take out 20% of your material and see what happens. Take out everything that you added 'just because' or material that now seems unnecessary. You can always put it back if it doesn't work. But can you imagine how much easier it will be to understand if it does work?

Being told that your speech was complicated, is a criticism and not a compliment. But someone saying that it was simple to understand and easy to follow, is a compliment. In my mind simple means adoptable, usable. A complicated idea is one that someone is not ready for yet. Give your audience an idea that they can take out of the box and use straight away. It's far more useful than giving a box filled with random parts that require self-assembly without an instruction manual.

Start Being Taken Seriously

At some point in our lives, we came to the conclusion that being vague was more beneficial to us than being specific. Instead of telling a friend, "I will be there at 2," we learnt that we would have more freedom by saying, "I will probably be there around 2," and almost total freedom with the phrase, "I might be there sometime in the afternoon." This example is known as 'hedging' which is one of the methods we use to construct vague sentences.

We got into the habit of using ambiguous sentences because at times they helped us get out of trouble, or granted us freedom and so we assumed that they would continue to benefit us. The truth is that when you are doing public speaking, you get taken seriously by being specific. The speaker who doesn't tell you how much evidence they have, what their examples are, or who their stories are even about — will look incompetent and inexperienced.

Vagueness used to be so deeply ingrained in my own language that I struggled to identify it, let alone replace it. I had learnt growing up that a direct answer was one that was easier to be called: "Wrong." If I said that fifty times sixty-seven was 3000, I would be slapped with a: "Wrong!" However, I learnt that by being artfully vague and saying that it would result in a number over 3000, I would escape the objection. But this came at the cost of discomfort and the fear of being exposed. Saying, "3350" would have been an open and shut case (and yes, you just learnt some maths).

By moving on from the fear of being called "Wrong," and believing in myself, my knowledge, and my experiences as a human being: I learnt to become more comfortable being specific. Audiences feel in safe hands when you're being specific. Replacing vagueness with specifics empowers your speaking.

I will now give you a brief introduction to vague language so you can find it in your own speeches. Once you start looking for ambiguous expressions, you will become less comfortable using them. Every time you replace one of your vague sentences with a specific sentence: you will strengthen your speech, and will be taken more seriously.

When I talk about vague language, I am talking about words and phrases that are not specific and can mean anything. If someone says that they have, "A lot of experience," they are not declaring a specific amount of experience. "A lot of experience," can mean two hours to one person, but to another, it might mean two decades.

A more critical audience is more likely to assume the worst. This is why you're doing yourself a disservice by being vague. It's just like submitting a CV., unless you said that you have worked at a company in a specific role, for a set length of time — you're going to be scrutinised and seen as a weak candidate.

Being specific and truthful is better than resorting to vague language. For whatever reason, if you don't want to bring up the truth — why are you talking about that topic at all? If you feel embarrassed that you don't sell much, don't talk about selling — talk about something that you do well. It's a far better alternative than using vague language which will make you and your audience feel uncomfortable: "We make a lot of sales. Several people are interested in what we sell. Many customers buy from us — quite regularly." Please don't do this, avoid vague language.

Below, are sentences which utilise vague words and phrases such as 'many', 'countless', 'later', and 'thing'. After each sentence I have written what an audience will likely think:

"I know many people who work in television..."

So she knows a couple of people who work in television. They're probably interns...

"I can give you countless reasons why I'm the best at what I do." That's hard to believe if she can't even give us a handful.

"At age eight I was awful at sports. But later in life, I realised that I had a talent for long jump."
When? When she was nine? When she was twenty? Last week?

"I have this thing, which makes me want to jump out of bed every morning."
An alarm clock? A dog? A personal chef? High blood pressure?

In the above examples, the vague language made the audience cynical and suspicious about the speaker's credibility. Even worse than that, using vague language made what she was saying completely open to interpretation. Now watch what happens when I remove the vague phrases and replace them with specific statements:

"Four of my friends work in television. One is Charles, the host of 'Bring Your Cod It's Dancey-Dancey-Dancey Time' and the others are camera operators who I met on the film 'He's Board of You — a Chess Player's Search for Love'"
Oh my gosh, he has such amazing friends, that's my aunt's favourite TV show! And I saw that film at the cinema. How interesting. (Please note, if the above titles actually exist, it is coincidental.)

"I am going to give you two reasons why I am the best at what I do. Firstly, I have 2000 customers, which is the highest number of customers in the sushi-carrier-bag-hat market." (Once more, if this product exists, it's purely coincidental.) "Secondly on a five-star scale for satisfaction I have never received less than three stars from any of my 2000 customers."

She's the real deal. With evidence like that, she must be the best.

"At age eight I was awful at sports. But my sporting prowess developed a decade later. At 18, I realised that I had a talent for long jump."
Wow, what a difference ten years can make.

"I have such a strong inner-drive to be productive and to do as much as I possibly can in a day. My inner-drive makes me want to jump out of bed every morning."
I wish I had that kind of drive!

As you can see, using specific statements not only strengthened the speeches but also changed the reactions from the audience. Audiences are less inclined to be critical or to misinterpret you when you avoid vague language. Specific statements are also more engaging and stimulating than empty, obscure words.

To become a stronger speaker: get into the habit of giving specific examples and developing them instead of assuming that your audience will be able to 'get the idea'. Your example can be a personal anecdote — how you have done or been affected by what you are describing, or something you've researched.

If you are using imagery: a comparison, metaphor, simile, or even an imaginative example that's a bit ridiculous — give specific details and examples. They will make the imagery so much stronger. Instead of saying: "Public speaking has the same learning experience as driving. You get used to it. Anyway as I was saying," expand on your imagery with specifics and develop them: "Public speaking is like driving. You're probably going to be a bit apprehensive about even getting in the car and belting up. You might experience the same hesitancy to deliver your first speech. You're going to be confused by all the things to pay attention to — what's a biting point? Why do I have to look at 3 different mirrors, and over my shoulder? Will other drivers be able to tell that I'm a beginner? As a speaker you will have just as many questions: how to write a speech, where to look, how loud to speak, how to look like a competent speaker. But after a year of driving: apprehension and confusion won't even enter your mind anymore. The same holds true for speaking." Giving specific examples in your imagery and developing them will highlight that you have thought things through and you will be likelier to captivate your audience.

The last point I would like to address on vague language is, 'who' you are talking about. (Please note that I will not be using the word 'whom' in this book, as I'm not a Victorian). It's easy for a speaker to forget that her audience will not know who she is talking about unless she tells them.

A speaker should refrain from using 'he', 'she', 'they', 'we', 'us' without first declaring who they are referring to. I personally think that being 'mysterious' about who you are referring to is more likely to confuse an audience than to entertain them. Consider how you introduce your characters: "On my birthday he gave me a block of soap. It was a strange gift for him to bring me but I thanked him, and he smiled. He was the only boy who cared about hygiene as much as me. He was the best dog I had ever had."
As a stand out joke, it's amusing. However, if it's part of a speech, it's more likely to confuse everyone.

The funny story could instead introduce the audience to all of the characters straight away, give specific details, and still be surprising and funny. To do this, you could simply re-structure the story like this: "I have had many dogs. My favourite dog was a golden-doodle called Blondie. On my birthday, Blondie brought me a really strange gift. I thanked him for it — and he smiled. It was a block of soap! He was the best dog I had ever had. And the only boy who cared about hygiene as much as me."

Personally, I prefer the second version because as well as having two funny payoffs at the end, the audience understands who is involved in the story and gets to laugh along as the story develops. And because the members of the audience were picturing a Goldendoodle with an upbeat name from the beginning, they had more time to start liking and caring about him.

Another trap is when a speaker uses a vague word to describe a group such as 'people'. Any couple of individuals can be called 'people' — who specifically are you referring to, and where appropriate — how many are there in the group? You might have noticed that when I write, I do my best to avoid saying phrases along the lines of: "When someone gives a speech, people will usually listen to them." Instead, I endeavour to be more specific, by using the context of my subject matter: "When a speaker gives a speech, her audience will usually listen to her." This is a straightforward adjustment to make, but it enhances the clarity of your communication.

My hope is that you will start to recognise vague language in your speeches and will instead filter it out and find more specific statements to replace it with. Doing this will strengthen not only your argument but also your credibility.

Look Like a Pro

When you see a live performance you might hear one of the following statements:
"Thank you. Now, what else can I tell you..."
"Let me just check my notes..."
"Maybe I should adjust this microphone stand before my next bit..."

These statements are signs that a speaker has not rehearsed her segues — how to transition from section to section. This is the peril of 'performing off the page'. The speaker tweaked and changed each section of her speech, but she gave no thought to what wasn't in her script — how she could transition from story to story or interact with her environment.

Great storytelling is smooth and clearly takes you from place to place. If you were telling a fairy-tale you wouldn't deliver it like this: "There was this girl with blonde hair. What else can I tell you? Oh yeah, there was this abandoned house. Sorry — I need to check my notes. Inside she ate some porridge, sat in a chair. Excuse me, I'm on the wrong side of the stage. Slept in a bed. Oh and then these bears showed up...which reminds me thanks for having me, hit me up on social media, you can find me at..."

To look like a professional, you must devote time while rehearsing to plan your transitions. If you don't, when you perform your speech you will forget what to say and will feel bewildered when you have to improvise a segue.

Planned segues are unsung heroes of your speech. Their job is to make your speech flow smoothly and to guide your audience from section to section of your speech. The reason why I called them unsung heroes is because a well-planned segue should not bring attention to itself. The best commute is the one that is straightforward, fast, and requires little attention. When we experience such a travelling experience we can focus more on the place we've just been to and on our destination, than on how we're getting there.

A one-line segue can sometimes be enough to bridge your sections together:
"That was the initial inspiration for my new idea..."
"The following day..."
"Unexpectedly, things escalated beyond my wildest dreams..."

I believe that when you know your transitions, you won't need your notes anymore. Think about it. When telling a story, you might forget details, but you will almost always remember the beginning, middle, and end. But when telling a string of tales, you're pretty likely to forget entire stories unless they link together in a way which is clear to you. When you have mighty iron links in your mind, your sections are going to be much harder to misplace mentally. For strong links: the stories should ideally be related and build on each other.

Below is a basic outline of six points which can be fleshed out into six parts. Notice how the segues create a smooth transition between each part and how the parts unify into one story under the heading:

'Why playing with my friend's power saw meant I missed work yesterday':

"1. Yesterday I went to my friend's house before work, but he was still in the shower...
Transition — Because I got bored waiting, I looked around.
2. I found he had a brand new power-saw...
Transition — I was intrigued by it and plugged it in.
3. I didn't realise I was holding the blade, it cut my hand off...
Transition — I screamed so loudly that my friend ran downstairs.
4. My friend got me in the car and drove me to the hospital...

Transition — There was a lot of traffic, and as time was of the essence he took me to a robotics lab which was closer.

5. Scientists spent hours creating a robotic hand for me and sent me home...

Transition — I realised it was now 5:30 and I had missed work.

6. I was shocked that I had missed work by playing with my friend's power-saw...

Transition — But I couldn't help but laugh because...

Technology had cut my hand off and given me a new one, all in the same day."

Now try reading the above story without the transitions: notice how disjointed it becomes. Without the links, the sequential chain of events becomes a random mess. Trust me, you don't want your performance to be a random mess!

To truly maximise your transitions, you also need to plan how to get to the right place on stage at the right time. If your first story ended with you on the right side of the room, and you need to be centre stage for your next story — you need to rehearse the transition.

You might think it's cute or quirky to announce: "Ha! I need to be on the other side of the stage now." It isn't. To position yourself in the right place on stage, move there during your segue. If your segue line contains action, your movement will enhance your message:

"That was when I decided to go on a journey."

"I went to the doctors."

"The next day as I got through the front door..."

Utilising your segue line to get ready for the next story demonstrates control and forethought, instead of broadcasting that you are unprepared. You must eliminate cringe-filled moments which subtract from your message.

I cannot stress enough just how much transitions can make or break a performance. If you're unsure about whether you are utilising your transitions effectively — film yourself. Scrutinise the moments between your stories and actively work on them.

Plan your segues: when you do, you will stop looking inexperienced and instead look like a seasoned pro.

Is Public Speaking an Art?

The most obvious thought that might enter your mind in response to the title is: "Does it matter if public speaking is an art or not?" I think that thought is justified. I wanted to share my opinion on this subject because although it's unlikely to stand up against a mob of scholars and academics, it will help me to show you why I approach public speaking with clarity and explicitness in mind.

There always seems to be a debate over whether something should be considered an art or not. To speak frankly, I don't know much about art, art history, or theory. Therefore I am not going to present an iron-clad case for academics to smile and nod along to. Instead I, a lover of public speaking am going to present my somewhat controversial opinion that public speaking is *not* an art. Although public speaking undoubtedly has *artistic elements* and unlimited potential for creativity, the goal seems to be different from art. Art is open to interpretation while public speaking gives answers and solutions. Even if the answer takes the form of a specific question.

When I was younger, I used to believe that 'art' was an accurate portrayal of the world around us. After hours of doing still life drawings of fruit at school, I thought that if a picture looked exactly like a banana — it was art. Similarly, I thought that a play should feel like seeing real events unfold in front of me. It wasn't until I started to see art galleries, more independent drama productions, and performed improv that I learnt that something did not have to strive to be realistic to be seen as art.

The impression of art that I have been left with is that 'art' needs ambiguity. Artwork has a reputation for being subjective in nature. Art lovers seem to enjoy looking at work and taking their own meaning from it. This can be seen clearly in our media consumption as well. The observer doesn't have to care about the artist's intentions or motives while she reads a book, she can interpret it in any way she wants. A painting created to symbolise the artist's anxieties and insecurities could be interpreted as: 'The story of a lovely day at a farmyard.' In my view, art is asking the observer: "What does this mean to you?"

My approach towards public speaking is to share a clear message. Of course, audiences can take different lessons and meanings away from my speeches — but I always have a salient message. I am a live speaker who is telling you exactly what my message is. I do not want my speech to be 'open to interpretation' and for no one to understand my message. If someone leaves thinking: "I wonder what his message was?" I have failed. And this is why in my opinion, public speaking is not an art.

When I started giving speeches, I focused more on my own self-expression than my audience's experience. At that time I treated public speaking like an art. Looking back, if I wanted to be expressive for expressiveness alone, I could have just shot a video of myself. However, I grew to realise that I needed to pay much more attention to my audience and what they wanted.

What my audiences wanted was to hear my unique perspective on things, to hear my ideas, and to apply them to similar situations and problems that they might be experiencing. I found that with a clear speech structure, actively avoiding ambiguity by focusing on explicit sentences and messages, audiences began to take me more seriously and tried to apply my ideas to their lives.

When you think of art — you think of emotion. This connection apparently throws a spanner in the works for my view on public speaking because I firmly believe in using feelings and inspiring my audiences to experience positive emotions. The reason why I think my conclusion still survives this is that I believe in linking the positive feelings with your words and messages in speeches. Instead of giving a primal roar and letting the emotion be interpreted in fifty different ways: I use emotions to bring life to my words and to reinforce my message.

As human beings we are sensitive to the feelings of others. This means that when we speak, we need to carefully consider our emotions because our audience will pick them up. As we can't filter out emotion and only focus on the words (like when we email each other), we need to be aware of our emotions so that they bring life to our words instead of giving them an additional, unintended meaning.

Feelings do not have to bring in ambiguity or hidden meaning, they can just highlight what you're saying and demonstrate that what you're saying works. If you said: "Buy this happiness pill, it really works," with a happy demeanour your emotions are not displaying a hidden meaning, they're serving as additional evidence. When I give a speech about public speaking being fun, my positive feelings reinforce that what I'm saying is true — because to me it is true!

By saying that public speaking is not an art I am not claiming that public speaking is not creative. This is partly because I think that creativity is not exclusive to artistic pursuits. You can use creativity in anything you do, from filing your expenses to stocking a fridge. Public speaking offers a lot of opportunities to be creative and strongly benefits from creativity. However, the goal when using creativity in public speaking should be to make your message clearer to your audience and not to introduce hidden meanings.

A speech with an explicit message can always be improved. When you understand what a speech is communicating, you can find how to deliver that message more effectively or visually. On the other hand, if you see a painting with an ambiguous message, it's challenging to offer improvements because it is unclear what the artist was trying to communicate. An 'improvement' could actually weaken the effectiveness of the painting unless you knew what the artist's intentions were. A speech must be clear with an explicit message.

When you start to think of public speaking as different from art, you can begin to understand why it thrives with clarity.

An Emotional Journey

A great speech not only has a structure that appeals to minds but also one that resonates with audiences' hearts. I want to be made to feel different emotions during a speech and to feel better at the end than I did at the beginning. I want to put my heart in safe hands and for my emotions to be taken on a ride.

I once read an idea from Taoist philosophy that sometimes you need to go down to go up, and vice versa. I firmly believe that this idea applies to an audience's emotions. If you tell an audience a sad story, then another tragic story, and then another one — the impact will continually soften. Not because the audience no longer cares, but because their emotional state can't go much lower.

If you told some jokes and positive stories and then a sad story — it will have a considerable impact because your audience has a higher emotional height to fall from. You might be wondering whether this idea works the other way round, whether jokes and positive stories can be made funnier by being preceded by a serious topic. I believe so, based on my own experience and observations. When you have had to watch something sad or severe, doesn't it feel like such a relief when you're allowed to laugh?

For me, the master of mixing opposite emotions in storytelling is Richard Curtis. I am a fan of his, and I always admire how he can combine laugh out loud comedy with such heavy and heartfelt moments. If you watch his comedy films closely: you will get an idea of how to create a compelling emotional journey.

I was discussing using humour in serious speeches with my friend Mary Robson (who is the backbone of Oxford Speaker's club and has always kept it running at such a high standard), and she told me about a time when using contrasting emotions hadn't worked. During one speech she saw: a speaker had included so many jokes that when he got to the serious moment, people laughed. I have also seen it (and earlier in my speaking journey, even experienced it), where a speaker was very jokey and delivered a serious line out of nowhere without changing his delivery, and the audience laughed. You might have been imagining this scenario, and so I want to share my advice to stop it from happening.

In an emotional journey where you are navigating your audience between two opposite emotions: there needs to be a crystal clear moment of transition. In films, they would usually utilise a hard-hitting surprise, a long pause, and then a reversal in tone.

This is how a film could transition from a positive angle to a negative one:
Near the end of the film, the high-school student protagonist would have finally won the respect of her mean maths teacher. Feel good music would start to play. In her hand would be her maths test with a big, red A+ written on it (which had taken the entire film and several montages for her to achieve). We feel so uplifted and know she's finally going to go on a date that night with her crush (who she had been shying away from until she had a moment of self-realisation). We see her skipping along outside, she drops her glasses case, bends over to pick it up
BAM!
She's hit by a car.

There's a long pause in complete silence.

You then see the driver get out of the car with a look of horror on his face and other concerned citizens swarm around the front of the car. The screen fades to black. And suddenly you hear solemn music and are shown a funeral.

The transition was planned so well, you would have to be unfeeling for your emotions not to change.

(Please note, safe driving is very important to me. If you drive, please obey the speed limit, give pedestrians and bikes enough room. And when in doubt whether you're up to driving: don't drive.)

Back to positivity-land everyone! As I have demonstrated, an effective transition can ensure that going from happy and upbeat, to sad and severe can be effective. I loved the upbeat tone of the story and how it conformed to the archetype of a high school-based comedy. The positive vibes meant that I couldn't help but care about the character because *her story made me feel good* and I had invested my emotions in it. It's because I had freely handed over my emotions that I was stung by the dark turn.

If you want to change the emotional tone of a story: you need a definite moment where things change. The pause at this moment must be long enough for your audience to catch up mentally and emotionally. When I was less experienced, I wasn't able to change the emotion in the room from happy to solemn because I rushed the transition. After the pause you must endeavour to completely change the tone of the story with your voice and physicality — it must be a stark contrast. Take your time with your transitions and make it clear that the mood of your speech has changed.

"What if I don't want to include anything sad in my speech? Can I still take my audience on an emotional journey?"

You definitely can. In fact, I think it's not the right tack to include a 'sad' bit in your speech, 'just because'. If you experienced a difficult time in your life or have an emotionally powerful example that supports your speech and message: use it. But don't try to invent a sad story or use one that has no relation to your message. Instead, make your audience feel something else. For instance, you could include a story filled with tension and suspense and then let your audience laugh and relax by following it up with a funny and relieving example. Or a funny story could suddenly become thrilling and have everyone on the edge of their seat.

I now want to give you a basic example of how an emotional journey can be planned for a speech. In the table below I wrote down how I want my audience to feel as my speech progresses. I want to ensure that there is variation so my audience will leave feeling uplifted and inspired. It's an example of an emotional journey that doesn't use any tearful examples or stories. Instead, it's based on the standard speech style: "I have a main message that will help you solve a problem you have."

Place In the speech	Audience's Mood
Beginning	Interested
Paragraph 1	Intrigued
Paragraph 2	Happy
Paragraph 3	Empathetic and reflective
Paragraph 4	Optimistic
Conclusion	Empowered
Ending	Inspired and uplifted

- Your first line is your chance to capture your audience's interest. By having a strong opening, communicating your main message, and briefly explaining how you are going to demonstrate your main message, (with perhaps a bit of suspense for good measure) your audience will become intrigued.

- With some humorous anecdotes and colourful examples: your audience will laugh and feel happy.

- When you discuss the problem and go into full detail about how the problem has affected you and the difficulties that everyone in the room has faced or might be facing, the mood will change. The room will become quieter, and your audience will empathise and become reflective.

- By reassuring everyone: "It's okay, my main message is the solution to this problem," you can provide examples of how your main message has helped people solve the problem. Your audience will become optimistic and think that maybe the solution could solve the problem for them too.

- With a conclusion that puts the power in the audience's hands: "If you use my main message, you can solve this problem for yourselves," your audience will become empowered.

- Your audience will then leave feeling uplifted because they have one less problem to worry about and empowered because they now have the knowledge to solve a problem that they couldn't have answered before.

I want to mention that the course of the emotional journey is different if you want to inspire an audience and not just uplift them. My belief is that to inspire an audience: you need to talk about the problem.

Glossing over or making fun of a problem can uplift an audience, but it won't inspire them. If you build to a point in your speech where you dig down deep into the problem and how it has affected you and the audience, your solution will not only uplift everyone — it will inspire people to solve the problem themselves or not to be as intimidated by it.

My advice is not to be afraid of being honest about a problem or expressing your pain. When I see speeches by people who have lived through physical or emotional injuries: I want them to make me understand and to feel their pain. What was it like: mentally, physically, and emotionally? Only then can I fully appreciate how powerful their message for dealing with it must be.

I believe that there are times when you must take your audience to hell in order to take them to heaven. After your audience feels like they have experienced your pain and sees this gigantic problem, they're going to look to you to guide them through it. That's your chance to inspire them.

The emotional journey always needs at least some variation — otherwise, the ride will stop, and people's feelings won't move. By considering how your speech will make your audience feel, you can plot the emotional course of your audience's experience.

When creating an emotional journey: make sure that your audience will experience more than one feeling based on what you present and speak about. If you are going between opposite emotions, practise your transition. Clearly plot out where you want to navigate your audience to on your shared emotional journey and how you will guide them there.

Preparations

"How on Earth Am I Meant to Practise?"

Public speaking states in its name that you need an audience to do it. However do not fear, because you do not need to hire a test audience. In fact you probably won't need to spend any money. What you will need to invest is time.

I will give you some guidelines to help you know what to focus on while practising to empower your speech. In this essay let's pretend that you have no budget, no empty theatre, and you have just finished writing your speech. When you hear people talking about a rehearsal you might start imagining practising on stage with a tech crew, a director, and others to assist you. If you have the budget for that — fantastic. Otherwise let's start simple with what you can do to practise at home.

If you're someone who is more comfortable writing out your entire speech first — print it out. Once it's printed, read it through. Then stand up and read it through again. If any lines don't sound right (you're going to find a fair few) either edit or delete them. Having your speech in your hand and then saying it, is a much better step towards learning how to present it than just staring at your computer screen. The goal is to put the paper down as quickly as possible (within five minutes if you're brave enough). Don't worry about learning your speech word for word. Instead, understand how your speech flows and memorise the key moments of your speech.

Alternatively, if you dislike writing out your entire speech and prefer to stick to the essentials (just like me): start verbalising. Instead of thinking: "Oh, I'll think of it when the time comes," start speaking now. If you do this, you'll run into any obvious pitfalls while you're at home. Then when it's time to deliver your speech, you will be able to avoid drifting between ideas or fumbling over your words. Make sure to organise your thoughts into a clear structure. Then repeat your speech until it sounds natural and your speech flows.

There is more to plan than just what you're going to say. Instead of spending your entire practice session planning: give yourself a time limit and time your speech while you deliver it from start to finish. Continually repeat your speech. With each repetition you can focus on a different area to improve it. For instance:

1) Give your speech while focusing on your breathing. Ensure you have enough breath to carry your words. Have you left enough time to breathe?

2) Think about your energy levels and expressiveness. How will they affect your audience? Will they wake-up an audience and keep them engaged?

3) Choreograph movements:
   - When does it make sense to move?
   - Where do you want to move to?
   - What motivation will you use to get back to the centre of the speaking area?
   - Choreograph how you will enter the speaking area and start your speech, and how you will end your speech and leave the speaking area.

4) Consider what gestures you're going to use. Try to communicate what you're saying with your hands and body.

5) Make yourself feel more powerful while you speak. Speak slower, hold your ground on stage and project your voice. Imagine yourself as a tiger or a proud lion. Feel in charge of your speaking area. It's yours!

6) Add more love to your speech. Imagine an audience and focus on how what you're saying is going to benefit them, because you care about your audience and want each person to succeed.

After this many repetitions, your speech will probably feel like it's of a good standard. Remember to check how long it took you to speak each time and to remove some content if it takes some pressure off of you.

Once you are satisfied with your speech: you can start rehearsing. This is where you try to deliver your speech in a similar way each time, so you can remember it and how it flows. When you rehearse, you can still make changes, but at this stage, you should feel quite happy with your speech. If you feel unhappy with it: be honest with yourself and find out why you're dissatisfied. If you need to: film yourself and watch it back or ask for help. It's never wrong to ask for help. Then make changes and continue to run through your speech until you are satisfied.

Once you are satisfied, it's time to transition into dress rehearsals.

If it's physically possible, try to rehearse in a space that is of a similar size to where you will be speaking. If that isn't possible: make as much room as you can (or go outside). This way, when you go to the real speaking area you will be prepared to fill the space. You just need a designated area to speak in and something to represent your audience (even if it's a wall).

Up to this point, you will probably have been saying to yourself: "Oh and that's when I'll use this prop," if you haven't already, get your props out. The problem with 'imaginary props' is that they can appear and disappear at will. When using real props, you need to constantly think about when you're going to get them and where you will put them once you're finished with them. You need your physical props to work these things out fully.

Set up your speaking area so it's the same as it will be on the night, with your props and any decorations you might have planned. If you need to use a table to put your props on, consider bringing a tablecloth for it. Also think of ways that you can hide your props from your audience until you need them (unless you want them to be visible, for dramatic effect).

Before you start your dress rehearsals, you need to know how you'll be dressed (obviously). It's helpful to wear the clothes you plan on wearing when you give your speech. You need to ensure that you are familiar with how you need to stand and walk in your shoes (this isn't a metaphor, I mean your literal shoes) and if anything you're wearing is going to restrict your movement. Otherwise, it will come as quite a surprise when you give your speech.

Consider your items of jewellery and accessories — will they make noise and will they tempt you to fiddle? If yes, go without them. You can also practise being able to take a prop smoothly out of your pocket without fumbling, and what movements complement the clothes you're wearing.

Now that you know your speech, what you're going to do, what props you will use and what you're going to wear, you are ready for dress rehearsals. If you want to set-up a camera to see how your speech looks, set-up a tripod or position your phone/camera on a surface (and don't be a doughnut like I have been many times before — press the record button). Also if you want to invite your partner or friend to watch it, you can.

Being able to focus on your audience and make eye contact with them when you give your speech will significantly raise their opinion of you as a speaker. For this reason, your objective while doing your dress rehearsals is to focus on your audience.

When rehearsing you need to ensure that you are giving enough attention to each place where people will be sitting. Imagine that your audience is in front of you while you speak. To help with this: set-up visual markers in your rehearsal space for you to focus on.

A visual marker can be anything, but I prefer using things that have eyes to look at. You can use pictures from magazines, figurines, soft toys, or if you some lying around — real people! These markers will represent your audience. If you are speaking in a rectangular room, put a visual marker on the left, in the centre, and on the right.

You have two tasks to rehearse when looking at your visual markers: 1) Make eye contact. Do this by ensuring that you don't just look straight forwards all the time. Look to your left and to your right. The movement from left to right is often slow so you can give each pair of eyes some attention as you work your way towards your visual marker in the centre and then as you slowly look towards the one on the right.

2) Observe and interact with your audience. Pay attention to how your audience is reacting to you and be prepared to change your energy based on how they are reacting.

Assuming you are using lifeless visual markers (or plants) imagine that an audience member looks bored (or yawning, on their phone, sleeping). You can now focus on getting their interest back. By practising this: you will be prepared for if it happens on the day. If an audience member stops paying attention, you won't take it personally because you would have prepared for it and will know what to do. Similarly, you can also try to ad-lib a line based on your observations of the audience. For instance: "I saw you strongly agreed with that point. Do you have experience with this problem?"

By this point, you will have practised your speech far more thoroughly than most other speakers. Your rehearsal process will likely differ to mine as you discover what things work for you.

I have given you a head-start, but to develop your own rehearsal process, you need to be honest with yourself. What things in public speaking are most important to you? And what about yourself do you most want to get across when you speak? By answering these questions honestly, you will start to think of extra elements that you want to practise before presenting your speech.

I want to commend you on taking practising seriously. Most speakers seem to spend most of their time constructing their speech and then the rest just reading it out loud. By practising thoroughly, you will truly empower your speeches.

Divorce Your Notes

In my last year of 6th form I took part in our drama class' Christmas pantomime. There were five of us performing a short comedy version of Charles Dickens' 'A Christmas Carol'. As it was just for fun (and not for a grade — thank goodness), we had little time to prepare it. To compensate for this, our drama teacher told us to read off the scripts when we performed.

I used to struggle when I read things out loud while performing, it was always a considerable trial to find my place when I looked back down at the script. As I expected, during the pantomime — I lost my place. Everyone watching had to wait while I spent ages looking to find which line we had got to. I could tell that the rest of the cast were a bit annoyed... I can't say that I blame them because I lost my place at least five times.

I made a joke of continually losing my place, and the audience was entertained by my antics — but I wasn't happy. I felt like I had let not only the other actors down, but the audience down. I knew that their experience would have been so much better if I wasn't using notes. That was the moment when I decided not to be dependent on notes. I wanted a divorce!

Not using notes is something that I have a reputation for. Whenever a lectern is present in the speaking area, the first thing I do is remove it. Over the years I have received a lot of questions about how I remember what I'm going to say or how to start speaking without notes. I am going to debunk a few myths and cover some common questions about my process.

"Do you not find it useful to write things down?"

I find it very useful to write things down, that's why you're reading this right now! Writing down my ideas has always been helpful to me. And having a lot of writing behind me really helps with efficient speech preparation (see '*How Writing Can Help Your Public Speaking*').

In day to day life, I write down details and exact quotes and phrasings that I know that I will forget. When I'm doing public speaking coaching, taking notes is useful because of times when I need to revisit ideas that happened to come up in conversation — a few weeks ago.

I like to write in notebooks when I'm thinking about things, my phone for key ideas (and when I'm out), and plain paper and coloured pens when working on other people's speeches. If I want to regularly refer to something I will likely type it up and then print it out.

Do you meditate?

The short answer is — no. I used to meditate as a teenager, and I took a Tai Chi course for a year or so. I keep hearing about lots of reasons to meditate, but it's something I still haven't got around to. However, I find running and going for walks helps me to 'get in the zone'. If I need to come up with ideas doing something that gets me moving seems to facilitate the thought process. If you're struggling to find an idea: go for a walk.

Do you use a memory system or technique?

I find memory systems fascinating. I am always flabbergasted when I see what incredible feats memory champions can pull off. I don't actively use a memory system, but I learnt about memory while studying for my psychology degree and have read about a fair few memorisation techniques. I have cherry-picked a few techniques and applied them to my life.

Two of the biggest takeaways I received from learning about memory have been to use my imagination and to engage all of my senses when memorising and recalling. I always recommend to speakers — pick up a book on memory! Learning more about how our memory works will change how you present your speeches. After all, we want our speeches to be as memorable as possible.

"You might be lucky enough to speak without notes, but I don't think I ever can..."

I can speak without notes because I forbid myself from using them. I had a feeling in the back of my mind that if I did some speeches with notes, it would be a challenge to give them up. To speak without notes: you have to make a commitment to yourself and then stick with it. It's not always going to be easy. You might experience times where you think: "There's way too much to remember, and I've only had five minutes to practise in my head, I wish I could use notes." By not giving in during these times, you will grow. The only way to speak without notes is to start. Just start. You will amaze yourself and others.

By not using notes you will start experimenting with ways to make things easier for yourself. Firstly, you're going to want to give yourself less to remember. A frequent public speaking mistake is when a speaker puts way too many details into her speech, causing her to frequently refer to her notes — which in turn means she has to rush. If there's too much content for the speaker to remember then there's definitely way too much for an audience to retain. Ensuring you can speak from memory is an excellent way to edit your speech so that it's more streamlined and easier for you and an audience to digest.

Instead of using notes — use your creativity. In acting it's a lot easier to remember your lines because you have cues. One actor says a line: "Good heavens, the fiend has a baking tray!" That line will cue you to say your line:

"Not if my diamond encrusted rolling pin has anything to say about it." If it helps, you can always give yourself cues in your speech. You can have a costume change (and truly earn my respect) which will help you transition into the next part of your speech, use a prop to trigger your memory or even pictures.

One of the more subtle ways I like to organise cues is by utilising stage positioning. If you know that you have to be in a certain place on stage when you deliver a specific line or section, it will make your speech a lot easier to remember. If you plan on standing still and delivering a speech, it's going to be tricky to remember everything. However, if you have planned your movements, you will know: "I stand here and talk about the cheese shop story. Then I walk over to there and talk about the history of cheese rolling. I then sit down in the chair to discuss how I was disqualified from all cheese related sports. Then I stand and whip off my coat, revealing my Camembert t-shirt and exclaim how I created my own cheese Olympics. I then walk to the front of the stage and end with: "Can you smell that? I am the future of cheese!"

"What are the advantages of not using notes?"

When I see someone using notes, it's like they're trying to manage an energetic and inquisitive dog while delivering a speech. The speaker is continually pulled away mid-sentence, keeps having to look away from the audience to pay attention to her notes, she can't move across the stage without being pulled back, and has to devote her hands and attention to her notes. If you can imagine giving a speech while having to look after an unruly four-legged-friend, that added difficulty is what your notes are giving you: mentally, physically, and emotionally without you realising. Without your notes, you can give the audience your full attention, use the stage and your body, and express yourself fully.

Those were my answers to some of the most common queries that I have received concerning my lack of notes. My advice to you is to promise yourself that you will stop using them. If you never stop using them, you will never start learning how to manage without them. It's incredible how much your speaking will develop once you divorce your notes.

Learn a Speech — Fast

One of the most common questions from new speakers is, "How do you memorise a speech?" The assumption is that you type up a speech and then read it out word for word as if you had an auto-cue. So when a speaker is told to speak without their printed speech in front of them, confusion occurs.

My solution to remembering a speech is to memorise your key points, and how your speech flows. It's usually better if you don't remember a speech word for word.

To learn a speech that you've written out, have it in front of you and start by highlighting the key points. These include: your main message, your introduction, the beginnings of your sections, your examples and your conclusion. Once you have highlighted these key points, you will realise that there is a lot less to remember than you initially thought. The plan is to polish these key parts while you practise and to let the rest of your speech rewrite itself through verbal practice.

When you have remembered your key points, (or have them on a cheat-sheet) time yourself and try to give your speech. You will notice that you can 'fill in the gaps' in a natural way. With each repetition, all you need to do is re-fill the gaps in a similar way to how you did it the previous times. After you have continually re-filled the gaps, your speech will sound natural to an audience and be easy for you to deliver. Most importantly — you won't need notes because you will be used to speaking from point to point.

An advantage of only memorising the key points and filling in the gaps is that you have more flexibility and you won't need to stress about being wordperfect. If you forget the odd line, no one will know but you. Whereas if you've memorised a speech word for word, if you forget one line, you'll lose your cue and you can become lost, "What on Earth do I say now?"

A second advantage is that you will be able to re-order or even remove sections of your speech while delivering it (which is invaluable if you become short on time). A speech that you can edit while speaking has what I call a 'floating structure'. As long as your main message is clear and running through your speech, you're free to move your sections. If you tried to edit a speech that was memorised word for word while speaking, it would take a considerable amount of mental effort!

If you want to blow the word for word memorisers out of the water: know your subject. Know it inside and out. If you planned a speech on how to make a toaster it could go down in one of two ways:

1. If you knew nothing about toasters but did a quick web-search and read about the assembly process: you would need to memorise what you found. You would have no idea what details were essential or even right.
2. Alternatively, if you had made some toasters before, often read around the subject and loved fixing them: you could easily describe the process with no script. When you know your subject, having some freedom in your structure will allow you to demonstrate this.

Freedom in your speech allows you to demonstrate experience because you can go into more detail when your audience is intrigued. If you give an example that gets the room buzzing, you might know a similar one to follow up with that you hadn't planned on sharing. If you had memorised your speech word for word, you would miss out on these kinds of opportunities. By allowing yourself some freedom: you can adjust your speech to your audience (for more on this subject, see '*Keep Your Speech Fresh*').

Fear not, for you do not need to memorise your speech word for word. Remember your key points and verbally fill in the gaps. By having more freedom in your speech: you will be able to survive mistakes, adapt to your audience and have more opportunities to demonstrate your expertise. Learning a speech doesn't have to be difficult or time consuming.

Always Do This Before You Speak

One of the most frequent errors that speakers make is not speaking to time. This is a mistake that both beginners and more experienced speakers make. Not speaking to time looks amateurish and it creates stress for the event organisers and ultimately annoys the audience. Timing your presentation and keeping to time is a sure-fire way to make you look like a pro.

The problem with both speakers and performers is that they only think about events from their own point of view. They think it's okay to go over time because they're enjoying it and their audience aren't protesting. What they fail to realise is that their tardiness is creating stress and work for the event organiser.

When you speak over time, there can be many repercussions. The event organiser could be panicked because the venue might only be booked until a specific time, agenda items might need to be moved about, and other speakers might have to miss out on some of their speaking time because you selfishly went over.

At many of the customer events which I helped organise, if a speaker went over time — a number of our attendees wouldn't stay until the end. They would leave when the agenda said the event would finish. By speaking over your allotted time you could prevent another speaker from even having an audience! Why would an event organiser want to recommend you or hire you again after causing her so much work? Whereas, if you speak to time and cause no problems — you will be an event organiser's dream.

I want to explain further why it's not a good idea to speak over your allotted time or too much under time:

"Oops, it appears that I've gone over by fifteen minutes..."

"Oh that's just Bob — he always goes over time..."

"I'm sorry everyone, we've run over so lunch will be a bit later today..."

"Hi to everyone who is still here. Sorry that we're running later than advertised..."

I have heard these phrases at many events. A few speakers will usually speak well beyond their designated time, and as a result, the entire event suffers. Audience members will feel antsy after listening to such a needlessly long presentation. Event organisers will be stressed about how they can make the time-up and still finish on time. Everyone will be annoyed at having a delayed/shorter lunch break. It's not worth going over time.

Speaking under-time can cause problems too. You might not always be required to speak for the full time-slot, but there will be times when you will be expected to. If you are asked to deliver a thirty-minute presentation — ensure you can present for thirty minutes (duh). Notice I did not say you need thirty minutes of content, you just need to be able to present for thirty minutes. If you have twenty-five minutes' worth of content, by using pauses, audience interaction, props and being expressive, you will fill the time. If you notice yourself speaking a lot faster than in rehearsal, slow down and take your time. It's not a race.

I warn you not to plan a twenty-minute presentation and to assume that you can fill the last ten minutes with questions and answers. There are three main reasons not to do this:

1) The tactic is transparent and clearly shows the event organiser that you were not prepared to speak for the full time.

2) At a lot of Q & As, very few questions (if any) are asked. If you have nothing else to say, you might just end your time on stage with a long silence where no one says anything.

3) Audience members are unlikely to ask you the questions that you want to answer. They might ask you about how you style your hair,

what you think of a competitor's ideas, or give you a long and complicated question that needs to be repeated five times.

The information that you want to get across to your audience has to be in your presentation. Q & As are just too unreliable to be used as a diving board for the key points that you forgot to tackle in your speech. They should be reserved for clarification, not explanation. Ensure you can fill the time you've been set.

Speaking to time will feel uncomfortable at first, but it's a skill that you will learn. It's crucial for me to mention two time-related issues that you might experience while learning to speak to time.

The first issue is that it takes speakers a fair bit of practise until they can accurately estimate how much material they can cover in a set amount of time. When you are new to public speaking, it's easy to go overboard and prepare too much material for your speech. After giving many speeches: you will come to realise how much content you can realistically cover in the time you've been set.

The second issue is that your perception of time on stage might differ from how you experienced time while practising your speech at home. On stage, time might go a lot faster, or slower. Be aware of any difference in time perception that you experience and bear it in mind during the construction of your speeches and during rehearsals.

When you rehearse, you should always time yourself. As soon as you begin practising: start the timer and then don't stop it until you have finished the presentation (no matter how long that takes). You will quickly find that how long you think a presentation will take will be very different from how long it will actually take. The reason I said not to stop timing is because you won't be able to stop or reset the clock when you present your speech. If you make a mistake: recover and carry on.

When you rehearse, and the timer reveals that you spoke under-time do not be in a rush to quickly add more content. Instead run through your speech again, except this time focus on speaking at a slower pace and allowing time to pause and most importantly — breathe. When a speaker seems to burn through content: it's usually because she's racing through her speech and then left with several minutes to fill but nothing to say.

If the timer is showing that you are speaking over time, don't panic. What often happens is that where you don't know your speech well enough, you have to stop and remember what comes next, or repeat a section. This can make you go over time in rehearsal. However, if you get through your speech without needing to stop and remember or repeat a section, and you're still going over time: you have too much content.

When you have too much content: look at your speech structure honestly. What parts could you delete or save for another speech? Are there sections that are not about or supporting your main message? There will likely be quite a few sections to delete.

Remove content until you can give your speech at a steady pace without rushing. If you detect that you are still rushing — remove some more. To feel powerful while giving your speech, you must be able to deliver your speech at a pace that you are comfortable with, where you can pause for effect and express yourself fully.

When you get to the stage that you can give your speech to time in rehearsal, you need to be honest with yourself:

1. Did you allow for time to set everything up?
2. Did you leave pauses for when your audience will interact with you: for laughter, shock and surprise, and for when you've asked them to do something, or for spontaneous applause?
3. Do you have sections that can be removed or skipped over at a moment's notice if it looks like you will overrun?
4. Do you have some extra evidence or supportive anecdotes that you can bring in in case you race through your presentation?

I would not expect you to have thought about making allowances for the above things. However, I would recommend doing so. When you present your speech: you don't know what's going to happen. When you give your speech at home you are speaking under perfect test conditions, the real world isn't like that, and so it's smart to make allowances.

When you go to give your speech: don't keep time in your head. After doing all of this work to speak to time, don't assume that you can adequately judge the time you've been speaking in your head (sorry, suprachiasmatic nucleus).

The most obvious way to keep time is to check your watch or your phone — but this can look like you've somewhere better to be. Instead, find more discreet ways of timing yourself. I sometimes set my phone to vibrate twice in my pocket when I have a few minutes left, my audience can't hear it, but I will know to draw things to a close. My favourite method is to conceal a clock on stage. All you need to do is hide a clock or phone somewhere visible to you but out of your audience's line of sight. For instance, behind a sign or banner. When in doubt you can always ask the event organiser for a discreet five-minute warning signal if there is no clock in the room. After all, you're a speaker and not a human clock.

Remember that speaking to time is essential because it will help you to speak powerfully and expressively without causing stress and extra work for event organisers. When you get the hang of speaking to time: you will be their dream speaker. And you will get to enjoy your speech without rushing or running out of content. Before you speak: Always set a timer.

The Breath of a Mighty Speaker

Growing up I suffered from asthma, and even now I have to pay attention to my breathing. For people without breathing difficulties, it must be pretty difficult to imagine what it's like. Breathing is meant to be something that we do without thinking. When I was young, there were times when I was mentally exhausted from having to think about my breathing so much. It hurt to breathe, and it was a struggle. I still experience pain when I breathe.

I always like to see an upside to things. With asthma I have to be honest — it was challenging to find one other than it forcing me to stay clear of smoke and rooms engulfed in a cloud of deodorant. That was until I noticed that speakers without asthma struggled with their breathing. I know — how ironic.

I am constantly alerted to whether I am breathing enough and how I am breathing. But when I talk to other speakers about their breathing, I often hear a phrase that is alien to me: "Oh, I forgot about my breathing." I'm not judgemental, if I didn't have asthma I would probably have never paid attention to my breathing either. But because I've had to, I can recognise when other speakers aren't breathing enough.

Why is breathing important in speaking? In my experience, if you want to be louder and to project more, you need to turn your attention to your breathing. Your breath supports your words. Breathing is what will bring life and power to your vocals.

I am not going to teach you how to breathe. Mainly because I don't want to be sued by someone reading this who tried it and somehow ended up with a screwdriver up his nose. If you want to learn to breathe like I do on stage: learn about the role of the diaphragm in breathing, and learn to use it. It took me some time to learn a new way to breathe, but it was a bit easier for me than most because I could use my pain while breathing as feedback to feel what was happening with my breath (see — an upside). I strongly recommend looking into using the diaphragm when breathing and making it a habit for when you speak.

One exercise I would like to give you is this: Pick up a book and read a paragraph out loud. While you do this, pay attention to your breathing. Find out: When do you breathe? And how much do you breathe in?

A common problem I see is that speakers do not give themselves enough time to breathe. They rush through their speeches with no breath to carry their words, because they don't let themselves stop. And then. Breathe. Speaking is not a race!

I also notice that when people speak off the cuff, in new situations, or to strangers they can feel pressured to rush, and so they restrict their breathing. You are important, and you always deserve the time to compose yourself and to breathe. The small change of giving yourself time to breathe will empower your voice with the roar of a lion.

Make your voice mighty by giving it plenty of breath.

Channelling Your Energy

I talk a lot about 'energy'. The energy we have as speakers and the energy we use to uplift others. What can be overlooked is how we channel our energy into our words.

The most common misconception is that to speak energetically means to speak rapidly. Of course you'll come across as lively and energetic if you quickly blurt your words out. But jabbering at that speed makes it difficult for an audience to understand you: "Hi everyone my name's Johnny and I like to speak very-very quickly without taking a gap for air and I speak at this rapid pace all the time and what makes it even harder to understand me is that I speak with a very thick accent, and I sometimes am making the mistakes with my grammar, and I feel like I have to speak quickly in order to show you that I am an enthusiastic person who is passionate about this subject."

I want you to keep that lively energy but to channel it into your words in other ways. To achieve this: learn to speak slower. What I discovered when I learnt acting was that on stage what you say and what you do has to be bigger and slower. You can't effectively control your words and make them bigger until you can manage your rate of delivery.

The first exercise I suggest to find the right rate of delivery for you to speak at is to pick up a book and to record yourself reading it out loud. At the end of every line: slow down your speed. Keep doing this until you are speaking painfully slowly. Then gradually increase your speed after each line. Listen to your recording and look for a rate which is slower than your average 'conversational' speed where you are clearly pronouncing each word. Practise speaking at this speed.

It will be challenging at first to speak at a speed which is slower than you're used to, but with practice you will use it in speeches without even thinking about it. When you feel like you've become comfortable with this new speed start playing with pauses.

A pause is not just there for when you forget what to say. A pause can change the feeling of a sentence and can create tension. Try short pauses, long pauses, and extra-long pauses. See what happens when you put them in different places. What you will find is that you can give sentences new meanings and feelings depending on where the pauses go:

"You really are one of the best in England," can become:
"You really are... one of the best in England," or,
"You really are one of...the best in England," perhaps,
"You really are one of the best...in England," or even,
"You really are...one of the best...in...England." Each sentence has such a slight (unwritten) variation, but they can really change how the sentences sound.

My belief is that if you can learn to stand still and in silence while on stage: your speaking will profoundly change. You will evolve from a speaker who has to fill every moment with noise and movement to one who chooses when to speak and move. Work on this after you've experimented with pauses. Just try standing still, slowly looking around, and smiling. You'll know when you've cracked this because the silence and inaction shouldn't phase you or make you buckle 'under the pressure'.

After following along to this point, you will have improved your control over your rate of delivery. By practising pauses: you will have started to see how to have fun with sentences by changing how they sound (without speaking faster). If you were brave and became comfortable standing in silence, you will have found a new level of control and inner-tranquility on stage. It's not until you feel relaxed enough to take your time while speaking that you will be able to turn your energy into real public speaking power.

The assumption that you might be making is that you should use your, "I need to speak fast," energy to speak louder. Sometimes you can, but that's only the tip of the iceberg. The goal now is to use your energy to become more expressive. Let's start breathing new life into your words.

One of my favourite drills is to take a sentence and getting the person I'm coaching to say it in several different ways — in quick succession. I like to do this because people usually understand volume, speed, and pitch but they don't often practise saying a sentence as different people or with different feelings or in other contexts. One phrase I like to use is: "Matt, I am so excited, let's go get a cheeseburger right now," you can say it many different ways. Try saying it now in the following ways:

- Say it with great excitement (without speeding up).
- Say it lazily as if you couldn't care less.
- Now say it like a mouse would.
- And now in a really deep voice.
- This time put a lot of emphasis on 'excited' and 'cheeseburger.'
- Sing the sentence like you're in a musical.
- Say it like a robot.

Now I would like you to try the sentence one more time. But this time we are going to align your thoughts with your words. As you begin the sentence: I want you to imagine a time when you felt unbelievably excited and to fully express that feeling as you say the word 'excited'. Next picture the tastiest cheeseburger (or nicest vegan meal) and how it must taste as you say the word 'cheeseburger'. You will find that you can express your energy in yet another way: by using your imagination.

I should point out that your movements on stage can really benefit from some extra energy — so don't feel pressured into putting all of your energy into your words. But at the same time, practising your speaking on its own (independent of movement) can be beneficial to you. When you synergise expressive speaking with expressive actions and movements, you will be a public speaking force to be reckoned with.

Congratulations on learning more about how to channel your energy. I hope that you now realise that jabbering is definitely not an effective way to show people your excitement or passion for a topic. Instead when you speak slower and have control over what you're saying you can use your energy to be incredibly expressive. It takes time — but in my opinion, it makes your public speaking not only more powerful but also more entertaining.

Flatten Your Emotions

I'm interested in how limitations can be helpful. Usually, a limitation is seen as a bad thing, however, when used intentionally, they can help improve our public speaking. By not allowing yourself to express your feelings while speaking, your performance will ignite once you remove the limitation.

When I ask speakers to be expressive, I'm always surprised when they say to me, "I am being expressive." To me it appears as if they are scoring two out of ten on the 'expression scale' but to them, they feel like they're delivering a solid nine if not a ten. This is when I get them to speak without any expression so we can get on the same page.

Imagine you have an 'expression scale'. At 10 you are uncontrollably expressive (like a firework display accompanied by five orchestras, on top of an erupting volcano, during a lightning storm). At 0 you're not expressive at all (no emotion or feeling, like you were three seconds away from falling asleep). My goal is to help speakers reach seven and above.

If a speaker can't get above what I perceive as a three or four, I call a time-out. I then ask them to turn their expressiveness down to zero. At this point: they usually look at me like I'm crazy. They especially think this when I ask them to remove all expression, emotion, and enthusiasm from their voice and to sound as bored as possible. After they have read out a few pages of a book sounding like that, there's usually a striking change when I end their 'fast on expression' by saying they can be expressive again. Suddenly they start speaking with great enthusiasm, energy, and an increased vocal range. Just like magic.

Sometimes you need to limit yourself to become aware of your true potential and how much you can do. I know from experience that whenever I have been sick (sometimes for months at a time), I would feel frustrated about not being able to do things. Then when I was well again, I would do all of the things that I wanted to do: I would go for a run, make some homemade bread, and have a balloon sword fight in a perfume shop with strangers... I believe that the same holds true with expressiveness. Until you stop yourself from being expressive at all, you might not realise just how effervescent and engaging you can be.

> To take your expressiveness to new heights: try going without expression. Pick up a book and find a few pages which are easy to read:
> 1. Read it out loud in your normal speaking voice all the way through.
> 2. Then read it a second time, turning your expressiveness down to zero. The only thing you are allowed to express is boredom. You don't have the willpower to smile or put any energy into the words. It's going to feel like a trudge — and it should. Feel yourself wanting so badly to be expressive, but deny yourself until you have finished reading.
> 3. Now read through a third time, expressing yourself as much as possible. Do not limit yourself in any way, have fun with the words and bring them to life in any way you like.

If your level of expression felt right to you, keep it. Otherwise, tone it down a little bit, but not too much or you'll need to do the exercise again!

If you find that you're not able to express yourself enough while rehearsing a speech: try speaking without expression. Or give yourself another kind of limit. Limiting ourselves can help us take our skills to new heights.

The Million Dollar Question

What would you do if you had five million pounds? Imagine it now: You've been given five million pounds that you must spend on your next speech. How will you spend it?

You could spend the money on:
- Show-stopping clothes (or even a specially designed costume).
- Your own green room.
- Incredible handouts and business cards, with professional headshots.
- An eye-catching backdrop.
- Custom made props.
- A Generation Game inspired conveyor-belt on stage.
- Mouth-watering slides created for you by a graphic designer.
- Exciting prizes to give-away.
- Music to play at key moments in your speech.
- Special effects and lighting.
- A camera crew.
- An assistant to walk into the audience with a microphone for when audience members ask questions.

Find a pen and paper and let your mind go wild: write as many ideas as you can.

Peruse your list and be honest with yourself. Do you really need five million pounds to have everything you wrote down? I know for the examples I gave — certainly not. And I'm sure (minus a few black-truffle oil and caviar filled bubble baths, parachute jumps, celebrity cameos, and limousines) your list probably doesn't need that much funding either. But notice how much bolder and more creative we seem to get when we imagine having such a humongous amount of money to invest.

I believe that we limit our ability to experiment and to try creative and exciting things on stage because of three fears:

1) **Fear of investing in ourselves**
2) **Fear of learning and trying something new**
3) **Fear of asking for help**

Let's break these fears down and see why they're holding you back.

A fear preventing you from investing in yourself can hinder many areas of your speaking. It will determine what clothes you wear on stage (which in turn has an effect on how you feel, and how your audience perceives you), the quality of your slides and photographs, the props you use and what you take on stage, and what you give-away. I think the fear partly comes from the false belief that by investing in yourself you have to pay so much money that you're going to go bankrupt or at least 'waste your money' by spending it on yourself.

You don't have to go to a top end designer and spend £2000 on a dress or a suit. But do give yourself a budget for your clothes. You don't have to buy a £10,000 backdrop, a fancy podium, or film-set props. Instead budget some money for more affordable equipment and props, and purchase some materials so you can make things yourself. One of my best giveaways was a collection of origami tissue paper roses I made. If I had thought: "Oooh £2 on tissue paper, that sounds like a waste of money," it wouldn't have happened.

When it comes to hiring people and buying things in general — don't be afraid to shop around. Instead of always wanting to buy 'the best' (the most expensive) be honest with yourself about what you're really looking for.

Often the thing you need to invest isn't money at all: it's time. Invest the time to make your dreams a reality. All you will need to do is learn or try something new.

From my own experience, fear can hold us back from learning and trying new things because:

A) We think that the subject is incredibly complicated and far beyond our understanding. If we can't understand it, how can we do it?
Let's get real here. Just learn the basics. They're called basics for a reason. I think the reason why we get caught up in thinking, "This is so complicated," is because we are afraid to say, "I'm a beginner, I've just started learning." Instead we want to become a master at something in two hours and end up feeling annoyed at ourselves for failing. We all want to run on stage as a Kung Fu master and not a Kung Fu beginner. In most disciplines I've seen, having a firm grasp of the basics is enough to impress people.

B) We don't want people to think we're stupid
The number one way to make people think you're incompetent is to ignore my previous advice — act like an expert in something you only started this week. If instead, you were to tell your audience, "I've been doing this for a week," and then show them what you've learnt, you'll likely get a round of applause. People love to say, "Wow, you've only been doing this for a week?"

If you're still nervous about how people will react to your new idea, remember this: Being seen as boring is far worse than being seen as stupid. The easiest way to be boring is never to try anything new. When you try something new, even if you fail — people will likely be there to advise you and to help you. Most likely, they will be amazed by your eagerness to try new things.

The third fear is asking for help. This fear comes back to the previous two fears, "What if they ask for money," and, "I don't want them to know that I'm a beginner." With these fears covered we are well on our way down Success Street. The main reason I think that we don't like to ask for help is that we don't want to impose on others or to feel selfish.

We can forget that a lot of people genuinely enjoy helping others. When I see people trying to take a selfie together in front of a landmark, I'll often ask them if they want me to take it for them. But why? For money? So they owe me a favour? So they'll take my photo? NO: I find it fun, and giving someone a great photograph makes me feel good (and also I get to pretend to be Nick Rhodes from Duran Duran).

If you want someone to film or photograph you on stage: just ask. Similarly, if you need an assistant for your presentation: ask around. If people say no at least you asked (which is far better than blindly assuming they will say no).

Look back at your list of ideas — and if you didn't make one (you know who you are) review my list. Without the fears of investing in yourself, learning or trying something new, and asking for help — how many of your ideas could you achieve?

Now you can picture just how much you can do on stage without these fears holding you back (and without the need for five million pounds) pick two creative ideas for your next speech and get to work on making them a reality.

One Rule When Choosing Props

I have shared my opinions on props for years. When I talk about props I am referring to: the objects you use, or that can be seen while you are speaking. This includes items used in a story, what you place on stage, what you drink out of, and what you hold or hang up. I see a prop as any object in the speaking area that is visible to your audience.

My most noted opinions on props usually concerned what made a good prop and what didn't. "Pens are not props!" used to be one of my catchphrases (as I hated it when speakers brought pens on stage). Also, I still shudder when I see a speaker using a sheet of A4 printer paper...

Instead of giving you a comprehensive list of what not to use as a prop, I have a rule which will serve you well for years to come. The rule will help you to find a prop that will get noticed by your audience.

My rule is: Select a prop that you would never find at the venue you're speaking at.

Over the years I have seen speakers who have used: wallets, pens, money, plastic cups, backpacks, printer paper, cutlery, and an assortment of other props which you could easily find at any venue. These 'props' do not show creativity, they're not noteworthy, and they communicate nothing about you or your message. This is because they're commonplace items at the venue and readily available.

Instead, if you were to bring a prop that would never be found at the venue (which I will now refer to as 'outside props'), your audience will react to it. Most importantly, an outside prop will communicate who you are and what you're saying.

I once made a cartoon bomb to use on stage (I painted a flower arranging ball, black). I asked: "Does anyone have a lighter I can borrow?" and then pulled out the black sphere with a fuse, you're not going to expect to find one of those inside a conference room! I started a workshop by making a hammer appear, "Well it is a workshop." By bringing unconventional and original outside props, I have been able to acquire sensational audience reactions. My props communicated my maverick attitude to the whole room. If I had fluttered around a piece of A4 paper with a grainy photo on it, no one would have blinked an eye.

At magic conventions: zealous autograph hunters beg famous magicians to sign their playing cards. Wow...playing cards — there are thousands of packs at a magic convention. Signing them is not remotely novel or interesting. At a magic convention I attended in January, I brought with me a castle made out of cardboard — the only one at the convention. Hundreds of magicians signed it, and people approached me all weekend, wanting to know more about my castle. I was the biggest mystery at the event!

During breakfast one morning, I was sat near a famous magic author. Each time people approached, he thought that people were going to ask him a question or for an autograph. Nope. Instead, they walked over to me, "Can I ask you about your castle?" I felt like a celebrity. The effort you spend on bringing an outside prop buys you people's attention.

I'm not saying that you have to find a prop that is particularly off the wall. Even if you bring a mug with your name printed on it, people will take note. If you happen to have some fake gold bars decorating your house, and you're doing a talk on money — use them. That's a far stronger visual image than using loose change. If you're discussing people's homes — why not put your front-door mat on stage? Your outside props will be noticed. When they support your theme and main message that's even better.

Bringing an outside prop will also improve your storytelling. Imagine the difference between these two examples:

1. "This reminds me of when I once ran into my favourite film star," the speaker reveals a sheet of A4 printer paper with a small picture of an actor's face. No one can see the picture, and the paper makes an annoying rustling sound, "That's right, I met Tom! Hello, Tom. How's it going?" Compared to:

2. "This reminds me of when I once ran into my favourite film star," she reveals a life-size cardboard cut-out of the actor. It's like the star is standing right next to her, "Hello, Tom. How's it going?"

The second example has so much potential. The speaker could even pretend to have a conversation with the actor if she wanted to. The speaker in the first example can't do much at all — people can barely see the picture, let alone work-out whose face it's meant to be of.

Assess your upcoming speech and list every prop that you will be using. Then be honest with yourself — how many of those props could you find at the venue? If your answer is more than zero, start thinking of outside props to replace them with. What alternatives do you have at home? What could you make? What can you borrow? What could you buy?

Once you follow the rule and realise the power of outside props, you will never look back.

There's Always a Better Way

When you think to yourself, "There's no other way of doing this speech," it's game over! If you can't even entertain the possibility that there might be a more creative way, a funnier way, or a more inspiring way to give your speech; you deny yourself the chance of ever discovering one.

When we watch a speech it can be tempting to think: "I can't see anything wrong with it — it must be perfect." If we do not notice any problems that we're familiar with, we stop analysing the speech and give up. When this happens while reviewing our own speech we become stuck until someone else gives us some help. We rely on being rescued by a fresh perspective.

Imagine what would happen if we believed with complete certainty that, "There's always a better way!" No matter how perfect, polished, and powerful a speech might be; when we believe that there has to be a better way of doing it — we'll find a way.

The areas of a speech that have been finely tuned can always be further improved by raising the bar on our desired outcomes. If there's a joke in your speech that's funny, how can you make it hilarious? If it's already side-splittingly funny, how can you evoke hysterical laughter? Or if there's a sad part in your speech, take it further. Consider how it can hit your audience in a way that changes the feeling from a sympathetic sadness, to an empathetic sadness. Think of ways to take it further so members in your audience cry.

For the areas of a speech that are often overlooked, the bar can be raised moderately and still give you substantial results. These moments can include your transitions, your movements (including how you will walk on and off the stage), and moments which aren't currently designed to influence your audience's emotions. Sure, you can walk on stage, but there's always a better way. Run on stage? Skateboard on stage? Crowd-surf on stage? Be carried on a throne onto the stage? There's always a better way!

Let's imagine that you want to start your speech by putting a briefcase on a table. Could you find a better way of doing this so your audience will react? Yes — there's always a better way. Here are three quick-fire suggestions, each to stimulate a different emotional reaction:

1. **Humour:** Lunge on stage with the briefcase, pretending that it's incredibly heavy. Stop to rest halfway across the speaking area. Feign hurting your back when lifting it onto the table. Open it and reveal that inside is a feather.
2. **Warmth:** Begin with the briefcase hidden from view. Tell a short story about someone you looked up to who always carried a briefcase (for instance, your grandfather) and how you always wanted one. Then explain how you got the money to pay for your first briefcase. Reveal the briefcase.
3. **Mystery:** Describe to your audience about how what's inside the case has a strange ability to alter people's fate. Describe who gave it to you and how it has affected other people. Open the case at the perfect moment.

Notice just how interesting we made a simple briefcase given the right introduction. We did it just by believing that there had to be a better way to walk on stage with a briefcase. There's always a better way.

I know that you're going to have a lot of fun using the belief that there's always a better way. It will make your presentations more original, more creative, and a lot more powerful. It's useful when watching other people's performances too. Knowing there is always a better way will stop you from getting star struck while watching a good speaker. Instead of thinking: "That's perfect. I could never do a speech better than that," you will start to think: "I've thought of several ways of performing that better."

You must remember that, "There's always a better way," is a bottomless hole. It goes on forever. While something can be continually improved, you must perform what you've been refining. In life, I strive to continuously improve and create. We improve our speech, and then we give life to it by sharing it. Continue improving your speech but also keep sharing it along the way.

Never Lose Sight of Reality

I talk a lot about concepts and new ways of seeing and approaching public speaking: Using power, positivity, love, beliefs, and ideas. One thing that I must stress to you as a public speaker is never to lose sight of reality.

There will be times when you build up a speech so much in your mind that you might feel a bit overwhelmed. You want it to go so well that you put enormous pressure on yourself. Or you could be so influenced by the venue and the other speakers that you feel some self-doubt creep into your mind. One of the greatest cures for this is a reality check.

This is advice for when you are feeling a bit overwhelmed. You want to be able to calm your mind and humble yourself before your next speech. You need to be able to stop seeing your speech as a humongous life event and from mentally insisting that it must go absolutely perfectly or your life and reputation will be ruined. When you feel like that, here are my five steps back to your calm and happy reality:

1) What's your message? What's your structure? And have you practised?

It's time to abandon your self-denial and be honest with yourself. Are you ready for your speech? If you're uncertain, work through the questions below:

What's your message?

You must be able to say what your main message is in a few sentences. If you can't do this yet, you need to spend time finding it and making sure it runs through your speech.

Does your speech have a clear structure?

Is your speech loaded with tangents, teases, and so much skipping about that it will cause motion sickness? If your speech doesn't have a clear structure: build one around your main message. Edit your content and remove anything that does not support your message.

Have you practised?

Practice can make or break a speech. You need to be honest with yourself about whether you have practised enough. If you are unsure, check how you have practised:

1. How many times have you timed yourself rehearsing your speech?

You need to rehearse without notes and reach the point where you can go from start to finish — smoothly.

2. Have you paid attention to your breathing?

You need to run through your speech to check that you are breathing enough so that you can project your voice. If you are not breathing enough, you might need to slow down your speech and give yourself more time to breathe.

3. Have you choreographed your movements?

This includes where and when you walk (including your entrance and exit), your gestures and your eye contact.

4. What have you done to stop your speech from being flat?

It's important to ensure that you are using your voice in different ways, utilising pauses, and using different emotions alongside your choreography.

5. Have you imagined performing for an audience?

When you imagine performing for a real audience, you will add pauses for their reactions. Also, you can work on your eye contact and how you will react to your audience.

6. Have you had a dress rehearsal?

You need to be acquainted with what you will be wearing and have a full run through, which will bring everything together.

If you have not done all of the above, stop worrying about your speech and take action. While you have the time to work on your speech, it's better to refine it instead of worrying about it.

If you have done all of the above, know that you have worked hard on your speech. You have done more than most speakers. If you have a few days before you give your speech: practise each day so that you maintain your high standard. But don't over practise because you don't want to exhaust yourself before your actual speech. Seriously — this can happen.

The night before your speech, it can be tempting to rehearse until the early hours. Resist this temptation. At this stage, it's better to make sure that you are well rested and feeling fresh the next day, than making more changes and tiring yourself out. Regardless of whether you feel like you have worked hard or not, getting enough sleep is what will help you the most. There is a lot you can do while presenting if you're feeling sharp and energised, but if you're tired and worn out your performance will suffer greatly. Remember to rest.

2) You and your audience will be safe and well after your speech. It's public speaking, not an emergency

Nothing terrible is going to happen if your speech doesn't go to plan. In my opinion, the worst thing that could happen is that your audience will find you so bland that they will forget about you.

If your speech is a 'complete disaster', no one's life will be any worse, none of your audience members will carry a lifelong pain as a result. The majority of your audience will probably forget about the experience — they will likely spend more time watching TV shows that night than they spent watching you. And if you're at a paid event where some people ask for a refund, does it really matter? Do you honestly think that the top public speakers don't get asked for refunds?

What you need to ask yourself is: "What would happen if I just sat down on the sofa all day instead?" because that's the alternative. No matter what happens when you speak, it's better than having wasted a day just sitting by yourself. At the very least, by going to give your speech, you will get your name out there. Even if you go on stage and talk for 30 seconds, some audience members will look you up.

If your speech did not feel good to you, audience members will admire you for having gone up on stage to begin with. So many people struggle with public speaking that a speaker will have admirers for going on stage and trying. And because you got to speak, it will give you authority and a celebrity-like shimmer which will help you to meet new people afterwards.

In your head: you need to be aware that the 'worst case scenario' isn't all that bad. Compared to the worst-case scenarios for an extreme sport or for the emergency services you have nothing to worry about.

3) You're so lucky getting to speak. You could be doing data entry

Whenever a speaker whines to me about how large the audience will be at their next presentation, I look them in the eyes and say, "I'm jealous. You're really lucky," and their eyes widen with surprise.

I can't tell you how many times I have longed to have a large audience to speak to. Whenever I get one I feel so grateful and excited to be able to share my ideas with so many people. When I hear speakers whinge about having a large audience, it makes me want to disguise myself as them and do it for them! To me, it's like someone complaining about being given a free lunch and expecting me to give them sympathy. It's near impossible to give someone sympathy when you're thinking: "Wow, can I have it instead of them?"

With public speaking, you can overthink a speech and forget how fun it will be to deliver. Public speaking is uplifting. You do it, and afterwards you and your audience will feel like you're on a high. Or at the very least you will feel a desire to do better next time. You're improving yourself by doing it.

Speaking is not soul destroying work. For me, 'soul-destroying work' is anything that you have to do as work that a machine could do in a fraction of the time. Data entry for me is the most boring thing on the planet. Why? Because it's repetitive, it's done in isolation with no use for creativity or humour, and it does not help you grow as a person. Oh, and a computer could do hours' worth of it in an instant, making the time you spend on it feel like a waste of your life. Public speaking is a social activity with the unlimited potential for being different, spontaneous, creative, funny, emotional, and expressive. A machine can't do it better than you: it makes you feel alive. Can't you see how incredible that is?

Public speaking is anything but boring. It's not a corporate office, it's a lit up amusement park. No audience is the same, and so it never has to be repetitive. You can express anything you want to and share your wonderful ideas. It's a fun activity, and you need to see that! There will be many times where you will stand before an audience and notice that it's composed of a group of bored individuals. They need you to uplift them. By knowing that public speaking is fun and exciting — you can give them the upliftment they need.

4) If you are hindered for this speech, you will be strengthened for the rest of your public speaking journey

When we speak, there will always be things that will hinder both our speaking and our effectiveness. When a hindrance pops up, most speakers can't cope with it. They do not see the bigger picture. It doesn't occur to them that they will go on to give many more speeches after this one. In later speeches, the speakers will likely be free of their current, temporary hindrances and as a result, their performance and belief in themselves will improve.

Imagine running a half-marathon while carrying a heavy backpack filled with rocks. This half-marathon is going to be a challenge, you're unlikely to run as fast as you usually do. Everyone always focuses on this part, this specific half-marathon. But what will happen afterwards?

Other runners and spectators won't tease you for being slower than you usually are, they'll be impressed: "You ran that entire thing while carrying a bag of rocks? Wow!" But what's more important is how your mind will grow. You would have just proven to yourself that you are capable of completing a half-marathon while running with a heavy backpack. If you have to do it again, you won't be worried because you will know that you have done it before.

No matter what new running course you try or new hindrance you experience while running: you will know that you have run with a bag of rocks on your back before. Not only would that experience have probably been harder than this new challenge, but you'll know that this time you have no bag of rocks attached to you. You can show everyone how much you can do without that hindrance!

Whenever something has hindered my public speaking, I have treated it as valuable experience. That way, no matter what the outcome was — I grew from it.

When I was first asked to give a speech with one minute's notice, I thought: "It probably won't be my best speech. But now every time I have more than one minute to prepare, I will know that I can do it. It will inspire me to make the most of that extra time, even if it's only one extra minute." After that speech I never felt phased when I was put on the spot and asked to speak — in fact, I sought out opportunities to do it more so that I could do it even better than the first time.

Once during a speech I was so unwell that I stopped being able to see halfway through: "This probably won't be my best display of good eye contact," I thought, "but from now on I will always know that I can perform without seeing," and the experience inspired me to perform an entire speech blindfolded, because I knew that I could speak without my sense of sight.

No matter what might hinder your next speech, see the bigger picture. You will grow from the experience: you will know that you can cope with that particular hindrance, and this will give you reassurance when you reach for greater heights.

5) See the room for what it is

When you arrive at the venue where you will be speaking, you might feel out of your depth because of the room you're in and the people around you. The room might be larger or fancier than what you're used to. You might be waiting around other speakers who are more well-known than you and are wearing clothes that are more expensive than yours. You might start to doubt if you are ready for this speech now you're actually here. You might even question whether you are good enough to be giving a speech here.

When you have built up the event so much in your mind and put so much pressure on yourself, you're going to lose touch with reality. You're going to see the venue as bigger and more intimidating than it actually is, and see the other speakers through rose coloured glasses. It's completely natural for this to happen. What I suggest is to open your eyes and see the reality.

Firstly, is the room really as big as your mind is telling you? Take a look and let your eyes adjust. Sometimes you can see the room shrink before your eyes. If it still looks big to you, that's okay. Just be aware of the walls and the back of the room. It's a room just like any other. So what if it's a bit bigger than you're used to? If anything you should feel liberated by being in a bigger room. A bigger room allows you to express yourself more on stage.

If you have a larger audience than usual, you can receive mightier reactions. I personally find it easier to perform for more people. This is because you get more energy back from a larger audience and so you don't need to give out as much energy.

If the venue is fancier than you're used to, take a second look. Why do you think it looks fancy? Is it an older location? Does it feel like a more expensive venue? The fanciness of the venue should not phase you. If anything a fancier venue gives you and your message more credibility: it's helping you.

If the fanciness of the venue is affecting you, it's probably because you're worried about your audience and what kind of people would go to a place like that. This is not a cause for concern. Once again, from my point of view, I would much prefer to speak to an audience who have gone to a somewhat luxurious venue, than to a football club's local pub on match night when their team has lost.

It's important to mention though that you can't judge an audience by the venue. Arriving at an expensive place does not automatically mean that you will have a stuffy or snooty audience. To see the reality: refer to the event organisers — they were the ones who thought you were a good fit. Why not go and meet some of the attendees yourself? Once you start to meet a few people, you will feel a lot more at home.

Don't let other speakers throw you off your game. If you meet speakers who dress like they've just popped out of a fashion magazine or who probably spent more on their suit than you did on your last five holidays — stop. It's time for a reality check.

How someone dresses does not make them better than you. If another speaker talks down to you or makes you feel bad: block them out. The best speakers I have ever met were kind, generous, and showed me respect. It was always the speakers who — how to put this delicately — weren't very good, who put me down.

The amazing speakers I've met knew they were good and didn't need to prove themselves. They wanted to enjoy the experience and to share a few laughs with me before they went on. I was a friend to them, not a threat.

The speakers who were unsure of themselves were threatened by me, and the speakers who were deluding themselves talked down to me to feed their egos. If anyone puts you down or tries to make you question yourself or your abilities as a speaker: ignore them — it's not the truth. The people who you should be listening to are those who want to build you up and who want you to do well. Not those who want to sabotage you.

At the venue, if you still have self-doubt: park it. You have to accept that right now, doubting yourself is not helpful. You have done everything possible, and now all you can do is to get in the right frame of mind to speak.

To park your self-doubt, you need to stop listening to it by focusing more on other people and on positive feelings. What I would recommend is to do things that will make you laugh and feel happy. Try to make a friend. Find someone fun to talk to, tell jokes to, or play a game with: even if it's something like rock-scissors-paper. Anything that will get your energy up will help you to focus more on other people than yourself, make you feel good, and burn away your self-doubt.

If you have to go to a green room and there's no one to talk to — make the best of things. Don't listen to sad or emotional music, I know speakers who do this and I personally think it's a bad idea. Instead, watch a video that will make you laugh out loud, listen to upbeat music that makes you want to dance, or message your friends. If you decide to message your friends, try to make your friends laugh. When you're feeling happy, you will be in the right headspace to share your message on stage.

Those were my five steps to escape that horrible feeling of being overwhelmed. You might discover more things that give you a reality check and help you to calm yourself and feel happy. Do what works for you. Just know that if you work hard at public speaking, you should never feel put off by self-doubt, the venue, other speakers, or anything else. You've worked hard, and you deserve to be able to share your message and to express yourself fully. Never lose sight of this reality.

Express Yourself

Feel Expressive While Speaking

We want to feel expressive while speaking because it gives us the freedom to share who we are, to connect with our audience, and to offer new experiences with life-changing messages.

One problem I find is that the majority of people have a misguided notion of what feeling expressive while speaking actually means. They might be imagining how great it must feel being able to: shout out their entire speech, wear an expensive dress or suit, or having a whole book full of witty one-liners and comebacks for hecklers.

Let me debunk all of the above notions. Shouting for extended periods isn't fun (for anyone). It's not the clothes that make a speaker expressive — it's the person wearing them. And rehearsed lines won't make an audience care about you. Making your audience feel appreciated (instead of trying to one-up them with old lines) is what will make them respond to you positively and enthusiastically, while further encouraging you to share the things that you love.

To be expressive, you need to feel expressive

To be expressive: develop an excitement to speak and to share your creativity. Feel love for your audience and use your time to celebrate your uniqueness while empowering those who listen. Know that you can communicate in such a way that audiences will pay attention to you and people will remember you and what you stand for. And feel a strong sense of purpose: know that you can change lives for the better. These feelings will make you want to share your ideas and passions.

If you want to feel expressive, here are seven points to follow. I have broken each one down to give you an introduction:

1. Develop an excitement to speak and to share your creativity

Public speaking is fun. You get to talk about something that you're dying to share with others, and you can do it as creatively as you like. You have total freedom of thought and expression. Every skill and talent you possess can be used to help you present. You can use any of your interests to help communicate who you are and what your message is.

You're given a room that is full of people, who will be quiet, and give you their attention. This is a priceless gift.

It would take a few hours to phone up (and get through) to each one of your friends and to share your message with them. Can you picture just how long and arduous it would be to cold call each and every person in an audience? Or to deliver a full presentation to each individual at a convention? Think of how many times you would need to get someone's attention and then repeat your speech as a rushed elevator pitch. Being able to give your presentation once to an attentive audience is a gift!

Conversation is sometimes compared to a game of tennis with all the back and forth exchanges. Public speaking is like playing tennis with someone who will only hit the ball back if you ask them to. When you speak on stage, you can keep serving as much as you like. No one's going to interrupt you and takeover, walk away, or hang up!

What I love about speaking in person is that you can share your energy with others. I believe that the energy you give out to people is returned to you sooner or later. If you are excited to see your audience — they will be more excited to see you. Before you know it, you will have rooms of people just as enthusiastic about your ideas as you are: listening to you.

2. Feeling love for your audience

The magician Howard Thurston was said to have repeated to himself that he loved his audience, before going on stage. If you go out on stage feeling fear towards your audience, they will sense it and feel uncomfortable. Love is a potent reliever of fear. If you go on stage and feel grateful that people are listening to you and feel a love for them: your audience will relax, smile, and listen to you.

Feel grateful that people have devoted time (that they will never get back) to listen to you. Value your audience as human beings and respect them and their time. It's easy to have enough of a speaker who is arrogant and insults her audience, but a speaker who loves her audience is difficult to dislike.

3. Using your time to celebrate your uniqueness

Public speaking is one of life's best opportunities to celebrate your uniqueness with other people: Do you have some interesting ideas? Have you got stories to tell? Or do you have something to try that you think could be hilarious? When you speak, you have permission to share.

4. While empowering those who listen

The worst speakers push their audiences out and break them down. The best speakers invite their audiences in and build them up. Having an honest connection with your audience and uplifting them creates trust and a fantastic atmosphere in the room.

In almost every magic show I have ever been to, no one wants to sit on the front row with me. People are scared of being asked up on stage, made to feel stupid, and humiliated. Paying money to be made to feel bad is not a fun night out. But when volunteers are made to feel like the hero instead of the clown and are made to feel great about themselves — people are queuing up to volunteer.

You want a member of your audience to leave feeling complemented, not insulted. Your treatment of audience members will influence how they will talk about you to their friends and family.

5. Knowing that you can communicate in a way that audiences will pay attention to you

When you believe in your speaking skills and pay attention to your audience, you can stop getting lost in your doubts.

Trusting that people will be able to hear your speech will free you from having to stop your flow to question, "I wonder if I'm speaking loud enough?" If at some point you're not speaking loud enough, the fastest way to be alerted and to then fix it is by paying attention to your audience.

When you've actively worked on your delivery, your movements, speech structure, use of visuals, and the changing energy in your speech — you will have a lot more focus and headspace to give to your audience. When you start focusing on your audience instead of niggling self-criticisms: you will be able to engage an audience's attention fully.

6. People will remember you and what you stand for

When you connect with your audience, keep your speech simple, and entertaining: they will remember you and what you stand for. You don't need to propose the most ground-breaking idea or provide thousands of case studies. You just need to present an idea, while having awareness of your audience, using a simple and easy to follow structure, in a way that makes your audience enjoy listening to you.

7. And feeling a strong sense of purpose that you can change lives for the better

When you see audiences who look happier after you've presented to them: you'll know you've uplifted them and improved their lives. But when you believe in your message, and you deliver it memorably: you'll know that lives will change for the better because of you and your beliefs.

Once you know that you and your beliefs will improve lives, it doesn't matter if people clap as you walk on stage. It doesn't matter if you don't get the reactions you were expecting. It doesn't even matter if no one comes up to you afterwards with a victory cake. Your belief in your message and the work you put into making your speech memorable is all you need to know that you will impact the lives of your audience for the better.

When following my view of how to feel expressive while speaking, there are areas to work on. If you want to enjoy public speaking: you are free to share my view that at its core, public speaking is positive and empowering both for the speaker and her audience. When you are filled with positive feelings and attitudes while speaking, you're going to want to express yourself.

It's Time to Show Us Who You Are

Knowing the reasons why it's important to express yourself is one thing, but how do you actually do it?

Imagine a dystopian future where the only way for people to communicate is by posting a standardised note. If you want to communicate with someone, you'll have to select a non-emotional sentence from a small book of 'approved sentences'. There's no choice of font, everyone must use the same typeface and size. And all note-senders must use identical formatting and the same type of paper.

As a species, we would be able to communicate information — but we wouldn't be able to express our emotions or our individuality; who we are.

Now imagine this — the same scenario (everyone can only communicate by notes) but different rules. This time you have no restrictions when it comes to what you write, what font you use, the formatting you choose, and what paper to write on. Because you now have options you can start to express yourself. You can convey your personal feelings and emotions. You can also express your individuality.

Some speakers are so focused on their message that they forget three critical things:
1. How their message makes them feel.
2. How they want their audience to feel and to react to them.
3. What choices they can make so that their speech is delivered in a way that is unique to them.

If you feel nothing for the message you're sharing you can't expect your audience to feel anything either. What many speakers have not grasped is that as well as communicating with words — we're communicating with our emotions. If you're telling us a sad story, you need to experience some of those feelings at key parts of the story, or it will come across as insincere.

If you're describing to an audience how you met your partner for the first time: you need to recreate the emotions that you felt. Your emotions are what people connect with. The easiest way of putting your emotions into your speech is to look at what adjectives you're using. If you're saying, "I was shocked," think about how you would have said it when you were shocked — recreate that feeling. The emotions you feel should match what you're saying.

Secondly, if you don't know how you want your audience to feel you won't know how to express yourself effectively. If you don't think about your audience's feelings — they're not going to become immersed in your speech.

Too often, I see speakers looking at their performance from their own perspective instead of looking at it from their audience's. Do you want your audience to feel excited? Profoundly inspired? Or maybe even, stunned? You need to ask yourself how you want them to feel so you can express yourself effectively.

If we were around a campfire telling ghost stories, you wouldn't tell the story in a deadpan manner. You would think: "How do I want other people to feel? Oh, I want them to feel tension, suspense, and moments of fear and uncertainty. I want them to be curious about what happens next — but equally scared to find out the answer..." Once you know how you want your audience to feel, you will understand how to merge your self-expression into a story. Your expression will then light up an emotional path for your audience instead of dazzling their view. Your audience will then experience the desired emotions and immerse themselves in your speech.

Once you know how your message makes you feel and how you want your audience to feel — you're ready to think about your choices. You know what you want to achieve on an emotional level and now you need to choose how to express yourself. If you're going to communicate the feeling of anger to your audience — you could shout. That is one choice. Instead, you might decide to beat a freshly made baguette against a wall. Or maybe you want to paint your face green and bend a steel bar in half. You have unlimited ways of expressing yourself.

The ways you decide to express yourself will inform your audience of who you are. Santa Claus will make an audience excited in a very different way to how a stuntman will excite them.

The way to find the best choice for you is through experimentation. When you try different ways of expressing yourself, you will eventually come across methods that you love. To you they'll be: flashy, hilarious, heart-breaking, or utterly profound.

Notice I said — to you. If someone else was giving the same speech, they might find other choices to be far superior. But that doesn't matter. What matters is that you make choices based on what resonates with you and what in your opinion will make your audience feel the way you intend them to. This is your speech, take ownership of it and trust in your choices.

I have discussed three ways a speaker can express herself.
1. How her message makes her feel.
2. How she wants her audience to feel and react to her.
3. How she can make choices — so that her speech is delivered in a way that is unique to her.

Let's run through a speech together to see how we can utilise all three:

A comedy speech about how you missed the bus because a 'life-hack' went wrong

"I slowly woke up after a late night's sleep. I got up slowly because I had used a life-hack that promised I would wake-up five minutes early. By calculating in increments of 90 minutes how long I would need to sleep to feel rested — I didn't need an alarm clock anymore.

I looked at my phone. I was horrified. I had overslept by an hour! I was going to miss the bus!

I raced around in a blind panic. My breakfast consisted of half a bagel — fresh out the bag, and some Parmesan cheese straight out of the pot.

When I got to the bus stop: I saw my bus pull away. I felt so disappointed in myself. And then so angry! I threw my bag into the road, dropped to my knees and as I looked up at the sky I cursed the life-hack website.

When I looked down from the sky, I noticed that another bus had pulled up. I had forgotten there was a second bus. I dusted the parmesan off of my collar in a composed manner. I calmly walked onto the bus like a distinguished executive. I had gotten away with it — it was like a normal morning. Until a cyclist came on the bus and shouted that a crazy person had hit him with her designer bag!"

1. **Some of the feelings the speaker felt when the events happened:** Sleepiness, cleverness, horror, panic, disappointment, anger, happiness, relief, and shock.
2. **Some of the feelings and reactions the speaker wants to evoke from the audience:**
   Laughter, tension in the room, surprise, support and a connection to the protagonist.

3. **Examples of choices:**

Doing all of the expressions and actions in an exaggerated way to create more laughter from the audience. Bending over and squinting while talking to portray tiredness at the start. Not eating a bagel on stage but pouring a large handful of Parmesan cheese and throwing it over herself to show she was too tired to aim for her mouth. Using long pauses when she wanted to express shock and surprise. Matching the level of tension in the speech with the intensity of her voice.

Knowing how you feel about your message and how you want your audience to react and feel are essential in any speech. But remember to pay attention to your choices — because they are what make your speech an expression of you and are what will make your speech memorable, or forgettable.

Orthopterophobia

The fear of being stuck in silence afflicts more speakers than you'd expect. They're worried about being stuck in a completely silent room and not knowing how to fill the silence. All while an audience is staring at them and not offering any help with the problem. Many speakers are scared of hearing crickets.

Some speakers cover up the fear of silence by speaking rapidly without stopping. Others refuse to tell jokes in case no one will laugh. People who want to work on their public speaking can be afraid to even try because they're so worried about 'awkward silences'. Equally, more experienced speakers might not play with silence or experiment with it because it makes them feel uncomfortable.

Silence is nothing to be feared, it's another part of public speaking to be embraced. Once you know how to 'break the silence', you can start to make silence work for you.

I first want to debunk the idea of an 'awkward silence'. You make silence awkward by seeing it as an 'awkward silence' and by acting awkwardly. When used properly, silence is one of a speaker's most powerful tools. It's when an audience sees you looking unsure of yourself and standing there nervously in the silence, that they will feel uncomfortable. You don't have 'awkward rainfall' or 'awkward sunshine', it's how you react that makes you appear uncomfortable or not.

The easy solution is to learn to enjoy silences. If the room is silent, but you're having a great time, your audience will not have a reason to feel uncomfortable. Or if you stretch out a pause to create drama and tension, that's what your audience will experience — not awkwardness.

One of the best things about silence is that by talking: you fill it. Funny that. You are always in control of silence. For this reason, during the times where you don't want there to be a lengthy silence, there doesn't have to be one.

A lengthy, 'inescapable' silence can sometimes occur if you forget what you're going to say, no one laughs at your chicken joke, or you go completely 'blank'. These are situations where the silence can be avoided altogether if desired. If you just let yourself enjoy the silence you will have a lot of options.

Let's be honest, if you forget what you planned to say — does it really matter? Probably not. What does matter is making sure you carry on instead of standing in silence for five minutes.

When it comes to forgetting what to say, I remember what I learnt from my primary school music teacher, Mr. Thomas. He taught us a lesson that has been invaluable to me over my life. If you make a mistake, it's okay because only you will know you made a mistake, your audience won't know. Your audience hasn't been rehearsing and practising with you, and so they don't know what is 'meant' to happen.

If you forget a line, don't worry about it. If you forget an entire paragraph, that's also okay. If you can find a way to re-incorporate what you missed, do so but if you can't, does it really matter? Similarly, if you forget what you were meant to say next: you can either skip a bit or cunningly repeat what you just said 'for your audience's benefit' so that you can re-find your place. The audience doesn't have a transcript of your speech!

Imagine you've been excited to tell a joke that you wrote, for a while now. You get up on stage and excitedly share your joke. There's no reaction. You stand there, stuck in complete silence.

What do you do? You fill the silence! You could comment on the joke or your audience's reaction to it: "Oh no! This club hates chickens — there go the other 500 of my jokes!" Alternatively you could jump straight into your next joke (if you have one) and when in doubt you can always just carry on. Most times simply carrying on and not calling attention to the joke that didn't make people laugh, is the best solution. Although, if you know how to play with tension: you can sometimes get laughs after telling jokes that no one found funny!

And now. Silence. Your audience is watching you with anticipation. It's like they're waiting to hear the most profound thought of all time to leave your mouth in the next few seconds. But your mind is blank. It's like your head has been emptied and there's not even a tumbleweed blowing through it, let alone a thought. In this moment, you will give anything to fill the silence, it's what the whole room is waiting for.

During the above situation, some speakers can't take the pressure and will bow out. They'll finish abruptly and then have a flood of ideas as they leave the stage (the wit of the staircase). Speakers who still use notes can check them, but it's this fear of going blank that sustains their dependency on having notes available. Unless you enjoy silence, going blank and even the fear of it can interfere with your growth as a speaker.

I have some thoughts to share with you that can help you to regain your thoughts and fill the silence...

Before I discuss solutions, I have a plea: When your mind goes blank, please avoid asking your audience, "What was I just saying?" Or stating: "I can't remember what I was going to say next..." You might disagree with me here, but in my opinion, announcing that you've forgotten what to say devalues your message. Telling your audience that you can't remember your speech might make them question whether you 'live' the message that you're sharing or whether you have been making it up as you go along. From my perspective, asking your audience to prompt you (even if you don't expect an answer) is the worst thing to do.

My main piece of advice to help you work-through the onset of 'blankness' is to know your main message. No matter where in your speech you go 'blank', knowing your main message will save you. This is because you will always have one line to say – your main message.

When my mind goes blank, it often requires me to have one thought to get the ball shooting again. Like a pinball, once I have one thought it ricochets around my brain and more thoughts illuminate. If you are giving a speech with the main message, 'Wash your lettuce for a tastier salad' you will always have that line to springboard off of: "These were some of the reasons to wash your lettuce...." Now my mind has gone blank, I can springboard off the main message: "As you can see so far, washing your lettuce results in it being tastier...What I haven't addressed is that you should be washing the lettuce with water. "

After using your main message as a springboard to get your thoughts back: capitalise on the moment. You can do this by using your skills to interact with your audience and to fill the silence. You didn't plan on going blank and creating silence. This means that right now you are going off script and are giving your audience something that no one else who has heard this speech has received: A spontaneous moment where you interact with them! Played right, these moments can turn out to be some of the best of your speech:

1) You could use humour, storytelling, impressions or anything that allows you to have some fun with your audience. You can tell a joke by observing your audience and adding your main message: "I see you're on your phone! You obviously can't wait until you get home to tell your friends why they should wash their lettuce. Let us have a

look. Will you let us? She's not going to let us, everyone. Thank you for telling your friends about lettuce!"

My advice when creating spontaneous humorous moments is to commit to them. If you want to move — move! If you want to try something a bit out there — go for it! Don't do it half-heartedly, commit to the moment. And your audience will be given a special, one of a kind experience.

2) If you're good at answering questions, you could ask one about your main message, "Who here washes their lettuce?" You can then follow up with, "Can you tell us why you wash it?" No matter what answer you get back, it will get your mind working again and permit new thoughts to flow.

While standing in silence with a blank mind, you might feel like a deer in the headlights, frozen in place. I find that if you ask an audience member a question, you will have a clear motivation to walk in their direction. Often a bit of movement is all you need to get your thoughts back, and an interaction is a motivated reason for moving.

3) When you have a strong feeling that you will need time and concentration to regain your thoughts, here is a method to buy you some time and to dissolve the pressure created by the silence. This method is more for longer speeches (over half an hour), but it's always there if you need it. Remember your main message (if a recent point is still in memory — use it instead) and perform a demonstration or set an exercise for your audience.

The demonstration or exercise can take the form of asking for volunteers: "Would you three, mind joining me on stage? A huge round of applause for my brave lettuce loving volunteers," and then demonstrating something or requesting: "Please turn to the person next to you. I want you to instruct one another how to make your favourite salad."

In a pinch, you can spontaneously invent your demonstration or exercise, but if you can — rehearse it. Rehearse a demo or exercise that can be used anytime in your speech. That way you will always have something in your back pocket to buy you time if needed. While your audience members are getting up, or interacting with one another, you have some time to think. Use the time to have a drink if you need to, move and if you must, refer to your plan. The best thing about this backup plan is that it will end the silence, your audience will make noise. All of the pressure will be taken off of you for a short time, allowing you to relax and for your thoughts to return.

Silence is nothing to be feared. Forgetting what you're going to say, doesn't matter. If no one laughs at your joke, you never have to stand there in silence. If you go completely 'blank', there are things that you can do to get your thoughts back.

Instead of worrying about a long, inescapable silence: I would like you to instead think about when you tend to experience long silences while speaking. Once you know when it happens, you can come up with your own methods to fill the silence and to get back on track. With a positive mindset of planning what to do when there is silence (instead of just freezing), you will never have to worry about being stuck in silence again.

Speak on the Spot — Straightaway

Impromptu speaking is a skill that seems to baffle a lot of people. How do you give a short speech without any preparation? How do you talk for a few minutes about a question you were given two seconds ago? And how do you prevent yourself from 'going blank' while on the spot?

The solution I would have given you five or more years ago would have been very different to what I would tell you today. What I have learnt in that time is that you don't have to be overly creative to create speeches on the spot, you just need to understand the ways of structuring a speech, and to choose a structure. That being said, I think the best impromptu speeches utilise a well built and reinforced structure which are brought to life with creative ideas and forms of expression.

What impromptu speaking advice would I have given you five years ago?

My approach to speaking used to involve selecting the most off the wall ideas that came to mind and then hoping they came out in an order that made sense. The positive side of this approach was that my speaking was unique and full of life — I always received great reactions. The downside was that my messages just weren't getting across and I couldn't seem to inspire people.

My advice to you would have been to learn to believe in the ideas that popped into your head, no matter how crazy they were. Not being afraid to express your 'strange' ideas and then running with them is a key technique in improv comedy. This advice still holds up, your speaking will always benefit from expressing your creativity. However, if you want to inspire people and have them remember your message, you need to learn different speech structures and how to choose one off the cuff.

Openings and structures for impromptu speaking

In impromptu speaking: it helps to have a strong opening and to tell your audience how you will structure your impromptu speech, or at the very least make your choice of structure clear to yourself. If you are on stage and someone asks you: "Please can you talk to us about trees," you can create a different structure depending on how you want to answer the question. The structure you decide upon will influence your opening – how you start.

Openings

Your opening is the first sentence that you will use for your impromptu speech. A positive, assertive, and well-chosen first sentence will prompt admiration from your audience and engage their attention. Here are some possible approaches to opening an impromptu speech:

1. Repeating the question

"I have been asked to talk to you about trees."
This is an example of paraphrasing the question back to your audience. Repeating the question is seen as good form if an audience member calls out a question, so everyone will be able to hear it and know what you are responding to. In other circumstances, starting by repeating the question is useful in a pinch, such as when your mind has gone blank. The mistake that speakers make is to try and 'wing it' by repeating a question and then not deciding on a structure. Instead, I recommend using your next sentence to advertise what structure you are going to use.

2. Intriguing openings

If you (and the entire audience) have heard the question, and you have an idea of how to approach it: begin your answer with intrigue. Starting with intrigue has a much greater impact on an audience than repeating the question.

To begin with intrigue, you need to decide on what structure you are going to use. Once you know what structure you will be using: make your first line count. Practise crafting opening sentences that grab the audience's attention and make them want to hear more.

Headlining
One method of getting everyone's attention is through headlining. Headline your impromptu speech by delivering a punchy, hard-hitting beginning — like a newspaper headline:

"This is the story of the best tree-house I ever built." By headlining a personal story, you will know that you need to follow a story structure. Essentially this means telling a tale with a beginning, middle, and an end. I recommend looking into how the stories in films and books are structured and adding this knowledge to your repertoire. Surprisingly, most works of fiction follow a particular structure depending on their genre — which is why most romantic comedies feel quite samey.

The second thing to notice in this example is that it's the best tree-house. Telling an audience that you will tell them the 'best', the 'worst', the 'scariest', 'funniest', 'first', 'oldest', 'most beautiful', or any other extreme will intrigue them and get them to pay attention. One humorous technique which is sometimes used is to tell people the 'second best' if you want a laugh — but be prepared to mention what the best was so you don't tease your audience.

The last thing to note about this beginning is that it says, "I ever built," it's a personal story. Personal stories work because as you were there at the time, you can provide a rich and accurate account of what happened. And people get to imagine the things having happened to you.

"Here's something that happened to my uncle Courtney on his annual golf trip," doesn't have the same impact as: "Here's something that happened to me on a golf trip." This is because we don't know your uncle Courtney! And we would much prefer to hear the full details from Courtney himself. Also when someone constantly mentions things that their friends or family have done, but little that they have done, I leave thinking:

"Wow, you must have a boring life, if you have no stories of your own!" It might sound unkind, but it's true.

Controversial opening

"Trees are the worst form of 'life', we need to burn them faster."
A controversial opening lends itself well to humour and intrigue but can also become a fascinating message. To use it: strongly declare the opposite opinion to what most people would expect you to say. This in itself is bold and will capture an audience's attention, because it's unexpected. I would advise deciding on what tone you want your impromptu speech to have before you declare the opening. Will it be tongue in cheek, or will it be thoughtful and enlightening?

Where speakers struggle with this beginning is that after such a compelling and surprising opening, they don't know how to develop it. My advice would be to utilise a structure to strengthen your impromptu speech. It might feel more challenging to think of reasons or a personal story to support a controversial claim rather than an obvious one, but when you pull it off, you will impress your audience.

If you are in need of time to think, you can always use audience interaction to support your cause while you formulate more of your argument: "Please, can I have a show of hands, who here has ever been hurt by a tree? And who has ever been hurt by something made of wood, (which incidentally comes from a tree)?"

If you think that the controversial opening sounds a bit too uncomfortable — you should try it. Sometimes taking the opposite side of an argument can be eye-opening. I think that you need to feel more comfortable defending a controversial opinion, so you will never be afraid to speak up for what you believe in.

Structures for impromptu speaking

After your intriguing opening, follow the structure you selected. I have eluded to a story structure (a story with a beginning, middle, and end) but I wanted to share some that you might not have used before. Below are three example structures that you can choose from while formulating an impromptu speech:

1. A set number of points to support a message

After an intriguing opening line, you go onto say: "I am going to tell you two reasons why trees are essential for our planet."
This is my favourite kind of structure. You begin by telling your audience your structure and clarifying your terms. You do this so that everyone will understand exactly what you're talking about and fully understand your point of view. If you only have two minutes to speak, you don't need to explain every small detail, but a straightforward explanation will ensure everyone is on the same page from the start.

In this example, you might want to go into some detail about what you mean by 'trees' (what kind of trees? Are you including bushes? How many trees?) And what you mean by 'essential' (that only trees can do the job and that there are no alternatives). You might even want to examine the relationship between the trees and our planet (that trees existed before us and if there is a correlation between the number of trees and the state of our world).

The next steps are to state your first reason for your claim and to support it with evidence (either personal, anecdotal, research, facts, or quotes). Then if possible smoothly transition into your second reason by having it relate to the first reason or by covering an important issue that the first reason ignored. You then give your second reason and support it with evidence.

To conclude: recap your two reasons by reminding your audience of them. Next, you deliver the key takeaway and call to action for people — what message do you want them to leave with? And what do you want them to go and do? Lastly, give a snappy and memorable one-liner to finish.

2. Diving into a personal story

"I have always loved trees."
This method does not advertise a structure — instead, it jumps straight into a personal story. Leaping headfirst into a personal story can be effective if you enjoy storytelling. Although it might not tell your audience about what structure to expect, it gives you one. You will know that you have to give a short story of your life (with a beginning, a middle, and an end) which features a consistent love of trees.

You can begin by retelling the first time you remember 'loving a tree' and how they were present at key milestones of your life. Finally, it needs to end with proof that you still love trees! To finish you can leave the audience with a heart-warming line that sums up your lifelong love of trees, you could also encourage your audience to appreciate trees too.

3. A comparison

"I'm going to show you why oak trees are superior to palm trees."
Using a comparative structure is difficult to pull off effectively off the cuff. However, comparing two things is an easy way to generate ideas. You can think about the features and advantages of two things and then discuss the differences and similarities.

I believe that you shouldn't be on the fence when comparing things:

openly speak in favour of one. People always care about what the best thing is, how something is more beneficial, or why we should care more about one thing than another. However, audiences rarely care about casual, directionless and meaningless differences and similarities:

"The prime minister has hair. I also have hair. Isn't that neat?!" No one will care about that observation.

"The prime minister's hair is not looked after as well as mine — here's why." This time you're saying that you look after your hair better than the prime minister — people will be intrigued to hear why.

When comparing things, always ensure you have a set destination, "Cheese is a better purchase than chalk!" Otherwise your audience will leave feeling confused over what thing is better and might buy a wheelbarrow full of limestone. You can of course discuss similarities, but make it clear through each comparison that your contender is the one that your audience should be backing.

Closing thoughts

My opinion is that when you become good at developing a structure off the cuff you can talk about anything in an impromptu speech. It will take practice to intuitively learn how to fit a structure into the time you've been given. Ideally, you don't want to have to rush any part of your structure, each section deserves its own time to shine. If you struggle to achieve this try not to cram content in. I think it's better to have less content but to deliver a clear and well-structured message than to try to fit in as many ideas as possible. Alternatively, if you are not speaking for long enough, focus on developing each part of your structure and try not to rush through it.

I used to think that letting my creativity run wild was the key to impromptu speaking. Now I know better. Yes! Let yourself be creative, but focus your creative energy by using a clear structure.

When you have a structure, you give yourself things to say and prevent yourself from 'going blank'.

How to Share Your Inner World

We all have a world inside our mind — if not an entire universe. We receive many sensory inputs from the outside world, but what happens inside our mind? Amongst many other inner workings, we have our experiences, our desires and aspirations, our feelings and empathy, imagination, and our own methods of solving problems. Between all of these inner workings, we have an uncountable number of associations. For instance, the smell of lemons might remind us of a childhood holiday we enjoyed, and make us smile.

Our inner workings are off-limits to anyone but us. No one can dive into another person's mind and extract a memory, a thought, a feeling or a solution. These workings can only be shared. We can express our inner workings through communication by talking, through our body, our writing and the words we choose to express ourselves. I want to help to increase your awareness of your inner workings so that you can express them. By doing so, you can share your inner world with your audiences.

If I were to present five English speakers with a chair and asked them to tell me what it was (simply), they would all say, "It's a chair." Unless a speaker decided to answer the question in an overly expressive manner, we would not get a glimpse at any of the speakers' inner workings. Similarly, if I asked them if I was taller than the chair, they would all agree. But what if I asked them a question that would allow them to share a part of their inner world:

- What do you notice about this chair?
- How does this chair make you feel?
- Who do you think this chair belonged to or should belong to?
- Would you buy a chair like this? Why?
- What kind of chairs have your friends and family owned? Can you think of a story that involved those chairs?

- This chair has a wonky leg. How would you fix it? Right here, right now!
- If you were a dog, would you enjoy biting this chair? Be honest.
- When you look at this chair, what does it remind you of?
- If this chair had a voice, what would it sound like?

The answers from each speaker would reveal something about their 'inner world'. The answers might not always be unique to each speaker, but they would certainly tell us a bit more about them. My favourite answers are the ones that make me think, "I would have never thought of that," because the speaker used their unique experiences, associations, and imagination to deliver an answer that is new to us.

When you prepare a speech: contemplate if you are sharing your inner world with others. It's one thing to state your idea or to generically categorise something that you have noticed: "You should be happy. And that's a cat next to you." But anyone could do that. Only you can open up your inner world and give us a taste of what these things would feel like if we were you. You can do this by explaining:

- Why should we be happy?
- Why is it important to you that we should be happy?
- What happened to you that made you value happiness?
- What are your solutions for being happy?
- When are you happiest, and what's one of your happiest memories?

And let's not forget the cat...

- Does the cat remind you of another cat/animal you've known?
- How does the cat make you feel?
- How would a person in your profession describe it?
- How would you have described it when you were younger?
- What do you want to do with the cat?
- What do you want to give to the cat?
- What do you think you can help the cat with?

The questions that you need to ask yourself might feel 'bizarre', to put it mildly. But the more freedom you allow yourself to ask unusual questions in reaction to an idea or stimulus, the more personal your insights and comments will be. Which is more personal:
"You should be happy. And that's a cat next to you." Or:
"I lost my job and was alone in a new city. The days I stayed inside feeling sorry for myself were horrendous. I couldn't even smile. I was at my breaking point until I made a conscious decision to allow myself to be happy. I started doing things to cheer myself up like dancing while I waited for the kettle to boil. Life itself started to look up. I got out of the house, made friends, and got a new, better job. I never want you to go through the isolation that I went through. Instead, I want you to be happy, and I'm going to show you how...

Oh, how exciting! A cat has walked in to see my speech. He's adorable, I just want to pick him up and cook him a fish dinner. But I think he wanted to go to the nightclub down the road instead, could someone show him out?"

One sticking point that you might have is finding something to question yourself about in the first place. If you were answering questions and a rather vein audience member called out, "Can you give me a compliment?" other than joking about his boldness or vanity, what could you say?

I've found that in every situation there is always something that will jump out at you. It doesn't matter if you are looking at a person, building, or a field: your eyes will fixate on something. Similarly, when you listen to someone, there will always be one part or something about their speech that you will particularly focus on and remember. (Even if it's, "He was incomprehensible!") The same holds true with the other senses and for ideas and concepts. Something will always make your brain click:

"Aha! I want to pay more attention to that part more than the rest."

The next question you need to ask yourself is: why does it jump out at you? Once you know why it jumps out, you can start asking yourself more imaginative questions so that you can present an answer that shares your inner world. In the case of our compliment seeking audience member, your thought process might go along these lines:

- What jumps out? His tie.
- Why does it stand out? It's huge and purple.
- How does it make me feel? It makes me feel warm and happy.
- What does it remind me of? My uncle, who used to wear ties just like it.

After recognising what jumped out at you and why, you could reply to the audience member: "I love your tie! As soon as I saw you, I got the warmest feeling. Not only are you smiling at me but your tie reminds me of my uncle who used to wear a tie just like it. Thank you for making my evening."

I must advise you to be tactful when mentioning things that jump out at you. If something jumps out at you, consider if it is politically acceptable to comment on and if it could hurt anyone's feelings. These are the fears that will prevent people from using this method.

Use your best judgment, and when you have any doubt find something else that jumps out at you. Even if one thing might distinctly jump out at you, it's always possible to find a second or third thing that is also prominent. Be kind and loving to those you are talking about, to your audience, and to their friends and families.

To discover and share your inner world you can use the following mental map:
1) What jumps out at you? Is it safe to discuss? If no, restart. If yes, carry on.
2) Why does it jump out at you?
3) Ask yourself a question or an unusual one. Repeat step 3 as much as desired.
4) Compile your answers.

Over time you will become accustomed to sharing your inner world without having to think much about the process. I have gone through the process in detail in case you have struggled with either the concept of an inner world or how to go about sharing what happens in your mind. To become a speaker who other people care about, connect to, and are fascinated by: you need to be able to share what makes you, you. We want to know what you experience in your mind. Share your world.

Going Back in Time

When we talk about being passionate, the first images that come to mind are chefs who make cooking into a fiery dance and the French. That's the problem. Speakers and authors talk about 'passion' all the time, but it can be tough for someone to understand how to be more 'passionate'. To help you work out what passion means to you, I want to explain how I see it.

For me, passion is not an intellectual exercise because it's something that you don't need to think about. In my view, when you have a passion for something, you spend time on it because you love it. You're not continually looking for rewards or approval from others — you would do it even if you never made a penny from it or if no one knew about it. When you have a passion for something you just couldn't imagine your life without it, it's such an essential part of your life. It will tire you out, occasionally cause stress and frustration but it won't ever feel like work does; where you need incentives.

My view is that there is a difference between having a passion and being passionate. The dictionary is not going to agree with me here, but when thinking of the word 'passionate' I think of another person saying, "You're so passionate about this," or me saying to them, "I am passionate about public speaking." I see being 'passionate' as a form of communication between people that expresses their love for their passion.

From my perspective, the key difference between having a passion and being passionate is that you can be on your own and have a passion, but to be passionate you need another person to communicate your love of the subject with. It's an interesting way of looking at the words, and I think it clears up the problem that someone can have a passion but not come across as passionate.

If Joe has a passion for trains (he spends the majority of his free time collecting miniature trains, organising a train club, and going trainspotting) he might not come across as passionate about trains. He could give a speech where he mumbles and just lists facts about trains. Trains are Joe's passion, but he would not come across as passionate about trains (fun fact, I also wrote this essay – on a train). When this happens, an audience can feel confused because they don't understand A) Why he does so much with trains if he doesn't seem to enjoy it and B) Why should they care about trains if Joe is not showing his love for them.

What's Joe to do? My answer is to go back in time and: "Express your love and excitement like when you were ten." I chose ten because it's an easy number to remember, you can select any childhood age you like as long as it's a childhood age.

A passion is not an intellectual exercise, and equally, neither is being passionate. To be passionate, you need to communicate positively on an emotional level. Children communicate on an emotional level all the time. When you were a child, you would be open about what you liked and what you didn't like. When you thought about the things you liked, you would not understand intellectually: "Oh this activity gives me a boost of dopamine upon completing this small game and it's a clever tongue in cheek look at society," you would just know which parts you loved and which parts excited you. Therefore, for children, it's incredibly easy to be passionate about the things they love.

As we grow up, so do our expectations. We develop a tendency to shut off our emotions to the things we notice unless they meet our high expectations. As we age, we tend to think: "Oh I've seen better, heard funnier and tasted nicer," but as a result that makes 99% of life a disappointment. We won't let ourselves laugh at bad jokes because we have developed a 'more refined' sense of humour.

We raise our threshold for an emotional reaction so that we can feel like we have matured and grown from our experience on Earth. But is it worth it if it means we don't get to laugh, smile, or enjoy life as much? Our audiences will suffer from us having expectations that are too high because we won't be as positive as we could be.

I used to only laugh at things that I found hilarious. But why? I felt miserable the rest of the time. What I decided to do was to lower my expectations. I started to let myself laugh at terrible jokes, random thoughts, or even inanimate objects. I felt much happier and cultivated a lot more positive energy to share during speeches. To truly express yourself like when you were younger: lower your expectations and allow yourself to feel, much more frequently.

Now you're all grown up, to show that you are passionate about something you need to express your love and excitement. If you have no idea how to do this, imagine how you would have talked about something you loved when you were a child. You would have expressed yourself from your heart and not analysed from your head.

If ever you go to a big firework display: look out for the difference in reactions after the display between the children and adults. An adult would either give the display a mild compliment or a criticism: "Was that it? It wasn't as good as last year's." But a child would just let their enthusiasm all out:
"Woah! Did you see that huge firework? It was the biggest one I've ever seen! It went porhhhhhcra-cra-cra it was amazing! They were the best fireworks in the world!" A child won't worry about being rational or objective, they will simply express their experience. They will speak passionately about the magic that they just witnessed.

To someone who doesn't share your passion, you have to admit that it can seem hard to understand. People who dislike public speaking don't automatically understand why I love it so much. People probably won't understand how Joe can have a passion for trains. Think about your passions, to someone who doesn't share them; they're probably hard to understand too: "Oh, you love cooking? Why it's so much work!" Unless they have a similar level of experience or knowledge as you with your passion, you could struggle to explain why you enjoy your passions logically. Not everyone will be able to understand your logical reasons, but everyone will be able to relate to your emotions. Therefore it makes sense to be passionate and to communicate why you love your passions at an emotional level.

When you want to communicate from your perspective what your passion is like, try being passionate and show your love and excitement for it like when you were ten.

I enjoy taking a logical approach towards speaking and giving easy to understand explanations. However when it comes to your passions, sometimes the only way to communicate why you care so much about them is to be passionate and to communicate at an emotional level.

"Where Should I Look?"

No public speaking book would be complete without a section on eye contact. One of the most commonly asked questions that future rock stars of public speakers ask is, "Where should I look?" It's a question that needs to be answered. I am going to briefly discuss my thoughts on the subject.

When speaking you communicate with your voice and with your body — this includes your eyes. I learnt about different applications of eye contact from public speaking, my psychology degree, drama, comedy, and also from studying and performing magic. There are many uses for eye contact in a speech. I am going to discuss four:

1) Engaging with your audience

"You have to make eye contact with your audience," is a piece of advice that's thrown around a lot. But what's not covered so often is 'why' and also 'how' to make eye contact with your audience.

The reason for making eye contact with members of your audience is to show that you are paying attention to them. Your audience is composed of individuals, it's not an amorphous blob. To speak effectively: you need to create the feeling that you are talking to each member of the audience. Like how I'm talking to you right now.

What I didn't understand when I started public speaking was that you also make eye contact to be receptive to your audience, not just to broadcast to them. By making eye contact with audience members, you are more likely to notice how they're feeling and what they're enjoying. This is what makes eye contact useful to you because it will allow you to receive feedback throughout your speech.

Learning how to make eye contact can be a personal process. I have to be honest with you, I didn't create a formal way to teach myself eye contact. At university, I was inspired by my lecturer, Mark Burgess who while lecturing would look to the left of the room, then the centre, and then the right, back to the centre, to the left. He didn't seem to notice he was doing it, but it meant that I got to make eye contact with him many times during each of his lectures. I thought that my lecturer had the right approach to eye contact and so I adopted it.

When I make eye contact with audience members, I gaze into their right eye (I find it difficult to look at two eyes at the same time). Some speakers look between the eyes, or at noses — but I never liked this. I'm a right eye, guy.

When I'm presenting, if I'm centre-stage and looking straight forward, that's my 'home' position. When in doubt that's where I return to. From 'home' I try to smoothly look to the left, making eye contact with individuals for a few moments at a time along the way. Then I gaze into the eyes of people I missed when I go back towards home. Then I look into the eyes of people as I look to the right, and finally I make eye contact with people I missed as I go back to home. You're unlikely to 'hit' everyone each time you do this, but the goal is to try to 'hit' everyone at least a few times during your speech. I know from being an audience member (many times) that I remember when I've been 'hit'.

I would just like to mention here that eye contact is not something to be rushed. If you look around frantically, you're going to find it hard to relax while speaking. Instead, take your time. You're not in 'nightclub mode', you're in 'greet everyone at Sunday breakfast mode'. Make eye contact with each audience member with the goal of sharing the love in your heart with them. Look around slowly and smoothly while feeling and sharing positive feelings.

Making eye contact might make you feel nervous. It's okay if it does because you're not going to stare straight at one person like in a stand-off during a Western, there's a lot of people to look at. When you make a habit of looking from person to person while you speak, you will start to do it without needing to think about it or over-analysing the process.

Not many speakers practise eye contact when they rehearse their speeches. This is simply because most speakers practise alone and forget to practise it. When I rehearse, I set-up visual markers to make eye contact with. Visual markers can be anything that has a pair of eyes such as statues, cardboard boxes, photographs or toys. I spread them out and use them as fixed points for me to look at while rehearsing. I also use my imagination to simulate different reactions from each visual marker, that way I can practise reacting to the feedback that I observe from my audience.

2) Directing your audience's attention

Quite simply, where you look is where other people will look. When you have a conversation with a friend, if at some point you stare at something, it's pretty likely that they will check out what you're looking at. This is probably a primal mechanism that has allowed us to communicate dangers and opportunities for our survival: "She's looking away from me. Has she spotted a lion? Is it a dinosaur? Oh, it's a funny picture of a rabbit taking a driving test." (The rabbit passed, with only one minor. He over-filled the glovebox with carrots).

Directing your audience's attention is invaluable when you're speaking. If you want your audience to look at a picture or a prop you're displaying, look at it yourself. This will direct everyone's attention to your picture/prop.

You don't want to show your audience something and for them to be so transfixed on you, that they don't look at it properly. This could happen if you're showing something small, or plain and unremarkable to look at. It might take a few seconds but look at something yourself, and your audience will follow your eyes.

3) Showing your audience what you're focusing on

In my opinion, one reason why gestures and miming can fall apart during speeches is that the speaker doesn't use her eyes. If you type on a computer, wouldn't you be looking at the screen? So when you mime it, why are you looking to the back of the room? By imagining a screen to look at and not just the keyboard, your physical communication will become so much more effective.

You don't need to focus your eyes during every gesture you make. But see what happens when you give a gesture while fixing your gaze on it. For instance, if you stick up three fingers and announce, "And now for my third point," if you stare at your fingers for a few seconds it will communicate that you are pondering it. Acquiring new ways to express different meanings using your eye contact is worth pursuing.

4) Doubling your laughs from physical and prop-based comedy

Using your eye contact to get a second laugh is an old idea and is present in a lot of comedy. Something happens without you seeing, the audience laughs, you then look at what happened and react to it, and this causes your audience to laugh again. Instead of receiving one laugh from a physical joke, by being blind to the joke and then looking at and reacting to the situation after the first set of laughter: you buy yourself a second laugh. For example, if you announce to your audience: "I've brought a bag of junk food with me," and then without looking remove broccoli from the bag, you will get a laugh. Then when you look at the broccoli and express surprise, you will receive a second laugh.

A similar comedic technique which uses eye contact is the classic 'double take'. To do this you look at something without reacting, you then pause, look again and this time react to it. Imagine yourself with a toaster on stage and announcing that it creates perfect toast every time. You then pop a piece of toast out, and glance at it — it's completely burnt/on fire. You face your audience, "A perfect piece of..." you then do a 'double take' by looking again at the toast and then reacting to it. If ever you want to make your comedy funnier in speeches, consider how you're using your eyes.

Eye contact is another form of communication. It's not a simple matter of knowing 'exactly where you should be looking'. That would be the same as telling you exactly what to say. Eye contact is fantastic for giving attention to each member of your audience and for being receptive to them. However, it also allows you to guide your audience, to bring your mime and gestures to life, and to improve your comedy.

Where you look is yet another tool that you can decide how to use. It's likely that you will find applications that I have not even considered. Have a think about how you use your eyes, are you underusing them?

Singing

In my teens, I got really confused by the concept of my voice 'breaking'. When will it happen? Will I speak deeply all the time? Will it hurt? I found the process confusing, and I had no idea what my 'natural voice' was afterwards. What helped me was singing.

I learnt from singing lessons that when I sing I have a somewhat deep voice (technical term) and I was taught where in my stomach to concentrate and tense to access it. At this point, I haven't had many lessons, but it didn't take long for me to find that when singing, I need to sing in a deeper voice. Discovering my singing voice and from that my public speaking voice, was one of my most empowering discoveries.

I decided not to speak in a deep voice all the time because I quite like having a lighter voice in conversation as I always saw it as friendlier. However when I need to get people's attention, or I'm speaking to a room I use my deeper voice because it carries a lot better. It also makes me feel a lot more powerful when I use it. Some people think that it's like a different person talking when I speak in a deep voice, but I know that to me, it's my real voice.

Speak Up!

The elephant in the room that most people don't want to acknowledge is: most speakers speak too quietly. New public speakers are often confused about how loudly they should speak and aren't used to projecting their voices. The funny thing (to me at least) is that they are worried about speaking too loudly. It's like listening to music on your earphones and worrying that your neighbours across the road might raise a noise complaint — you don't need to worry!

The majority of speakers can benefit from speaking louder and clearer. Your words might seem loud to you, but they need to travel. Some rooms have terrible acoustics, others have ambient noise, and if the audience members listening to you are older than you, their ears might not be as sensitive as yours. When people with hearing difficulties have been in the audience, they often come up and thank me for actually being able to hear a speech for once!

Listening to your speech should not feel like work to your audience. If your audience is straining to hear you, they will be tempted to stop listening. They need to be able to relax and enjoy the performance. Also in my experience of consuming content, if something is easy to hear and euphonious, you're more likely to agree with it.

If you're still sceptical, here's what I want you to do. Set-up a camera (better yet, get a friend to help) and walk a good ten to fifteen metres away and then:

1) Speak at your normal 'presentation volume'.
2) Imagine the camera is your audience, and speak to the camera.
3) Speak louder.
4) Deepen your voice and speak louder.
5) Continue to increase your volume until you feel you're slightly too loud.
6) Speak a bit louder.
7) Review the footage.

Unless you have a camera with a fantastic microphone, you will find that your voice in steps 3-6 was far clearer and easier to hear than your usual step 1 volume. If you had a friend to help, ask them for their feedback. Don't worry about speaking too loudly (as long as you weren't shouting or straining your voice) the problem is usually that you are too quiet. By following this exercise you will be encouraged to speak up!

You might be hoping to hear some of my advice on how to reach the right volume for you. Great news, I'm going to share some with you.

I learnt how to project my voice from acting and singing. In acting, you're taught to get your voice to hit the back wall. If it helps you can pretend someone is sitting at the back of the room. I recommend taking a singing lesson to learn to project your voice properly. In my experience, it's not about pushing your voice to the back of the room, it's more about using your breath to throw it. Take a singing lesson!

When I speak, I endeavour to get my voice to fill the room that I'm in. This means that in some rooms I need to be louder than others (due to acoustics, the size of the audience, and how far away they are). But I can't stress enough — your voice should fill the room. No matter where anyone decides to sit, they should hear you. Even fill the room if you're speaking in a small presentation room. When I speak, I want to fill the entire room with my warmth, and I do that by filling it with my voice.

When you're speaking you need to pay attention to your breathing, where you're speaking from, and your pitch. If you're not breathing in enough air, it becomes challenging to speak. The next thing that I advise you to think about is where you're speaking from. As you probably guessed, you should be using your diaphragm. I also recommend speaking in a deeper voice while presenting as it's easier to hear, and serves as a reminder for you to utilise your diaphragm.

When I first saw Martin Taylor (the hypnotist — not the guitar player!) perform, I was amazed by how he could speak loudly but in a relaxed manner. The following year when I was at one of his lectures I asked him afterwards how he did it. He gave me the most helpful piece of advice on how to achieve a higher volume when speaking.

Martin told me that he tried to say things like he was singing them. Not only did he burst into song at that point, singing about the entire periodic table, but he gave another striking example: "It's what market traders do," he said, and then he sang: "Banaaaaanaaaas, baaaaanaaaanaaaas, get your baaaanaaaanaaas!" A light bulb went off in my head. If I were to continuously shout, "Bananas," my voice would quickly get tired, but I could sing it for a long time.

If I want to warm up a room and say good evening, I don't shout, "GOOD EVENING!" Instead I try to make a smooth curve with my voice like I'm singing it, "Goood eeeeveniiingg!" Give it a try.

One question you might be wondering is if I speak like a presenter all the time. No — I don't. I might use my public speaking voice when I need to get people's attention, but I never use it in conversation. So don't worry, you don't need to make a humongous life change. Just work on your volume while presenting. You will likely speak clearer in everyday conversation anyway from working on your breathing.

Remember when you present to project more and speak louder. You want to fill the room with your energy. Even if it's strange at first, you will be amazed at how much easier it is to win over an audience when they can actually hear what you're saying!

Deactivate Your Robot Voice

In 6th form our teacher would say: "Okay we need to get through five pages from the textbook," everyone would sigh. Our teacher would then come back with, "What if I got Matt to read it to you?" Suddenly everyone would get excited. I'm not making this up! My classmates enjoyed me reading dull textbooks to them because I:

- Added energy and enthusiasm to my voice.
- Played around with the energy I projected — going from bouncy to dull, to manic.
- Used accents and different voices when reading quotes.
- Changed my volume according to what I was reading.
- Added dramatic pauses and looked around at everyone.
- Came at dry subjects with a slightly tongue in cheek attitude — which made them exciting and easier to understand.

As you can imagine, being asked to read out loud for the class was my favourite part of school (behind being invited to present to the class of course).

In contrast, the majority of other pupils read things out in class like a robot whose battery was running out. They said to me that they could never read like I did because they weren't confident enough. This baffled me. I felt like I wasn't confident enough to read like they did, it looked so cringe-worthy and painful!

Whenever I heard someone read or present with no expression, no inflection and none of their own personality, it felt like nails on a chalkboard to me. I could never understand how my peers could take such a fun opportunity and turn it into the most socially awkward experience of all time. No wonder they hated reading in class.

Learning how to make factual writing sound entertaining gave me strong public speaking foundations. "The words alone are nothing without the right energy to carry them," was continually hammered home to me through experience.

Here's an exercise to try. Take a book and find a random page:
1) Read the page out loud.
2) Reread it, but pretend to be the world expert on the subject.
3) Read it while pretending to be someone who hates the subject.
4) Read it — pretending to be the biggest fan of the subject.
5) Read each paragraph in a different voice or accent.
6) Repeat step five and insert pauses and volume changes.
7) Freestyle!

The exercise is meant to be fun. If you found it a chore, either find a different page or try to enjoy yourself more. It's a re-learning experience. You're learning to entertain yourself and others by reading.

After completing the exercise, you will have discovered how entertaining you can make any subject. All you needed to do was to approach something you have done countless times (like reading out loud) from a different angle. Instead of being a robotic fact relaying machine — you were an entertainer and an engaging story-teller.

"But I just want to talk normally..."
Often when people speak of 'talking normally' they mean talking without energy in a rather compressed and emotionally flat manner, like a pancake. When speaking like this — audiences stop listening. It doesn't matter what you're saying, it will just be too easy to lose focus.

I believe that because of habituation, when a listener becomes accustomed to a speaker's voice they will stop paying as much attention. Their mind will wander. Instead of her speaking like a pancake, imagine if the speaker's delivery style had as much variety as a breakfast from an international buffet (rice, cereal, croissants, salami, baked beans, soup — the works). Every time the speaker changed her voice in any way, people would have to listen. When done entertainingly throughout a speech she would continually conduct her audience's full attention.

If you want to make your voice less robotic, ask yourself, "How can I be more entertaining?" You have a different voice and a different appreciation of entertainment to me — and from anyone. So by asking yourself how to make your speech more entertaining, you can come up with unique ways to make the driest piece of content an absolute delight to listen to.

"But I'm a serious speaker — I don't want to be 'entertaining'."

Entertainment comes in many different forms. Think of how many genres of films you can have: thriller, drama, action, comedy, romance, horror, documentary — they're all entertaining in their own way. If you have to present some content which is more sensitive, you might not want to use too much humour, but you can use your voice to create suspense, shock, power, and tenderness. You can utilise different tones and emotions to encourage your audience to care about the people involved.

If you're a speaker who wants to be taken seriously, being a flat pancake is not the way to go about it. When presenting to an audience, being passionate triumphs. People want to see that you believe in what you're saying and that you are passionate about your message and your subject (if you're not, why should they be?). We fully communicate our love through vocally projecting our energy with a rich and textured delivery.

Practise reading entertainingly as often as you can. When reading a recipe, a film description, an email, an article, or a blog post. The more you practise, the more you will expand your vocabulary of vocal delivery and discover just how exciting your voice can be. Consider your robotic voice — powered down.

Motivate Your Movements

One of the top three 'mistakes' that I see speakers make is moving aimlessly around on stage. They do not have an aim when they move. During a speech do you know why you're moving?

As a teenager, Stanislavski's theories blew my mind. You've probably consumed some of them without even knowing it. Especially from the acting joke: if an actor is asked to do something, she asks, "What's my motivation?" Stanislavski's work taught me that characters don't just move about for no reason. Characters always have goals, they want to achieve something at all times during a performance. It should be the same for public speakers.

Imagine being a mighty oak tree on stage, with solid roots supporting you. By rooting yourself on stage, you will appear to be in control of your speaking area. When you're in control of your speaking area — your audience can relax and feel like they're in the safe hands of an expert. As the expert, you decide when you want to move.

When you want to move, you need to know — what do you want to achieve by moving? If you have no answer to this, you are moving aimlessly (literally, without an aim). The most common unmotivated movements I see are speakers walking, leaning, curtseying, moving one leg in front of the other, or shifting their weight for no reason.

It's not enough to think: "I've been still for a long time, I should probably move." That might be true, but to move without motivation is to move without power. Instead, you need to retrain yourself into thinking: "I need to move over there soon – **because**..." If you find a reason for moving, you will empower your movements on stage.

You can plan or create a reason to move

You can form a motivation to move by strategically placing a prop at a different part of the stage to you. At some point in your speech you will have to move so you can interact with it. You can also plan a reason to move by including verbs in your speech. While talking about walking or running if you move at the same time, you will bring your story to life.

You can create a reason to move by engaging with your audience. If you interact with a specific audience member, for instance, asking her for a high-five, you will have a reason for walking towards her. Another reason to move is when you are bringing a story to life through movement. Instead of describing a story, try making it an immersive experience by using your body to make it feel like the events are happening in front of the audience's eyes.

Get ready to stand up and practise this with me now. Let's imagine that you've finished a section of your speech where you have stood in one spot like a mighty tree. You now want to move to another spot to wake up your audience and to make them move their heads. The last line of your previous section was: "And that's why I called my dog, Charlie." Say the line each time and pick a motivation below for moving (try them all).

"And that's why I called my dog, Charlie…"

- "Who here has a dog?" Imagine that an audience member lifts her hand, walk closer to her, "What did you call your dog?"
- "Of course Charlie's favourite game," walk towards your prop (a stick) located somewhere else on stage while talking "…is to play fetch."
- "Charlie ran away the other day." Run along the stage while exclaiming, "So I had to run after him!"

- "I took Charlie on a lovely walk yesterday," mime holding a dog lead and walk along the stage while talking.
- "When I was a child and lived at home with my parents..." walk to another part of the stage and squat down while talking, "...I always wanted my own dog."

After trying each of the above motivations and movements, you should have a good idea of how to insert movement into your speeches.

As you saw with the second one (moving for a prop), you can plan movements in advance. This is particularly useful when you're planning a speech, and you notice that you are standing in one spot for too long. Prepare a motivation for you to move. Your speech structure must give you moments that motivate movement. If it doesn't, you need to add more action into your plan.

Final request: Please don't shift your weight or 'go for a little walk' without a reason. It's so easy to either plan or to create a reason to move. Here's an instant example, you need to get up and practise this lesson. Now you have your reason to move — so move!

Gestures: The Untold Story

Over the years, one thing that I have been consistently complimented on in my public speaking is my use of gestures. The reason why I want to discuss this topic is because I see a lot of bad advice about gestures being thrown around: "Make these five gestures, and it will fix everything," or: "Learn these five gestures to look confident." Please don't fall for these kinds of claims.

My opinion on gestures is the same as with public speaking in general — your approach comes first. What approach do I recommend for gestures? That you use a gesture to create a visual image of what you're saying, to reinforce your point, and to make it memorable.

Anything that you can say with your words, you can communicate with your gestures — without using sign language!

Think of an animal. How could you show me what animal you're thinking of through gesturing? Think about it. I want you to think of your own ideas first, and then you can see what I thought of. Only use my ideas if you need help getting started or by some chance we came up with the same gesture.

What gesture/body language could you use to say you were thinking of an:
1. Elephant
2. Bird
3. Rabbit
4. Gorilla
5. Spider

Think for a little while about this. Remember, you want your gesture and body to create a visual image of the chosen animal and to be memorable. Use actions, space, your emotions, even sound effects if they help. Don't limit yourself. If you need to, stop reading and come back to this a bit later.

Welcome back. What answers did you come up with? My answers aren't necessarily right, they are simply what my mind came up with.

1. Elephant

My idea was to use my arm as a trunk, to lean over and have it wag across my face as I walked. I also thought that it could be funny to pretend to audibly 'suck' things up the trunk such as an audience member's pen, snacks, or water.

2. Bird

In my speech on motivation, I used a sock puppet to act like a bird, with a cloth serviette to look like wings. Without using a prop, the hands are great for imitating wings, or the arms can do the classic 'chicken wings'. Another idea was to pretend to pick a bird up with cupped hands and to mime throwing it into the air. I like that one a lot because it's a powerful and recognisable motion that could make people flinch: "Is he throwing a bird at me?" Or the audience will follow the bird's trajectory with their eyes.

3. Rabbit

There's the classic, hands behind the head and then hopping around routine. I've used that a fair few times! I also thought that you could mime eating a carrot, like a certain famous, wise-cracking rabbit. You could even mime removing a top hat and then pulling a rabbit out of it. Top hats instantly make audiences think, "Rabbit!"

4. Gorilla

Gorillas are imposing, and so I would use large, primal body language, space under the arms and a wide stance. A slight hunch and of course chest beating always helps. My second idea was to mime a cage and to pretend that a gorilla has you by the arm and is pulling you in. By putting your hand in upwards, it will communicate that a tall animal is inside. You could even mime peeling a banana and sticking that inside the cage first.

5. Spider

I'm sure you've noticed that your hand can move like a spider does. I would have my hand act spidery and rest on my back, moving while I try to brush it off. My second idea was to mime holding a glass and to pretend to catch a spider on the wall using it. If you wanted to create a small scare, use a real glass...and I'll leave the rest of this evil idea up to you, so I don't get blamed for it.

How did our ideas compare? Did you do better than me? If so — well done!

Notice the process that we used for devising our gestures. We had an idea that we wanted to communicate visually (in this case an animal) and then we thought about how we could use our bodies to communicate it. We did not sit around and think: "What gestures do I know? Oh, I know how to wiggle my thumb, so it looks like a lit stick of dynamite. I'll use the word dynamite in my speech!" or: "I only know five gestures, I hope an appropriate sentence pops up when I can use them." Having a limited set of gestures is the ineffective method of thinking that is constantly being blown around. When we worked with the image first and asked ourselves how we could use gestures to bring the image to life — the sky was the limit.

It's important to remind you that you can communicate anything with your gestures and your body. You can show people where in the world you are: a hot place, cold place, a jungle, a city, a farm, inside a fish tank, in an office (life's aquarium), or perhaps even outer-space. You can also communicate your feelings visually, you can portray excitement or sadness using your body. You can literally communicate ANYTHING you want to.

There have been times where I've not been able to talk for a few weeks because of laryngitis or ulcers (ewww) but I always used those times as a chance to practise gesturing. Once you've bought a bus ticket with gestures, placed a food order, asked for directions, and for a photo with a stranger, you start to get the hang of gesturing. It was these experiences that taught me that gestures aren't useful just because they give your hands something to do. They are another channel of communication.

If you want to get better at gestures, get into the habit of bringing your words and ideas to life with your body. When you've written a speech, why not write a list of your key images and work through the list as we did together? If you do this, your gestures will not only reinforce your messages, but they will also capture your audience's imagination.

I have more to say about using gestures, particularly points that speakers overlook and some that speakers worry about.

What should I do with my hands?
When giving a speech, you want to have a relaxed body. If you constantly use gestures, they will become ineffective. That's why when you're not gesturing, your hands should go down by your sides (this is the neutral position). Ideally, your hands should not be touching anything while at your sides so that they can spring up and gesture at a moment's notice. I like to keep my upper frame relaxed so that my hands are a short distance away from my legs. If your hands naturally brush your legs, that's okay just try not to actively touch your legs. Remember — when you're not gesturing, your hands go back to the neutral position.

When you're speaking (and not holding anything) your hands are either gesturing or down at your sides. If you stick to this way of thinking you will never have to worry about hand clasping, fiddling, having your hands on your hips, or in your pockets. Either gesture or have them by your sides. Case closed.

Don't copy other speakers' gestures

A gesture is powerful because it holds an emotional meaning to the speaker, or it's their interpretation of something. Therefore it doesn't make sense for you to note down and pinch another speaker's gestures.

If you want to find inspiration for new gestures, here are some ideas:

- Research and analyse how something works or an action is performed. For instance, if you want to perform a drinking gesture, think about how you hold a glass. How heavy is it? How quickly do you drink it? And how do you fiddle with it or use it when you're not drinking with it? You can analyse anything in this way, and the gestures you discover will be unique to you.

  Similarly, if you want to mime something that you don't normally do (for me this would include digging a hole and mountain climbing) watch video footage of someone doing it. When you understand how the action should look, gesturing will become a lot easier. If possible go beyond imitation by learning why an action has to be performed a certain way: Learn the mechanics of the gesture. Think about what physical laws and forces might be affecting you in that situation.

- Read books on mime and watch mimes and silent performers. I haven't been formally trained on how to mime, but by reading books on the subject, I came to learn some of the ideas and principles. Watching mimes opened my eyes to what could be achieved on stage without using the voice. Sometimes that's all you need to get your creativity firing.

- When in doubt, look to the arts. Films, TV shows, theatre, dance, comic books — anything artistic can give you new ideas about how to gesture and use your body. I mainly look for ideas that make me feel something. For instance, a sharp movement that feels powerful to me or a way of moving that makes me laugh out loud.

Gesture from your audience's perspective

When delivering a speech, it can be easy to forget that you are facing a different way to your audience. As I have learnt through practising magic, if something looks great from your perspective: check to see what it looks like from the audience's. So often I would think that I mastered a coin vanish — to me, it looked amazing. But the second I stood in front of my mirror I was shown that it never disappeared from the audience's view at all!

Filming yourself helps with the problem of perspective because you will be able to see your movements from the audience's view. It's easy to forget sometimes that your audience can't see what you can. A gesture might look good when you're looking down at it, but to your audience, it might be difficult to see. If you made a gun with your fingers and pointed it straight at someone, you would see a gun, but he would only see the tips of your fingers! Turning the finger-gun so that it's at an angle will allow him to see the entire gesture and to recognise what it's representing. One training idea is to set up your camera at different angles while you practise your gestures so you can see it from multiple points of view.

Remember to mirror your gestures where appropriate. Your audience is facing a different direction from you. That means that if you are trying to indicate going from left to right, you will need to gesture from right to left. It might sound confusing, but when you film yourself, you will see how simple this is to do.

Big and small gestures

People seem to accept that being open and taking up more space is a 'confident' physical display. Therefore shouldn't gestures and movements be more open, larger, and take up more space? If you want to inject more energy into a speech — open gestures get the job done. However, my advice is not to overuse open gestures because they will start to lose their 'punch'.

Don't write off smaller gestures. Smaller, space-saving gestures can be effective when used correctly and can create an interesting contrast to the larger gestures. When using smaller gestures: always exaggerate them to increase their visibility and recognisability. For instance, if you were miming a coin toss don't just slightly raise your thumb. Make it clear that you're resting a coin on your thumb, then spring your thumb all the way up and immediately look up and follow the imaginary coin with your eyes. Then mime catching the coin and slapping it down onto the back of your hand. It's a relatively small gesture but the exaggeration and commitment make what you are doing much more recognisable.

What words do you say the most?

Find the words you say the most while speaking. As speakers, we use numbers a lot, "Here are my three main points," or: "Reason number two!" Almost everyone overuses their usual set of compliments. You might be inclined to say,
"I loved it," or, "I really like your clothes." It makes sense to devise unique gestures for these frequently used words and phrases. Write down the words you use most alongside a few different gestures that you have devised for them. Need some inspiration?

When you say: "Here are my three main points," how do you signal that there are THREE main points? Do you put three fingers up or count your fingers? So does everybody else! Think up new ways of communicating numbers with your body. You could jump three times (making 3 loud bangs) or do three karate chops (one in each direction) or sandwich and lift your foot between your two hands. Come up with something original.

If you say: "I loved it!" all the time, how do you normally communicate this phrase with your body? Do you put two thumbs up? I thought so. How else could you communicate with your body that you love something? You could pretend your heart was beating out of your chest, that you were mesmerised, part of a Shakespearean tragedy, or even salivating over a fishcake — be inventive!

If you're the sort of person who likes to compliment a person's clothes: "I really like your clothes," how do you do it? Do you gesture to your own clothes? What else could you do? One idea I had was to mime picking up a hanger off the rack and to either pretend to put the clothes on or to mime putting them in a bag while asking the follow-up question, "Where did you buy them?"

Now think about the words that you say the most. Think up some original gestures, from your own creative mind.

Please remember: The most important thing with gestures is to know why you're gesturing. You're gesturing to reinforce your words by communicating them visually. Knowing this should be liberating. Please resist the urge to 'learn gestures' from articles, videos, and books. Your words are unique to you — your gestures should be too.

Is It a Performance or a Speech?

A comment that I have received a fair number of times about my speeches is: "That wasn't just a speech, it was a performance." I take that as a compliment. The people who have made the comment are usually those who are new to my style of speaking and are just starting to see the possibilities of what makes a 'live' speech such an extraordinary experience.

For those who are familiar with my style of presenting — a speech is also a performance. Your job as a speaker is not just to deliver information: it's to engage, entertain, and to inspire the people listening. Otherwise you will be talking, but no one will be listening. People seem mostly ignorant of this fact. They pretend to ignore that as experienced information consumers we no longer have the attention spans or the time for a speaker to pour out barrel loads of dry, unflavoured, and unseasoned information.

When people who are new to public speaking think of what a speech is: they conjure up images of political leaders, someone standing behind a podium and talking. They imagine this because this style of speaking is what their leaders do and have always done. But the truth is, the world and the ways we learn have evolved.

It's funny reading books from the 80's where authors preach about how much the world had changed thanks to television and those 'distracted youths' with their music videos and their arcade games. It's laughable because these authors had no idea how that was the tip of the iceberg and our world would change so much more in the coming decades. How could anyone foresee that we would live on a racetrack of information uploading and downloading?

To get a feel for how much we now crave constant stimulation and a fast pace, watch the beginnings of older films. Notice how long the opening credits last. In some films, they last a good five minutes. No one would have time for that now, they would fast forward, pull out their phone, or maybe even put on another film. Older films also contain stretched out scenes with little action to create an atmosphere like in a play. Again — the phone comes out.

Our films today are usually streamlined, we want each scene to fit into the genre's story structure and for every scene to progress the story. The scenes take us from place to place, action to action; at a fast pace. I am not saying that this focus on speed and progression makes our contemporary films better. I enjoy a lot of the subtle nuances in atmospheric storytelling, that's why I love the theatre. But the reality is that the majority of audience members need content delivered to them in ways that understand and play to the changes in our media consumption.

Over the years the sheer amount of information and media that we are bombarded with each day from our phones alone has been increasing exponentially. There's just too much content and too much competition for our time.

We need our content to be intriguing, fast, rich, and hard-hitting. Intrigue draws us in: "10 hacks to lose weight in two seconds." A quickly consumable piece of content stops us from getting bored and looking at something else. And a hard-hitting message means that we will remember and talk about what we learnt. With phones in their pockets, our audiences can access limitless information and entertainment in an instant — and as speakers, we have to compete with that.

As technology has progressed so much, why do we even have live speeches today? You can go online and stream enough speeches and presentations to last several lifetimes. Here are a few of my ideas why people want the real thing instead of a recording or a live-stream:

1. For an experience

People want to be wowed and to leave with memories that they can always remember and share with others: "The day I went to see Matt, I was sitting in the second row. I didn't know what exactly was going to happen — and then the lights went down and..."

2. To see the speaker in person

Some people might want to meet the speaker, others might just want to see what the speaker looks like in real life. When you only see someone on a screen, seeing them in real life makes their message so much stronger because you'll think: "Wow! They're real. Their life's real. It makes sense that what they're saying can also be real. It certainly looks like it is."

People want to see that you are a real person and that you embody what you talk about. If you're a happiness coach — they will be looking to see if you look happy, especially when things go wrong.

3. Trust

It's the reason why people still have face to face meetings. People want to see a real person on stage. Someone without notes who is an expert on what they're talking about.

When speaking to a camera, you could easily be lying about yourself and your life. Anyone can say that they're a memory champion on camera. They could have notes written behind the camera or secretly try several takes. But if someone stands in front of an audience and memorises and recites a phone book, the penny drops: "Wow she really is a memory champion."

When I give a speech, I ensure that my audience really learns from our time together. But I want it to be an experience — I want people to have a great time and to leave with stories to tell.

I love meeting audience members after a speech and asking how they're speaking's going, and I love using the ideas I talk about. I use my interests and express myself to the max on stage so that others can feel inspired enough to express themselves more. It's funny when people mention how loud I am. Or they're amazed that I don't use notes and how instead I look into their eyes during a speech. Their eyes widen when they see that my energy fills the room and they feel how exciting it is when anything could happen. They learnt from my speech, and they were moved by my performance. All of these things have a far stronger impact in real life — than they do on camera.

I have a question for the traditionalists, those who see a speech and a performance as two separate entities that should never be brought into contact with one another. The people out there who think that a speech should just be standing and talking like a politician or reading off a slideshow: "Why do you even need to be there in person?"

If you're not creating an experience for your audience, showing them that your life embodies your message or proving to them that you are the expert you say you are — why turn up? Is it for the money? Do you refuse to 'perform' and entertain because you are scared to update how you communicate? Maybe you're reluctant to let slip your facade of: "Oh I'm a professional, I'm above performing and entertaining my audience. I can just hide behind my job title and deliver page after page of dry information."

Here is my advice to people who want to 'update' their speaking style and who want to create amazing live experiences: express yourself more, see yourself as a performer and a speaker. A speech should be a performance to you. You need to consider your audience and all the performance elements that can engage them, and not just 'what you say'. Do this, and you will get the reactions that your message deserves and you will rock live events.

When someone says to me: "That wasn't just a speech, it was a performance," I take it as a compliment because I wanted them to have a fantastic experience. I wanted them to see who I am and to discover that I live what I talk about. I am both a public speaker, and a performer — a video of my speech will never come close to what it felt like in person.

Befriend and Understand Your Audience

Everyone Is a Friend

One thing about me that not many people know is that as a teenager I had my visual memory tested. The test revealed that my visual memory was far below average which explained why I found visual learning so difficult. It also explained another one of my difficulties — remembering and recognising faces.

I used to find it strange when someone would come up to me and start talking to me when I had no idea who they were. Eventually, the unrecognisable person would say something that would help me to work out their identity. I felt so bad every time it happened, and I never wanted to hurt anyone's feelings. That's when I taught myself to treat everyone I met like a friend, that way no one would ever get offended if I didn't recognise them.

The interesting thing that sometimes happened as a result of treating everyone like a friend was that it became easier to make friends. When you see everyone as a friend, it not only helps you relax but it also makes you want to cheer everyone up instead of wanting to shuffle off and hide somewhere.

When I give a speech: I like to imagine that everyone in the audience is a friend of mine. This is a helpful mindset. When you think that everyone wants you to do well, it becomes a lot easier for you to powerfully deliver your speech and to share who you are. Next time you speak: seek friendship by searching for smiles and kind looks. By searching for them, you will be much likelier to find them!

If you are feeling a bit down about things and feel afraid of audiences. Try seeing everyone as a friend. You might be surprised by what happens.

Feel Great Before You Speak

I find it interesting to hear what different speakers do before they speak. There are many pre-speech rituals that people do. Some speakers meditate, some sit still and drink coffee, and others isolate themselves to 'get in the zone'. If none of those things sound appealing to you, keep reading!

There are some things to do before a speech that I think you have to do, and others that I think you should do.

In my view, the essentials before a speech include: drinking water, relieving yourself, and warming up your voice.

1. Staying hydrated is essential if you want to get the most out of your voice and to avoid some of the unpleasant dry mouth noises that microphones pick up.
2. Going to the toilet is rather self-explanatory, you want to think about your speech, not your bladder.
3. I believe that a vocal warm-up is also something you have to do, but be savvy about it. If you want to be energetic and expressive with your voice — you need to warm up first. If you don't warm up, you could self-inflict vocal damage or at least struggle to speak the next day. You don't have to be a prima donna and do vocal warm-ups in front of people. Go somewhere private and warm up, or sing in the car. After you have tried warming up your voice, I'm sure you will find how much easier and more comfortable it is to be more vocally expressive.

Most speakers I see: sit by themselves and obsess over what they're about to say. Shouldn't they already know what they're going to say? A quick five-minute recap is fine, but don't spend an hour freaking yourself out. It's not doing you any favours. What do I think you should do before a speech?

I personally like to 'get in costume' and make sure that all of my props are ready to go (it's the magician in me) and to check that the technology is all ready — and working. I also like to ensure that I have some water to have on stage if I need it and that I have discussed what I need to with the host (for instance, how I'm going to be introduced). If I'm planning on throwing some cards or doing anything that requires dexterity, I will shoot some cards out and have a quick practise to get my hands and coordination all ready to go.

I make sure that I know when I need to be ready to go on and ensure that I'm where I need to be in good time. Then I stop. I let myself relax and forbid myself from running my speech over and over in my mind until my brain hurts. The rest of the time I'm letting myself feel happy, making people smile and having fun.

"Woah, woah, woah! Did you say *fun*?"

Having fun, making people smile, and sharing excitement are what makes my approach different from most people's pre-speech routines. Most people are so concerned with 'calming down' that when they walk on stage, they feel a bit down or emotionally flat. If your body feels excited, trying to force yourself to feel calm will likely cause inner-conflict.

If you have told some jokes, shared some laughs, and in general made lots of people smile — you're in the perfect frame of mind to present. You can go on stage feeling like you have been super-charged with positivity (because you have been). An added bonus is that the people who you made smile will support you and want for you to do well before you set foot on stage (and they will smile at you during your speech). You won't ever hear crickets again.

When I wrote my first book on public speaking, I included an entire chapter on the importance of making people smile before a presentation and how to do it. It's just that important to me. I feel that too many speakers are so concerned with being seen as 'a professional expert' that they forget to loosen up and make friends. I'm talking about in a genuine way — not a sales manager style: "Mwah ha ha, I wonder what I can get out of this chump."

Go and have fun with people. I love giving people gifts and smiles. Sure you can be Miss. Professional, sit by yourself, and act all important — but you will likely get locked inside your head and start doubting yourself. To prevent this from happening you can give to others and make other people feel amazing. You will be made to feel like a major celebrity as people remember you, smile at you and sometimes even give you things!

If you like the idea of feeling incredibly happy and positive before your speech: try my way. Go and cheer some people up, have some fun, share some laughs and give them a smile. It might just change your whole outlook on public speaking.

Uplift Everyone

I often stress that every audience member should feel just as happy if not happier after watching you speak. It's one of my core beliefs for public speaking.

I have been described as a positive person, "Some people are naturally happy," is the line I often hear. I really do have a lot in my life to be grateful for. However, for me, positivity is something I have to work for.

When I say that I have to 'work' for positivity, I mean that there are things I need to do to not only feel positive but also to stay that way. I try to stick to entertainment that is intended to make me laugh or feel happy and I avoid the news! These things aren't hard to stick to, the difficult part is not to indulge negative thoughts that appear. I am acutely aware of my own thoughts, and I'm constantly challenging them. It's partly because of this that I know how disastrous entertaining or dwelling on negative thoughts can be.

It took me longer than I would like to admit to learn the simple lesson that it's not 'stuff' that makes me happy but the people I spend time with. Whenever I think back to my favourite memories, they all involve other people. Initially, when you look back, you might think: "Oh it was the place I went to for my holiday that made me happy. It was eating half of that ice cream. It was that board game I got to play, that piece of technology, that I bought," for me, it was never the stuff, it was the people I spent time with that made the memories magical. I see some public speakers who admit that they only speak to promote their business, that's their only reason for doing it. This makes me shake my head because they should also do it because they love speaking to audiences and being able to help people.

I love having friends who are so kind and positive. The great thing about having friends like that is you can be optimistic and energetic without feeling out of place. At the same time, if there comes a day when I'm not my usual self, they're there to inspire me to be positive.

My friend Kasia and I became friends within minutes of meeting each other. I thought: "Oh my gosh, she's the most positive person I've ever met!" And not many people are open-minded enough to befriend a guy wearing a bright orange scarf that went down to his ankles. I would like to thank Kasia for making studying for our psychology degrees so much fun.

Our study sessions were the best. When everyone Kasia and I studied with got annoyed at me for making a rowing boat out of cheesecake or for building a tree out of newspapers, she always saw the funny side of my antics. That's how life should be when you try to be a positive person. When you get to spend time with other positive people you can enjoy and treasure the memory of anything you do together. That's what I want to share with everyone who comes to see me speak.

While you're speaking to an audience, everyone is connected. Everyone is in the same place, experiencing the same thing. In this room, everyone is part of a group. Watching a speech is not the same as watching television by yourself. I want people to experience the warmth of friendship so that no matter where they have to go once they leave the room, they have a fond memory to take with them, which contains a message that will help them.

Are They Even Listening?

Imagine — you're in the zone, you have grand plans for your next speech. You convince yourself that it's going to be the best you've given so far. You find yourself smiling at all the clever parts coming up. You go out to give your speech and then, "Meh," your audience doesn't pay much attention to you. When you talk to people afterwards, no one can tell you what you just spoke about. Isn't that the worst?!

I am all about being creative and sharing who you are with others. But there's always a point when planning your speech that you have to stop looking at it from your perspective. You need to shift your vision and see things from your audience's point of view. It's not until you start doing this that you will learn to structure your speeches with clarity and begin to turn areas where attention levels dip into moments of intrigue.

Speeches need clarity like plants need sunlight. If what you're talking about isn't abundantly clear, your audience is going to feel lost.

I think all speakers start with a sort of vanity (which often translates into nervousness) and believe that their audience is going to give them 100% laser-focused attention and remember every word they said:
"Thanks for the speech. I just have to say though — I didn't understand why you started talking about Frisbees after your introduction about staplers,"
"Weren't you listening? I explained why I used that metaphor during the 213th line!"
No one gives you that much attention in the real world. I'm not sure if an audience even has the capacity for that much attention.

Your speech is not a Shakespearean play that will be analysed word for word. It's not a university essay where someone experienced in the subject can slowly look through your structure. You're presenting to people who will lose focus and will not remember every section — let alone every line you said. That's why I hammer on so much about having a main message, some audience members might only remember a single thing from your talk!

Paying attention for an extended period of time is hard work. People's thoughts will wander for parts of your speech, and you have to accept that. This is why clarity is so important. If you introduce your speech by saying what your main message is, your audience will be able to re-join the story after they 'drop off' for a short time in the middle. If you don't have a robust main message that connects with every section, your audience will be lost when they re-join and have to navigate amongst a hubbub of mini-messages.

Contrast these two examples:
"Today I'm going to tell you why Spain is amazing and that you should go on holiday there."
Compared to...
"Today I'm going to tell you about why Spain is amazing, Germany is also amazing, my new kitchen is spacious, the food in Poland is pretty interesting, I buy two seats when I go to the cinema, how I got a cool hat from America once and how I met a dog in India. Oh, and why holidays are good — but not always."

I feel sorry for the audience in the second example. Because there is no overarching main message, if the audience loses focus for even a minute — there is no way they will be able to know what's going on. Whereas in the first example they can lose focus several times and still think: "Oh cool, another reason why Spain is amazing, and I should go on holiday there."

Clarity, clarity, clarity. Have a clear main message and make sure all of your sections support it or reinforce it. If your speech is a dish at a restaurant and you advertise it as a burger on the menu — that's what you serve them. You don't have an item on the menu called: "I don't really have a name for this," and then serve your customer half a croissant dipped in lasagne with chocolate sauce, a burger bun, a can of soup-without the soup, some cocktail cherries, and a hiking boot. Keep your message simple and keep it clear throughout your speech.

As I'm talking about your audience's perspective, I need to recap my opinion on the idea of 'value'. I hear the word value being thrown around all over the place: "I want to deliver a speech that's of value to my audience." In public speaking, I see value as 'value for time'. To provide excellent value in exchange for your audience's time, learn as much as you can about your audience. Then cover the questions and topics that will be most relevant and interesting to them. Of course an audience will tune out if what you're saying has no bearing on their life!

If you've tailored your speech to your audience but you're still losing attention due to boredom — that's when you need intrigue. Essentially, you want to have moments in your speech that draw your audience in. I'm talking about the moments where your audience leans in to hear more and thinks, "I wonder what's going to happen?" You can ask an interesting question, say you're going to tell them a secret, create a sense of mystery, introduce your audience to something they're not familiar with or do something unconventional. Anything that will make your audience watch and listen with anticipation or excitement.

People who are finding a speech boring are most likely thinking that they've sussed out the structure, have heard it all before or that the content doesn't apply to them and so they're just going to zone out. Having a moment where the audience is in the dark, a moment where they think, "Oh my — I wasn't expecting that!" or where they see something unfamiliar that they need to evaluate (to see what it is and if it's of interest to them) makes them focus. If you have these moments strategically placed in your speech, no one can switch off out of boredom while you speak.

Below are some examples of how intrigue can wake-up an audience and grab hold of their attention. Imagine that you are sitting and watching a speech about how important it is to eat fruit and vegetables. You think you're wasting your time and begin thinking about what you're going to do when you get home — then suddenly:

- "Question for you. If you are marooned on a desert island, what fruit can save your life?"
- "Let me tell you a secret that the health and fitness industry doesn't want you to know about vegetables..."
- "Underneath your chairs is a picture of a fruit. If your picture matches the fruit inside this bag — you win a prize. Make sure to memorise your fruit, because I'll be opening the bag very soon."
- "In a second I'm going to show you a rare vegetable that you wouldn't have heard of, let alone seen before. Very few people get to see one. And I'm going to let you taste it."
- "Of course the real question we have to ask about fruit and vegetables is: who can throw them the best? I need two people to come on stage and throw some fruit and veg with me!"

I encourage you to think-up some moments of intrigue for your next speech.

When devising moments of intrigue you don't have to go nuts. Like with a lot of things, it's not just what you do — it's your attitude. If you're asking an interesting question ask it intriguingly and enthusiastically. But if you're sharing a 'secret' lower your volume, or whisper it loudly. If you're going to do something unconventional, make sure that the moment feels unexpected. If you announce: "In five minutes time I will stand on this table, is everyone okay with that?" you lose your moment of rebellion.

As soon as your speech feels 'ready to go' — imagine being an audience member watching. Film your speech and highlight the parts where your mind wanders, or you feel a bit bored. Is there clarity throughout your speech? Is it what your audience wants/ needs to hear? Are there moments of intrigue — and in the right places? By getting in-tune with your audience, you will help them to listen to you and remember your message.

Compensate for Their Lack of Energy

You're welcomed on stage with half-hearted applause, you look out at your audience and feel that the energy levels in the room are low. What should you do?

Some people might think that you are meant to 'mirror' your audience and to speak at a similar energy level to them. What do I think?

Forget that!

I feel disappointed when I see a speaker who copies the low level of energy that their audience has given to them, in their own delivery. The speaker then struggles to get their audience to pay attention or to engage with them. It's like speaking to a cold audience instead of a warm audience. I'm disappointed in the speaker for not warming up her audience!

The problem with a cold audience is that they won't give you the reactions that you deserve. Your jokes will not get much laughter, your points will not be met with as much enthusiasm, and you will not receive loud applause when you finish. All because your audience started off cold and you didn't warm them up.

If I happen to be sitting amongst a cold audience watching a speaker who is mirroring said audience: I try to help. I laugh loudly at the speaker's jokes and clap as loudly as I can and give a cheer, "Wooo!" when they come on stage. Doing these things warms up the rest of the audience for the speaker and gives the other audience members permission to react and to be livelier. As you probably guessed, if the speaker had higher energy levels to begin with — I wouldn't need to help them. Being more expressive than your audience and making an effort to raise the energy level in the room will make it a lot easier to obtain the reactions you desire.

What I am about to say might sound pretentious, but to me, it communicates to your audience that you have standards and you expect a certain amount of energy and enthusiasm. If you receive a round of applause as you walk to the speaking area, and you're not happy with it, don't be afraid to ask for more applause. The reason why it might sound pretentious is that you're probably imagining the cringe-worthy pantomime style of announcing: "That was terrible. This time I want you to give a round of applause so loud that my socks fall off!"

My favourite way to ask for more applause is to encourage my audiences to clap with me for someone else. This can be the emcee, the organiser, or even themselves. Asking an audience to clap for someone else does two things: it makes them like you, and it trains them to clap. A lot of the time audiences will overlook your applause cues later on if you've not taught them how to clap.

You don't need to communicate that you want more applause verbally if you don't want to. You can gesture towards your ear while your audience is clapping until the volume goes up, or you can gesture 'raise the volume, clap louder'. If you want to ask for more applause, try doing it funnily or cheekily. Another method I've used is to enter to music, it will pump the room with energy (seriously, many performers swear by it). By doing these things, you are doing the introducer/emcee's job, by ensuring that you start with enough energy in the room. Being unafraid to set a standard will end your reliance on how you've been introduced to energise your audience and to give you momentum.

I need to express that I personally dislike it when speakers begin their speech by getting their audience to stand up and do things. If you do this, you're squandering the beginning of your speech (see '*Public Speaking Is About Waves*', for more information on this) and making everyone resent you. No one enjoys being ordered to stand up and to do ridiculous warm-up exercises — sorry. Not to be a sourpuss, but I also dislike it when speakers ask people to get up and dance or touch people during a speech. Unless you're discussing the importance of touch or dancing — these exercises are out of context and distracting.

What can you do while speaking to an audience to raise their energy? Here are a few suggestions:

1) 'Raise the bar' by projecting more energy than the room expects from you

When you speak louder or more enthusiastically than people expect, or you express yourself more than they anticipated — you will raise the bar. When I talk about 'raising the bar' I am referring to the level of acceptable energy and expression in the room, where the bar has been set. When you defy your audience's expectations of how high a level of energy and expression is 'acceptable' you raise the bar.

Social psychology studies have shown that it only takes one person to do something for others to follow. People are scared of being the first. But once one person has written something on a bridge or a wall, several other people will do the same (we've all seen it — unfortunately). On a week-long drama course I went on: everyone sat in silence every morning. Then once I burst in and started joking around, the other dramatists began talking to each other. It takes one person to raise the bar and to change what's seen as acceptable.

When the bar is raised, everyone else feels like they have been given permission to react and express themselves more (this includes speakers who come on after you).

2) Interact with your audience

Pay attention to your audience and respond accordingly. If you notice that your audience is falling asleep (it really does happen), do something to wake them up. Or if they're giving you their attention but have their arms folded and they look reserved, tell a joke or do something to get them laughing.

If you are giving a longer speech and the energy in the room is low or flagging, you can take a more direct approach by asking a question. When you get an answer back, lead a loud round of applause. As a result, the energy in the room will increase. Leading applause for another person is a useful tool for when you need to pick up the energy levels in the room.

No matter how low on the energy scale your audience appears to be when you enter the speaking area, do not give in to 'peer pressure' and feel like you have to mirror them. You have the power to 'raise the bar' and to increase the energy levels inside the room. By doing so, you will get the reactions to your speech that you deserve.

Public Speaking Is About Waves

Many public speakers seem to assume that audiences have inexhaustible attention spans. If I drew a line graph of this perception of attention, it would be on a constant high. Most speakers don't stop to consider their audience's state of mind. They think that they can deliver a continuous stream of information and their audience will absorb every last detail.

Attention spans are not infinite! Audience members get tired. Their concentration levels dip. And their attention...wanders. Attention levels are never static horizontal lines, and so we shouldn't present audiences with an unrelenting barrage of information. Instead, we should synchronise the amount of information we share, and our energy levels with our audience's attention spans. Instead of thinking about our audience's attention spans as solid lines: we should picture them as waves.

When you speak, do you deliver a continuous stream of information? Does your speech require your audience to have remembered every single thing you've said for the next point to make sense? If so, your audience will tune out.

One way to break up the stream of information that I discussed in, '*Your Speech Is Like an Essay*', is to make parts of your speech stand out through highlighting. Making parts of your speech stand out, will relieve the pressure from your audience, by removing the necessity to pay active attention to every single word in the speech. However, you might still feel confused about where to highlight if you have not thought about how attention levels fluctuate.

I believe that when you see attention levels and your speaking as waves: understanding and anticipating attention levels will become intuitive.

Whenever I studied for exams, I followed the advice from the memory books I read, to take regular breaks. If I didn't, I would find my mind wandering. In fact, I can't remember a single study session where my brain didn't stray at some point. No matter what class I was in, when I listened to a teacher or lecturer, I would try my best to listen and then I would zone out. My mind would think about other things. Then when I paid attention again, I had already missed out on a lot of important information that wasn't written on the board or in my textbook. The worst part was when we were then told to go off and do the thing by ourselves. Do what thing?

Knowing that I would always zone out, I thought that it must happen to other students as well. That's why when I delivered presentations to my classmates, I would include plenty of summaries and wouldn't take it personally if they needed a minute or two to switch-off and think about something else. I also tried to change my energy levels during the presentation so that it was more engaging for them. My style seemed to work, and so I kept it.

What I have learnt over the years is that it's not just students who need to let their minds wander — everyone does! When giving a speech to an adult audience, I tend to find that attention levels continually dip and go back up.

Below is what I would expect to see during a short speech (seven minutes or less):

Paragraph number	Audience's attention levels
Introduction	10/10
1	8/10
2	6/10
3	4/10
4	6/10
5	8/10
Conclusion	10/10

Attention levels start on a high (I marked it as 10 for clarity) but then they rapidly drop. The audience's high attention levels at the start of the speech are why I say not to make your introduction too lengthy! Otherwise, by the time you get to the 'meat' of your speech, your audience's attention will have been depleted. However, attention levels do recover (as long as the speaker is interesting).

What I have noticed as an audience member is that the decline of my attention levels can be sped up. Some causes include being bombarded with too much information (it tires me out), not liking the speaker (why should I pay attention?), and if the speech does not offer me any value or emotionally engage me (why should I be interested?). If you were to plot the audience's energy levels on a graph, you would get a U-shaped curve. A speech that is longer than ten minutes could consist of more than one of these curves — and hence it will be made of waves.

Now I have armed you with my perspective that an audience's attention consists of waves, here are some things to take note of and to consider:

1) Your introduction and conclusion are critically important

The first line of your speech should make the most of your audience's high attention levels and grab them! Your introduction needs to serve as a guide to your speech so that when your audience 'dip out' while you speak, they can work out what they've missed and what point you're now covering. It also needs to be concise.

Your conclusion is composed of three parts: a summary, a call to action, and a snappy one-liner. The summary needs to summarise your speech and re-deliver the key points. Don't assume that everyone will 'just remember' your key points. You receive a lot of attention during your conclusion — capitalise on it. The call to action will tell your audience what to do next (in case it wasn't obvious). Your ending, snappy one-liner will encapsulate your speech in a thought-provoking and easy to swallow line.

2) Plan where you want to place your most important points

Your main message must run all the way through your speech (no one can miss it that way), but figure out how you can most effectively deliver your other points and examples based on your audience's fluctuating attention spans.

3) What can you do when your audience's attention spans are low?

Using more energy can help to get an audience's attention back. But remember that your audience will need mental breaks. I recommend using interesting anecdotes and examples during these times. Audience members still listening will enjoy the experience, but those who are zoning out will not miss anything too important. I think you would much prefer someone to miss out on one example rather than a key point of your speech.

4) When attention spans start to rise, what can you do to speed up the process and to awaken audience members who don't want to refocus on you?

Involving your audience is a sure-fire way to awaken them and to refocus them on you. Ask a rhetorical question or one that involves an arm raise. Or you can always use good-old intrigue!

5) How can you repeat the information you share?

There is much more that you can do than blatant repetition. Consider how you could weave in callbacks, reminders, and the odd recap into your structure.

6) How can you become aware of your audience's attention levels while you speak?

When you are making eye contact with audience members: pay attention to their energy levels and responses to you. Are they nodding along and smiling? Or are they yawning and staring at the ceiling? Cater your delivery to what you observe and synchronise what you say to achieve harmony with your audience.

When you speak, it's essential to calibrate your delivery to your audience's attention levels. Pay attention to your audience when you speak. Make a habit of this and you will notice that there will be times when members of your audience look a bit distracted. You can do something to get their attention back, "Who wants to win a prize?" Or you can synchronise your speech with how you predict your audience's attention levels will flow. Essentially: You can deliver your key points when attention levels are higher and provide interesting anecdotes and examples when they are lower. Plan to use more energy to slow down the decrease in attention or to speed up the increase. Lowering your energy is for when you want your audience to have a break and to relax.

I firmly believe that once you start thinking about an audience's attention levels, you will improve at creating and delivering speeches. It's something that I haven't seen talked about — but it's incredibly apparent to me when a speaker isn't aware of her audience's fluctuating attention levels. Pay attention to your audience and ride the waves!

Why Do You Speak?

What Fuels You?

What motivates you to give a speech? What do you need to pump yourself up enough to say, "I want to speak?" Is it a reward? Do you have anxiety: an uncomfortable feeling inside yourself that doesn't go away until you give your next speech? Or do you get angry and mentally punish yourself until you get up and speak? I think delivering speeches would be a lot easier if you decided to speak because you enjoyed it.

Many speakers need some form of motivation to speak. My issue with this is that I feel that relying on external motivations is ineffective and results in a constant mental tug of war. If you don't like public speaking, it's going to feel unpleasant and like work. On the other hand, if you enjoy giving speeches, it will feel like fun. You need motivation to work, you don't need it to have fun.

The way I see it, most speakers see speaking as work. As a result of this, they use business strategies to help them to 'get their work done'. I want to discuss why these forms of motivation are ineffective until you realise what you want to achieve with your speaking. I also want to stress that public speaking is not a roadblock — it's there to help you. As soon as you have these realisations, you can stop seeing public speaking as work and start seeing it as fun.

I find it shocking, looking at traditional business advice on ways to 'motivate' employees to work. The three which I see and hear the most are: more praise, more money, and more responsibility. None of these factors address the key issue: if you don't like or even believe in the work, then you're doing it because you have to or because you've been persuaded to — not because you want to. I think that the traditional motivations are most effective when someone's aspirations line-up with the work they're doing.

Imagine you love the idea of space travel, you want to be an astronaut but you currently work on a bean farm. Your job is to harvest beans — but you hate the job, and your bosses want to motivate you to work harder. Their first attempt to motivate you is to give you lots of praise. If you dream every day of being an astronaut and hate farming, it doesn't matter how often someone calls you the 'best bean harvester'. You don't care about that, you want to be called the best astronaut. In fact, every time they give you praise for being a bean harvester, it stamps on your dreams of being an astronaut.

Your bosses move onto their next tactic. This time they offer you a bonus to make you work harder.

Bonuses for someone who hates the work can feel like blackmail. If you don't work harder at the job you hate and harvest enough beans, you won't get your bonus. Not getting your bonus will affect your home-life. You will look bad in front of your family for not being able to afford the holiday they're expecting from you because of your steady 'well-paying' job. Now if you don't work hard enough you're not just letting the company down and yourself down but your family as well.

Alternatively, if you have enough money to live on and everything you need — why would you need more? To buy more stuff that doesn't make you happy? No thanks. Does a bit more money that you're not even going to spend make up for being miserable all day and unfulfilled all night?

Your bosses bargain on one last attempt to motivate you. They thrust more responsibility upon you. However, because you hate the job, you just see added responsibility as more work to do and more to be blamed for when things go wrong. Each of these 'motivations' has only added more stress to your job and actually 'demotivated' you.

How would things be different if instead of hating it, you loved farming and wanted to be the best bean harvester in the country? Every compliment and bit of praise you receive would make you swell with pride. Being offered more money for something you love doing would be a symbol of your excellence and make things more comfortable for you. Being offered more responsibility would be exciting because you're already motivated to learn as much as you can about your job, and now you get to learn about brand new areas of the bean business. And for the cherry on top: you get more recognition for the farm's successes.

Traditional motivations can make us feel even better about a job we already enjoy doing. However, when what we're doing feels like it has no relation to our aspirations and our sense of purpose and feels meaningless — no amount of motivation will make us enjoy it.

If you need a source of motivation to do public speaking outside of, "I just love doing it," — I think you need to re-evaluate what public speaking represents to you. Giving a speech is not the same as harvesting beans so you can survive long enough to one day be an astronaut. Public speaking is not standing in the way of your life having meaning. It's there to help you to find and share your aspirations and what you love. Public speaking allows you to express yourself, who you are, and how you want to change the world.

Public speaking is not stopping you: "Oh I want to get a promotion but my public speaking is getting in the way!" Instead public speaking is there to help you: "I want to get a promotion, and my public speaking is going to help me share my exciting new ideas and why I am uniquely suited for the job."

If I were to take away the nuts and bolts of public speaking and you could communicate telepathically with a room full of people, what will you be doing? Sharing your ideas and who you are. So many people forget that. They focus so much on the speaking side of things, they forget the purpose of speaking.

When you speak, it's your ideas and your uniqueness that you're sharing. Why are you sharing them? To help your ideas, yourself, and your audience — to grow. It's this growth that should excite you. Knowing that you are going to end your speech empowering your ideas and everyone present; should give you such a rush.

When you acknowledge that public speaking is there to support your aspirations and the things you love and not to stand in the way of them, you can appreciate the many growth opportunities that it offers. When you accept that public speaking is going to help you and your audiences, and will allow your ideas to spread and grow; you won't be dependent on other motivations to entice you to speak.

Instead of asking yourself, "How can I reward myself for speaking?" find out what your aspirations are. Learn what things you love talking about and what excites you. Then public speaking will stop being your mountain to climb and will start being your cable-car ride up the mountain.

Why They Quit?

You're looking at public speaking the right way when you're enjoying it and you see it as the horse carrying you over a hurdle instead of as a big hurdle to jump over. Yet over the years, I have met about one hundred public speakers who really got into speaking and then hit a slump and quit. They got off the horse and didn't have any incentive to get back on it. They had the ability, they enjoyed speaking, but then it was like they lost their drive to share.

My opinion on this matter is that when you start something new, it's novel and exciting. You might doubt yourself, but prevailing, and round-house kicking your self-doubt will give you a tremendous high. But then when you know you can do it — the challenge evaporates. The challenge becomes a medal so you can show off to others about your achievement.

Once the trial has been completed, you continue if you loved the activity or you quit if you just enjoyed trying something new and challenging. You might not want to carry on if you have claimed your reason to boast or ticked off an item from your list of ambitions: "Oh yeah, I've given a speech to several hundred people," is where it ends for many speakers. They have their prize, now they want to move on.

I have nothing against challenges. But for most people, a challenge is to do something:
"I want to give ten speeches." And then probably quit.
"I want to run the London marathon!" And then never going running again.
"I want to lose one stone in weight." And then put it on again.
"I want to hug a panda." And then ignore endangered pandas forever.

Once the challenge has been completed, most people drop out — they're done. That does not mean that what they have achieved is meaningless. What it does mean is that the challenge has not impacted their future goals and their long-term way of living.

You probably know just how much I LOVE public speaking and I'm aware that most people don't feel the same way. For this reason, I'm going to tell you my approach to doing new things and sustaining them over the long-term, so you can apply it to your public speaking.

"What would happen if..." That's the magic phrase right there. I ask myself that question when I'm unsatisfied with things, and then I test it out. I don't like following challenges that other people set for me — they bore me. Instead, I like to ask myself an interesting question and then fully commit to it.

My motivation is pure curiosity: to discover the truth for myself. We live in a digital world where everyone is telling us to do things, and we have no way of knowing what works and what doesn't. The only way we will know is by asking ourselves a question and finding out the answer through experience.

"What would happen if I actually made the recipes in cookbooks I've bought? What if I put stickers on each recipe I've completed so I can try to finish new cookbooks?" I learnt to cook. I am not afraid to use new recipes, and try a new one every week.
"What would happen if I regularly read books?" I learnt a lot, picked up a lot of inspiration and found a lot more ways to connect with other people.
"What would happen if I gave up wasting time on pointless videos, mobile apps, and games for a year?" GREAT things.

By asking a question, you receive a self-proven answer. That means that you change your thinking and opinions on the subject. A challenge will tell you that you can run a marathon, but a question will tell you what will happen if you do. This means that as the challengers think: "I ran the marathon, done it! Now I've finished I can go home and eat lots of cake," the askers will think:

"My life has improved so much from all of this running. I feel so much better physically and emotionally, and I love being a runner. It's just common sense to keep it up."

What I love about asking myself a question is that I'm driven by my own curiosity. When you take part in a challenge — let's be honest it's usually to show off. Either you want to put a picture of you and your medal online, or you want to tell everyone what you've achieved. In contrast, when you're doing something because you're curious about how you're going to grow and what you're going to learn — you're self-motivated.

The elephant in the room is how to keep up the running, cooking, and not wasting time when it's all down to you. So many people have been preaching about the perks of being accountable to someone else when trying to improve at things. My response is — sure that can work. But in my opinion, that's living life as a series of challenges. You're not learning or developing the mindset of: "I'm doing this because I love doing it, I'm great at it or because it makes my life so amazing," you're doing it so other people don't make you feel guilty. Being in another person's power like that is not the way I want to live.

Get curious. Ask yourself a question about public speaking. "What would happen if I…"

The Ultimate Escape Plan

When you listen to exercise coaches, you might hear the word 'plateau' pop up every now and then. It comes into the conversation when a gym enthusiast has been improving steadily and then once they reach a certain level — that's it, the improvements stop. It's like your body saying, "I'm not going to improve anymore."

Obviously, reaching a plateau is a huge problem because people aren't going to be anywhere near as motivated to work hard if they're no longer going to improve (they might even quit). It falls on the exercise coach to give solutions for the plateau and how the gym goer can start making improvements again.

Public speakers will also reach a plateau. I've seen it over and over again. Once they have control of their body, structure their speeches and can warmly speak to a room of people: they hit a plateau. If you can identify with this, you shouldn't feel guilty because it's not your fault.

The reason why I say that the speakers aren't to blame for coming to a plateau is because everyone will encounter it. On top of this (but still very flatly — this is a plateau), most speakers seem perfectly content to be at a plateau. They don't want to change anything, not knowing how to improve seems to give them reassurance: "I'm perfect, there's no way for me to improve, hooray!" It's because most speakers don't search for greater heights that there are few speakers to look up to for inspiration. This then affects the feedback speakers receive from others:
"I don't know how you can improve on that," because the road of public speaking looks like a hike and not a lifelong journey.

When I hit my public speaking plateau, I felt great. "Finally," I thought "I've made it!" I was getting floods of compliments and very little criticism. I felt like a master of public speaking. Most people seem to hold onto this great feeling. I lost it on the walk home, straight after I got it.

My triumphant feeling dissolved into boredom! Just like with people who exercise, I needed to improve. My whole life philosophy is based around improving myself every day. Not being able to improve at public speaking was draining my excitement to speak. I'd had enough.

When you begin studying a new way of doing things — the floodgates open and your brain is submerged in new ideas and learning. For me, it's always been an adrenaline rush. I love being able to learn a book-full of new ideas and then to run off and test them out and experiment. This is the feeling I wanted to have forever with my public speaking. It was this feeling that showed me a way to escape my public speaking plateau.

I didn't see any speakers who were so powerful that I felt compelled to study them. Watching other speakers to improve my own speaking did not spark an adrenaline rush like when I learnt something new. Other speakers perhaps had more years of speaking under their belt, but they didn't have any raw public speaking skills that I could truly be in awe of. I am very thankful that I didn't feel in awe of them. I say this because what I did instead: opened up the doors to the lifelong journey that I needed.

I studied people I admired from other disciplines and applied what I learnt into my speaking. I took notes from magicians, comedians, actors, directors, musicians, designers, copywriters, marketers, debaters, chefs, mimes, puppeteers, variety performers and hosts, dancers, politicians, philosophers, filmmakers, artists — to name a few (I'm not kidding). I wanted to know enough about them, so I could imagine how they would deliver my next speech.

Studying such a diverse range of orators and performers helped me to think about public speaking and to grow. I could synthesise strong performance ideas from anyone by combining their work, mindsets, and methods with my imagination. Learning from other disciplines is not a new idea, but it is an underused one. I had opened up my source of learning, exponentially. Public speaking was more exciting than ever because I had a whole world of knowledge and experience to help me grow.

As no one else had studied the same sources as me, I stopped relying on other people's feedback and started relying on my own evaluations of my performances. I still listened to other people's feedback, but I stopped depending on it. Audiences were continuously saying to me that I was great, it was up to me to ask: "Two parts of my speech could have had more of an impact. How would someone I've studied have performed them?" It's incredibly liberating once you get to the point where you are your own best critic.

But don't take the role of being your own best critic lightly. It comes with responsibility. It's your responsibility to devote time to learn and study. It's then up to you to take your new ideas and test them out. You must see if the ideas actually work or if they can be improved. Then your final duty is to strive to be honest with yourself, to stay humble, and to know you have a lot to learn still.

Everyone on this planet has a lot more to learn — without exception. But not everyone wants to continue learning. As I said, many people reach their public speaking plateau, and they're happy staying there. They don't want to experiment or take risks with new ideas. They just want to play it safe. They choose to sentence themselves to a never-ending plateau, if not a gradual decline.

But not you. For reading this far, I trust that you want to keep learning. You want public speaking to always be exciting and fresh. If that's what you want, and that's what you work towards — it will be.

If you have hit your public speaking plateau: try what I started all those years ago. Study sources outside of public speaking. Try-out your new ideas. If they don't work FANTASTIC, you have generated something to work on and improve. If they do work, have a victory dance and go try some more new ideas.

If you have not hit your public speaking plateau yet, don't fear it: look forward to it. When it comes, you will feel great, and now you know what to do you will be ready for the real beginning of your lifelong public speaking journey.

An Introduction to Feedback in Public Speaking

Positive Feedback Is Paramount

There is never a shortage of critics. You could take someone to Mars and they would complain that the space shuttle didn't have a swimming pool. People enjoy criticising others. Why? Because it takes no effort to criticise, but it makes you feel important and knowledgeable by doing it.

Blunt criticism: "You did that wrong. You messed up there. Oh, and your fly was down the entire time," is the worst thing to give to a speaker who has just finished her speech and is on a 'speaker's high' and feeling great (if you are the speaker in this situation, refer to *'Distance Yourself*). Instead of criticising a speaker, give her positive feedback and build her up. Instead of sharing a blunt criticism: consider giving a positively framed optional enhancement.

For me 'positive feedback' has a dual meaning. Of course, it means to approach feedback with optimism and cheerful energy, but to me, it also means to give and not to take away. A blunt criticism takes away a speaker's positive vibes and can rob them of an idea. Saying, "That was bad. I didn't like that," does not offer anything to the speaker, all it does is write off that moment of their speech. On the other hand, if you offer a suggestion, you are giving to the speaker and empowering them: "A solution here would be to add a costume change." I see this as different to 'constructive criticism' because constructive criticism contains a criticism! Your suggestion should feel like a possible enhancement, not a criticism.

To give genuinely positive feedback, I believe in combining both of my positive meanings into one mega-positive method of feedback. The formula is to reflect on the speech by showing what you liked about it and to offer your enhancement (as opposed to a fix, which suggests that the speech was broken) by framing it in this style: "I liked this, and I think that if you want to make your speech even better next time, you can enhance it by trying this..." That way the enhancement is optional, and it's up to the speaker to decide if she wants to use the feedback or not. The most important thing to notice is that the feedback is positively framed as an optional enhancement — and not a definite criticism.

When I was the president of Oxford Speakers club (and before that vice president of education), I had an important mission. My mission was to keep membership up and to set the tone of the club. What I noticed was that if guests or new members were given feedback that contained a criticism or feedback with a negative feel to it, they wouldn't come back. The member had told a speaker these things to be helpful and to point out an area of improvement but if the guest/new member never came back, was it worth it? No, because if a guest/new member did not come back, that meant that they had given up trying to improve at public speaking. When people stop trying, they stop improving.

As the president, I knew that it was my job to create a positive and supportive atmosphere. I did my best to ensure that everyone offered positive feedback and had a delightful public speaking experience. I did this by making every guest feel special by interviewing each of them at the start and end of the meeting. I gave each speaker recognition and added my own positive comments about their performance if the feedback they were given wasn't positive enough for my liking. I also kept the energy and enthusiasm up in the room (if I wasn't satisfied with the level of applause that a speaker received, I ensured it improved, or that he got a second round). Doing this encouraged both guests and members to come back to the club and to continue with public speaking. When they did, they continued to improve.

If you have read, '*Do, you need motivation to speak*', you might think that giving positive feedback to speakers is nice but unnecessary. The reality is that the majority of speakers haven't learnt to self-motivate themselves and will continue to need some form of motivation to speak. Knowing how to positively frame feedback as an 'optional enhancement' will make anyone more receptive to your opinions. This is why by default it's essential for us to give positive feedback to speakers.

What should you avoid when giving feedback?

A positively framed optional enhancement is the ideal method of feedback for me. To show you why, I would like to address some issues that I've seen feedback givers struggle with.

There is one word that will automatically change the tone of your feedback from positive to negative. Guess what it might be. The word you were looking for was 'but'.

'But' is the three letter killer that makes everyone's heart sink when they hear it during feedback: "I really liked your choice of language. I liked your suit. And I liked your gestures. BUT... I hated your tie, hated your message, was bored during most of it, and I found your voice annoying."

'But' releases the hounds during feedback. It's as if the feedback giver is saying positive things, and with each compliment she delivers, her negative comments become hungrier and more determined to get out. And then finally she says 'but' and the criticisms fly out.

If you practise positively framing what you didn't like and say it as an optional enhancement, your feedback can be positive all the way through. If your feedback is all positive, you won't need to have a, "Stuff I liked," half and a "Criticism," half with a 'but' in between.

There is one method of feedback (other than using 'but') that I have a strong distaste for. Parodying the speaker. When giving feedback, some people find it funny to parody the speaker's movements or voice. It's a cheap laugh, and it's unlikely that the speaker will find it amusing. A lot of speakers are insecure about how they come across and being parodied will be humiliating to them. It's best to simply say: "To look more powerful, you can try standing still in one place and moving when you have a reason to move," instead of imitating a drunkard and exclaiming, "This is what you looked like!"

It can be tempting to give one speaker a lot of suggestions, "I recommend that you fix these nine things!" When you provide a speaker with some feedback try to stick to a few optional enhancements and not a truckload. If you give more than a few, the speaker will become overwhelmed and will be less likely to try your idea than if you had given one suggestion.

If you know the speaker and they have asked you for a thorough report, you can offer several suggestions but tread carefully. You might think that you know a speaker and how they will take a piece of feedback — but you might not. For all you know they are having the worst day ever and just want what they did to be perfect. There have been times when I have received bad reactions to my more in-depth feedback, and each occasion has been a learning experience. Whenever you're in doubt — stick to one optional enhancement.

Feedback givers often neglect to clarify that what they're saying is their opinion. When a feedback giver says, "This is what you should do," or, "You must do this," they don't realise that it comes across as aggressive and that there is a possibility that their advice might not be right for that speaker. Instead, if you say to a speaker, "What I would do is," or, "One thing you could try is," or a sentence with that tone, your suggestions will come across as a fresh perspective instead of an order.

Hearing how different people would approach the same problem is fascinating and inspiring. However, being told that there is only one way of doing things can be both intimidating and demoralising. When giving suggestions make it clear that you are sharing your opinion. You are not weakening your feedback by framing it as your opinion. In fact, you will be more likely to uplift and inspire the speaker.

Positive feedback is crucial because it encourages a speaker to persevere with their public speaking and to continue to give speeches. Although delivered with helpful intentions, other kinds of feedback can demoralise a speaker and make her want to give up. With positive feedback: we can uplift the speaker and give her both reassurance and an optional enhancement to make her speech even more powerful next time. That way our good intentions will serve the speaker and not just ourselves.

Distance Yourself

I am always telling you to put feeling into your speeches and to share who you are by opening yourself up. When you first start doing that you might be afraid of criticism. You might particularly feel afraid of other people's negative feedback because they are now evaluating YOU. They're not criticising a cold, impersonal performance. They're dissecting who you are and how you express yourself. They will be picking apart a speech that you are proud of and maybe a bit in love with.

For a newcomer to expressive public speaking, criticism can feel daunting. That's a natural way to feel. By learning to take a step back from your speech for a few minutes, your work can be criticised and altered without you needing to experience emotional pain.

When I wrote my first book on public speaking one of the hardest things for me to do was to reflect on a chapter I had just written. I would look at it — and to me it was great. I looked at what I had written, and it made me happy. A few days later I would look back and heartlessly delete the chapter. Why? Time had given me the distance I needed to be objective. After a few days had passed it felt like I wasn't in a relationship with that page anymore. That meant that the break-up was easy: "I'm sorry, but you're not helping my message, delete."

The problem when people criticise our speeches is that the criticism rarely comes a few days afterwards — when we're thinking about it more objectively. The criticism almost always comes at times when we feel happy with what we've done. I refer to the feeling you get after speaking as your 'speaker's high' because you feel great after giving your speech.

If you feel like your speech has a ground-breaking message, but someone says to you during your speaker's high, "Your speech didn't make sense to me," it can be heart-breaking. I once received that comment and later found out that it was because he didn't like my one time use of the word, 'strategy' (I am not proud to admit that I reacted to this by reading several hefty tomes on the subject). Or if you deliver a speech and feel like you have seriously impacted your audience and one person runs up to you afterwards and blurts: "I got lost after the introduction. You need a better structure," your feelings of victory can turn into stings of defeat.

You must develop the skill of being able to distance yourself from your work and to protect your heart from other people's opinions. Essentially you need to switch from using your feelings (which you use on stage) to using logic.

If someone runs up to you the second you walk off the stage and says, "I didn't understand any of that," you need to be able to switch from using your feelings to thinking logically in an instant. If you don't switch, you will take the comment personally. Whereas, if you think about it logically you will know that this one person could be an exception (you can't please everyone) and the rest of your audience could have understood your speech.

By thinking logically, you can ask your critic what he didn't understand. He might say that English is not his first language (this has happened to me more often than you might imagine). He might say that he believes in something different to you (again — you can't please everyone). Or he might confirm your fear and say that your speaking style was hard to understand. You might receive some useful feedback. Once you have taken on that feedback and rationalised it, you can switch back to focusing on your feelings and feel great about everything that went well in your speech.

It's vital for me to stress to you that not all suggestions are good suggestions. There will be plenty of times when someone will not really understand who you are, what you're about, or they will have had a different experience with speaking to you and might give you inappropriate advice. Do not take other people's opinions as fact. Play with suggestions and suss out if they line up with what you want to achieve. Even if you're given an excellent piece of advice, which just isn't right for what you're going for — you have no obligation to use it.

When I give feedback: I avoid telling people what they 'should do' but instead open their mind to what they 'could do'. That way the speaker can improve, but through her choices and in a way that fits her style.

If you're finding it difficult to take-on criticism during the planning/writing/rehearsal process of your speech, take a step back. When you create you're going to feel attached to your ideas — you created them. However, there's always going to be a story or an idea in your speech that doesn't belong there, but you love it so much you can't remove it. You need to be able to think logically, remove your tangents and confusing bits of business and stick with what supports your message.

If you're in love with an idea but it doesn't fit, you don't have to delete it for all eternity. Save the idea somewhere. Then in a few months, you can review it, use it in a more appropriate speech or perhaps even create a speech around it.

When you receive feedback (even self-criticism) practise distancing yourself: Think logically and evaluate the advice you are being given and why it is being given to you. Not all advice is good advice. When you can present with feeling but then edit and evaluate objectively, you can improve and grow without the fear of getting hurt.

How to Critique and Evaluate

People in general (not just speakers) seem to struggle with critiquing and evaluating speeches and performances. They're great at saying, "I liked this," or, "Oh no, I hated that," but why? What specific moments did you like? Or what did you take from a speech that didn't sit right with you?

When watching a speech: a lot of people struggle to analyse it and to understand what the speaker did well, and what needs improvement. I have heard countless audience members watch a speech and then say, "I can't think of any recommendations." No matter whose speech I'm watching I can always find room for improvement — without fail. This is because I can critique and evaluate speeches.

In my own public speaking journey, being able to critique and evaluate has helped me to work out who I wanted to be. When I saw a speech I didn't like, I broke it down and saw why it didn't work. That way I avoided the same mistakes. I also examined how I felt after watching the speech and what impressions I was left with. When you make a habit of critiquing and evaluating, your understanding of yourself and how you want to speak and present will grow with every speech you see and deliver.

When I use the word, critique I am talking about paying attention to all of the small points and moments during a speech. Did they work? Are they hindering the speaker and her message? I go over these points in detail while coaching — but probably wouldn't mention them to another speaker in conversation. My reason for this is that a speaker is more likely to reflect on broader points that will apply to her future public speaking endeavours.

When I evaluate, I am talking about weighing up a speech in a more general sense. How did the speech make me feel? On what level was the speaker communicating? What jumped out? What messages did the speaker give off: with her words, focus, voice, body, movements, and interactions with the audience?

To make my definitions easy to remember: Critiquing focuses on the fine points like a highly concentrated laser-beam while an evaluation deals with the overall impressions you took from a speech, like a giant fishing net.

Every performance is made up of small moments. A critique carefully assesses these moments to judge their value and what effect they have on the audience. The first question you might have for me is: "What's the point of critiquing? If you're looking at such a fine level of detail, do the small points even matter?" They certainly do matter. Not only do audiences notice these moments (even if they don't actively notice) but small moments stack on top of each other.

Everything you do while speaking is a form of communication and each moment holds a micro-message. Eventually, all of these little messages will pile up, leaving the audience with a more significant message in the form of an impression: "There was something off about that speech."
"I wanted to like the speaker, but something wasn't quite right."
"I had a sense that she wasn't prepared."
"I couldn't seem to connect with her and what she was saying."

How do you critique?

To begin critiquing: start paying attention to each moment in a speech. This is not limited to the moments when a speaker is talking, it includes when she has paused or when she is moving, picking up a prop/drink/chair, searching her pockets, looking at notes or her slides, listening to a question, and waiting for an audience response such as laughter or applause. Every moment in front of an audience counts — not just when the speaker's lips are moving.

Naturally, you will not be able to critique the vast majority of moments on your first viewing. This is why, to successfully critique you need to be able to re-watch a speech. If possible, record the speech and then watch it back. You will critique a speech much better once you have seen a speech before and know where it's going (just like rewatching a film). If you have seen a speech before, you know what the moments are building towards and therefore what micro-messages they should be giving off. You can critique on a first watch by spotting moments that give off the wrong message. However to offer appropriate solutions you will likely need to see the entire speech.

When looking at each moment, you must be both honest and experimental. Your honesty will allow you to decide whether you thought a specific moment supported the speaker and her message.

Allow me to show you what I mean by using honesty. Firstly, what was the purpose of the moment? If she dropped a tissue on stage to express a specific message — did that come across? Did the moment fulfil its purpose? And could it have been more effective?

The real 'meat' of an honest critique is deciding if a moment makes a speaker look powerful and if it gives off a good impression. By powerful, I am referring to a speaker demonstrating that she is in control of her audience, speaking area, props and furniture, and her speech, and that she can express energy. By 'giving off a good impression', I am referring to how the audience will perceive her. At a basic level, this includes rapport with her audience and her likeability.

The impressions that the speaker gives off from moment to moment should also be consistent with her message and values. This is to create a feeling of consistency. No one wants to hear a speech on being calm, from a speaker who bounces when she's not talking and looks frustrated when an audience member takes too long to ask a question.

If a speaker quickly, and effortlessly brought a chair over from the side of the stage without breaking eye contact or her rapport with the audience, she would look powerful and give off a good impression. On the other hand, if she turned her back to her audience, fumbled around while lifting a chair, had a grumble, and lost her audience's attention, you could instantly tell that at that moment she didn't look powerful or give off a good impression.

It's important to note that a moment won't always appear to be both/neither powerful and favourable. If the speaker lobbed the chair to the front of the stage and it crashed down — she would look powerful but it would not give off a favourable impression to her audience. Equally a speaker could maintain humour and rapport while getting the chair, but make a big song and dance out of getting it (the fumbling kind, not the Broadway kind. The Broadway kind would be sensational: "Oh I'm gonna get this chair. But it's all the way – over there," and then an orchestra plays, backup dancers arrive with chairs, there's a dramatic costume change...).

After coming to a conclusion about whether a moment is powerful and if it gives off a good impression: you can remedy or enhance it by being experimental and using a, 'What if' approach to the problem. In your own speech, you might not instantly know how to adjust a moment so that it makes you look more powerful, or gives off a better impression of you. That's completely fine. Instead of refusing to think and declaring, "I don't know what do," experiment and try out different ideas.

Let's imagine that there's a moment in your speech where you want to capture your audience's full attention, "Have a look at this?" To critique this moment we start by being honest:

- What was the main message of the speech?

The importance of spending five minutes a day learning something new.

- What was the purpose of this moment?

To capture the audience's full attention.

- Did the moment fulfil this purpose?

Not really, the majority of the audience didn't pay attention.

- Could the moment have been more effective?

Yes, there are many ways that I could have received a lot more attention from my audience.

- Did the speaker look powerful in this moment?

No, I came across as uncertain, the audience didn't know if I was telling them or asking them to look.

- Did the speaker give off a good impression?

No. I made no eye contact towards my audience while trying to capture their attention, it was like I was presenting to myself. It was also like I didn't believe in what I was trying to show the audience. I gave the impression that what I was going to show the audience would not benefit them or have any impact on their life — even though it would.

- Was this moment consistent with her main message?

No. I was talking about the importance of spending time each day learning something new, and when it came to me showing the audience something new — I failed to express the importance or the need/urgency to pay attention.

This is the part of critiquing where most people leave things. They're honest but not inventive or helpful, and this makes them feel awful about their performance. Some 'delightful' individuals critique another speaker's performance and give them nothing but criticisms — 1000 pin pricks to the heart.

Now we know the problems we can work on them by being experimental and coming up with solutions. This is what changes a critique from a painful 'blow by blow' review into helpful guidance. Look how many opportunities for greatness your speech has!

When being inventive there are no wrong answers, but you will need to play around with your answers until you find one that is the 'right' fit for the speaker and the speech. Using the above, honest feedback, I will use 'what if' and 'how could I' questions to generate solutions that can be experimented with:

Saying, "Have a look at this," was meant to capture the audience's attention, but didn't...

What five things have I seen or used before that have captured an audience's attention?
A change in volume, surprise, the word 'now', a sense of urgency, and audience interaction.

What if I used one of these things in this moment? I could...
1. Raise my volume when saying, "Have a look at this!"
2. Surprise my audience by raising my volume — unexpectedly.
3. Use the word 'now', "And now, have a look at this."
4. Create a sense of urgency by saying: "Daily learning is something that you must implement as soon as possible. Have a look at this."
5. Use audience interaction to gain attention: "Please raise your hand if you dedicate at least five minutes a day to learning

something new. Have a look at this."

Out of the five, I want to experiment with number 3: the word 'now' and number five: using audience interaction to solve the specific problems with this moment.

Problem one: I did not come across as powerful — I came across as uncertain, the audience didn't know if I was telling them or asking them to look.

How could I clarify that I am giving a direction and not asking a question?

I could pay attention to my intonation and ensure that it sounds like a direction and not a question. I could also reword it slightly so that it's clear that I want my audience to do something.

Problem two: I gave off an unfavourable impression, with no eye contact towards the audience it was like I was presenting to myself.

How can I improve my rapport with my audience and make it clear that I am presenting to them?

I could ensure that I make eye contact with members of the audience while I give the direction and then turn to face the projector screen before I reveal the slide. I could also gesture at my audience while speaking and then point towards the screen just before the slide appears. By using the word 'you' my audience will know that I am talking to them. "I want you to look at this," is better but 'want' sounds too dictatorial, I will replace I want you to, with 'please': "Please look at this."

Problem three: I did not convey my belief in what I was about to show, or its value to my audience.

Is what I am about to show going to be valuable to my audience?
Yes, it will help them learn a lot in only five minutes.

How can I express that it will be valuable?
I can tell them: "I am going to show you how to learn more in five minutes than you ever thought was possible." Or I could highlight that this is the most valuable part of the speech: "I now want to share with you my most important and life-changing finding." Both of these intrigue the audience and make them want to see what I am about to show them. Saying a line like this will convey that I believe in the value of what I am about to show.

Problem four: This moment was inconsistent with my main message about the importance of spending five minutes a day learning something new because — I did not convey this importance when I was about to share something new!

How could I reinforce my main message in this moment?
I could create a sense of importance to my message by lowering my voice and speaking from the heart. I could ensure that I don't waste time while presenting and that I become more time efficient. Or I could make it clear that what I'm showing counts as learning. I like the first idea.

Our combined experimental solution is to replace: "Have a look at this?" while not making eye contact with: "Please raise your hand if you dedicate at least five minutes a day to learning something new. Thank you." Speaking lower and from the heart, I gesture towards my audience: "I am now going to show you how to learn more in five minutes than you ever thought was possible. Please look at this." I move my eyes and hand towards the projector screen. Then the slide appears.

The moment now fulfils its objective while conveying power, a favourable impression, and it reinforces the main message. This is the result of a thorough critique.

Realistically, you are not going to have a detailed critique which improves each moment of your speech. Instead, you will probably want to iron out the creases and then focus on enhancing a few moments. I wanted to demonstrate an in-depth critique so you could see that there is always room for improvement. I also wanted to show you that the worst part of your speech has the potential to become the best part of your speech. I personally find this prospect incredibly exciting.

Please remember that when you critique: being honest is important, but it's only half the job. Generating solutions and finding what works is what will transform the 'not so great' moments of your speech. Your inventive and practical solutions will make your message and what you're conveying to your audience both consistent and effective.

How do you evaluate?

Your evaluation consists of your overall impressions that you took from a speech. Critiquing was like a fine laser that lit up each moment, an evaluation is more like a giant net. When you have finished watching a speech, what do you have left in your net? Ask yourself:

- How do you feel?
- What impressions have you been left with?
- What level did the speaker communicate at?
- What jumped out at you?

- What messages are you left with that the speaker gave off — with her words, focus, voice, body, movement, and interaction with the audience?
- What's left in your net?

An evaluation is what you're left with after a speech. You might have given someone your assessment without even noticing: "The speech you gave just now, inspired me. You really talked to me on an emotional level. I particularly remember the part where you carefully arranged thirty pairs of shoes that belonged to your friends at the front of the stage. I can tell that you really care about your friends and other people. When you spoke, I felt like you cared about me too. You inspired me to make friends and care about people." This is an entirely positive reaction. When someone has just given a speech and is on their speaker's high, this is what they want to hear.

If you're evaluating yourself or someone else: your goal will likely be growth and improvement. To look for improvements, compare what is left in your net with what could be in there.

You have just finished watching a speech...
How do you feel? What emotions are you currently experiencing? Consider whether you feel different now compared to before the speech. Also, contemplate the 'emotional journey' that you were taken on during the speech. Did you feel different emotions and feelings while watching? What feeling most stood out to you?

When evaluating: it's essential to think about your emotions and how they were affected during and after the speech. If you felt little or no change in emotion during the speech, then the speaker was not fully engaging you. Either you were listening to something that was not relevant to you (but you listened to be polite) or the speaker was not passionate when talking about the subject and didn't connect with her audience.

Enthusiasm is contagious. If a speaker is passionate about her subject and puts her emotions into her speech, it's likely that the audience will mirror some of these feelings. This might happen because the speaker's emotions are broadcast so openly that we become influenced by them. When you are around a fun and positive person, your mood can't help but be uplifted. When the speaker does a particularly good job of expressing herself, we can experience empathy and imagine ourselves in the speaker's position.

If you experienced different emotions during the speech, do you think they were the ones that the speaker wanted you to feel? And were they in the right places?

Sometimes a speaker can make an audience experience the opposite emotions to those that he had intended. For instance, if he is so determined to be severe and to be taken seriously, an audience might misinterpret the speaker's intentions and conclude that it's dry humour. Or an audience might feel so tense throughout the speech because of the stoic disciplinarian approach that they will burst out laughing if anything goes wrong.

How strong were the emotions you experienced during and after the speech? Could you have experienced any of these emotions more intensely, if the speaker had done things differently? The answer to this last question is almost always, "Yes!" Trust your gut feeling, if you felt this emotion as a 5 out of ten, how could the speaker have increased it to a six? To an eight? And how about to a ten?

In my opinion, the best speakers take an audience on an emotional journey and leave them feeling more positive than before the speech. If a speaker did not give you this emotional experience, ask yourself — why not and what went wrong? Think broadly here:

- How could the speaker have made you emotionally invest in the topic?

- Had he neglected the audience's emotions?
- Did he fail to empathise with his audience?
- Or did he need to go back and understand what feelings he wanted his speech to communicate and how to structure these expressions?
- If the speaker did not leave you feeling uplifted, what could he have done differently to uplift you?

One other consideration after a speech is to ask yourself if you feel disappointed. If you feel disappointed, then the speaker might have failed to deliver something, or he might not have given you an answer that satisfied you: "I'm going to tell you how to have lots of money in your bank account...and the answer is: never to spend anything."

A reason why I sometimes feel disappointed after watching a speech is that I saw a lot of potential for greatness, and the speech didn't meet my expectations (just like when you go to the cinema). A feeling of disappointment is like an emotional signal that you know a speech could have been better.

When you can look at a speech as more than just a transmission of thoughts, but also as a sharing of emotions, you can evaluate much more effectively. How an audience feels after a speech will determine whether they apply the speaker's message to their life or if they ever want to see the speaker again. Never overlook emotions when you evaluate.

What impressions have you been left with?

Now that you have seen the speech, ask, "What do I think?" Specifically:

- Did you like the speech?
- Why did you like/not like the speech?
- How long would it have taken for that speech to be created and rehearsed?
- Do you see the speaker any differently after the speech, and if so, how?
- Do you remember the main message from the speech?
- Have you been left with a positive or a negative impression of the speaker and his topic?
- Would you recommend the speaker to someone else?

The impressions you have been left with are vital because you cannot relive what you've just experienced. All you have left is what's in your net. You will use your impressions to remember the story, through your self-narrative.

In the future when you think back to the speech, the story in your mind will either be: "I remember when I saw that speaker giving the rushed and ill-prepared speech — I can't even remember *what* it was about, it was terrible," or it will be "I remember when I saw the speaker giving that wonderful speech on why we should walk every day, I loved how he made us all laugh — that was such a good speech."

Remember, that the impressions you are left with will determine how you tell the story when you replay the memory!

What level did the speaker communicate at?

I will first explain what I mean by communicating at different levels. To explain it simply: imagine that you spent last Saturday having a fun day out. Today you are going to give a speech, telling me about last

Saturday. How you tell the story will determine what level you are communicating at:

Level One — Describing

If you only describe what happened last Saturday, you're speaking at the descriptive level. This level is impartial because you're just repeating what happened.

"Last Saturday I got up at seven. I drove to the city and played some early morning miniature golf with my friends. I then went to the sandwich shop and ate a tuna sandwich."

Level Two — Sharing Opinions

If you want to upgrade from level one, you need to also share your opinions with us, and the views of those around you. This will stop your story from being impartial and directionless.

"Last Saturday I got up at seven — I don't like getting up that early. I thought the fastest way to the city was by car, so I drove to the city. I played miniature golf with my friends, even though they don't think I'm very good at it. I like sandwiches, so I went to the sandwich shop and ate my favourite sandwich, tuna."

Level Three — Through Your Eyes

To take the speech to level three, it needs to be personalised. You were the one who had a fun day last Saturday, let us experience it through your eyes.

When telling us the story through your eyes, you are painting the outer world for us so that we can experience your story.

"Last Saturday morning I was awoken by a chirping. It was my alarm clock. I clawed my way out of bed – it was seven, I don't like getting up that early. I stared in front of the mirror, looking like I was about to fall asleep and thought the fastest way to the city was by car, so I drove. I played miniature golf with my friends. I stood there with my club, falling over my own feet. I covered up my poor performance by showing lots of enthusiasm. Afterwards, I marched to the sandwich shop and ferociously devoured my favourite sandwich, tuna.

Level Four — Sharing Emotions and Feelings
It's one thing to share opinions and how you see the world, but to level up: you need to include emotions and feelings. Be daring and venture into how an event made you feel and how you were affected emotionally.

Often when speakers recount an experience or analyse something, they don't reach this level. A lot of speakers can say what happened, what they liked, and describe the event from their own perspective but they do not express their feelings.

Sharing emotions and feelings opens the speaker up and gives her speech so much life and authenticity — not to mention the potential for her audience to empathise with her. I always encourage speakers to get to this level because the change in how they present will be profound.

"Last Saturday morning I was awoken by a chirping. It was my alarm clock. I clawed my way out of my comfortable bed - it was seven, and I was feeling exhausted, I don't like getting up that early. I stared in front of the mirror, looking like a zombie — I felt hideous! I thought the fastest way to the city was by car so I drove — I'm so happy I did. I played miniature golf with my friends. I stood there with my club, falling over my own feet. My friends found it hilarious watching me play golf — I felt a bit embarrassed by my poor performance, to be honest, but I covered it up by showing lots of enthusiasm. I was starving afterwards, so I marched to the sandwich shop and ferociously devoured my favourite sandwich, tuna."

Level Five — Personal Guided Tour

Level five includes everything from the previous levels but this time you share your inner world. Even if we can see through your eyes and know how you felt: we are missing your essence, the thing that truly makes the story personal. In writing, I would call this 'your voice'. It's not just what you saw and what happened, but how you interpreted the events and how you chose to tell the tale. You can share your sense of humour, your ambitions, and your thoughts— anything from inside your mind. Its level five for a reason: it's telling the story like only you can!

I call it a personal guided tour because you are not only guiding your audience through the story, but you are sharing your spin on things and your personality as you go through. You can put in extra details for comic effect, give interesting descriptions — whatever you want to guide your audience.

"Last Saturday morning I was awoken by a chirping. No, it wasn't a bird. It was my £9.99 alarm clock. I clawed my way out of my comfortable bed — it was seven, and I was feeling exhausted, for a second I thought that my head was going to fall off. I don't like getting up that early. I stared in front of the mirror, looking like a zombie — I felt hideous! I thought the fastest way to the city was by car, so I drove — I'm so happy I did, and I had my favourite car tunes blaring. I played miniature golf with my friends. I would love to tell you that they now call me: "The almighty overlord of miniature golf," but in reality I stood there with my club, falling over my own feet like a zebra learning to tap-dance. My friends found it hilarious watching me play golf — because they're horrible people. Only joking. They're really horrible! I felt a bit embarrassed by my poor performance, to be honest, but I covered it up by showing lots of enthusiasm. I was starving afterwards, so I marched to the sandwich shop because a) I like sandwiches and b) it was nearby. Did I calmly eat my tuna sandwich? Nope! I ferociously devoured my sandwich in 30 seconds flat."

Now you understand the levels you will be able to judge what level someone is speaking at when they give a speech or present feedback. Most people who I see presenting feedback — speak no higher than the first few levels. You might think that level five is inappropriate for giving feedback. I would disagree because your personal experience and your voice are unique to you. If you give feedback at level five, you will do so in a way that no one else can. Give people the opportunity to learn from your unique approach to life.

When you're evaluating a speech, assessing what level they communicated on will help you to see how personal their speech was. 'Use personal stories' is a popular 'top tip' in public speaking. But a personal story is not always presented personally (as we have seen). Judge what level the speaker spoke at and then you can understand how personal the speaker was and what they need to do to 'level up'.

What jumped out at you?
Evaluating is so much easier when you ask yourself, "What jumped out?" When you ask yourself this, you will be able to find a memorable part of the speech that you liked. This could be your favourite moment, something you found clever, or a particular skill that you thought the speaker was good at.

By waiting a few extra seconds, something you didn't like will also jump out. If something had felt off to you — the reason why might jump out. Similarly, if the speech was missing or lacking something (energy, humour, eye contact, breathing) it will likely jump out at you.

If you need to give someone feedback on the spot, this method of evaluating lets you come up with feedback in seconds: "What jumped out? The section when she started singing and put on a sombrero made me laugh and caught my attention. And what else? She never made eye contact with me — that's why I lost focus in the first place."

Once you know what jumped out at you, the next step is to work out why those things jumped out at you and either how to make them jump out more - or how to stop them jumping out: "When you sang, some backing music and maracas would have had me laughing with delight. If you make eye contact with everyone present, your audience will feel like you're talking to them and will give you more attention." Of course, you can go in any direction you like with the things that jumped out, you don't necessarily need to think of suggestions if you don't want to.

When in doubt ask yourself, "What jumped out?"

What messages are you left with that the speaker gave off with her: words, focus, voice, body, movements, and interaction with the audience?
After looking at what jumped out, you can be a little more specific with your evaluation. You can do this by looking at each component of the speech and asking yourself what message it gave off.

The most straightforward component is the speaker's words. What was the speaker saying? Did her words communicate anything that they shouldn't have? For instance:
- "I don't know my topic well enough to explain it simply, so I'm hiding behind jargon."
- "I found this complicated word in a book, I'm not sure what it means."
- "I don't know what to say — so I'm going to keep repeating the word 'so'."

Ideally, we want a speaker's words to be focused on her main message and to show her in a favourable light.

On my drama course, I learnt some interesting ways of rehearsing. One of the methods involved running through a play in complete silence. This meant that as actors we had to become aware of what messages we were giving off with our bodies. If you can imagine that the speaker was only communicating with her body, what message would you have taken away? If it was: "I don't know what I'm doing up here in front of all these people," do you think that was what she wanted to communicate?

You might find it peculiar for me to suggest that a speaker's focus can send out messages. In reality, it's a straightforward reason. A speaker's focus communicates what she is focusing on. Is the speaker focusing on her audience and therefore communicating that she is trying to connect with them? Or is she focusing on her slides, the back of the room, her watch, her shoes, what she's going to cook for dinner, or what to say next? Each focus communicates a different message.

How a speaker interacts with her audience sends out a lot of messages. It communicates her experience with the topic and public speaking, her personality and likeability, and even her feelings towards her audience. No matter how good a speaker is, her message will be undermined if her style of audience interaction communicates the message: "I don't like any of you, you disgust me."

When you look at the various messages that a speaker gives off during a speech, you can see whether they are consistent. If not they need to be synchronised. Rehearsing each component of a speech is an excellent way to achieve this.

What's left in your net?

After going through this evaluation process, you might be surprised to discover that there are still things left in your net. Each speech is different, and everyone who evaluates is unique. Therefore no matter what process you use to evaluate, and how thorough you think you've been — have a final check. Is there anything left in your net?

Your unique set of experiences will make you look at the world in an entirely different way to me. Use them. If you're a scientist and you think: "I never got to use this new scientific analysis on the speech," use it! If you're a dancer and you are an expert on choreography, use that knowledge. You need to be aware of what makes you unique and to use that when you assess speeches. My recommendation is to create your own process for critiquing and evaluating, and in the meantime — check your net.

The final thing to do is to compile all of your unique observations and answers. This particular essay dealt with how to critique and how to evaluate as opposed to how to deliver a critique and an evaluation. How you decide to deliver your findings is up to you. My advice when delivering feedback to an audience is to stay positive and to use a clear structure. In essence, giving feedback should feel like a miniature speech. At least that's how I always approached it.

I appreciate that there's a lot of information to take in about how to critique and evaluate. When I do it in my head, it's a straightforward process. It wasn't until I put my process on paper that I went: "Oh my gosh. I think in a complicated way!"

I wanted to share how I analyse speeches because my way of doing things can seem alien to other speakers. You might be surprised to hear that even more processes fire-off in my brain when I critique and evaluate! Even if you don't want to follow my way of critical thinking, I believe that having heard it will still help you.

What I want to leave you with is that every speech can always be improved. There's never an endpoint when a speech is entirely perfect. Avoid the trap of assuming that a speech can't be improved, because it most certainly can be.

Beyond Your Speech

My Rock Star Image

This year I got to meet two performers who I admired for their sense of style. They always look like they are dressed to kill. And they're not afraid to dress differently to everyone else. Before I met them, I would look at their photos and think: "One day I will be able to dress as cool as they do." I have always had difficulty with feeling good about how I look.

For some people, style comes naturally. I wasn't one of those people! At age eleven all I knew was that if films had taught me anything, if you wanted to be cool, you needed a leather jacket. Because I was asthmatic and needed to carry my bulky medication for it, my first requirement used to be pockets and not style. I overcompensated with either a farmer style jacket with pockets that could house a brick, or trousers with at least half a dozen compartments. Oh boy.

But soon, Japanese animation — anime captured my imagination. Suddenly I was obsessed with long coats and gravity-defying hairstyles. I couldn't find any stylish long coats in Salisbury town centre, but I could at least style my hair.

As a teenager, I was determined to impress a particular girl in school (you knew this was coming). It turned out that she loved bands who were a bit on the dark side. There was a little more to it than that — but my takeaway was: "They wear black all the time!" I was starting to get more into music, especially rock music — so I went for it. I started wearing black all the time. What I wasn't expecting was that I liked it, it made me feel different and a little bit 'edgy'.

It was at this time that I had started to grow my hair. I had never liked the shape of my face but somehow when my hair grew I began to feel more comfortable with how I looked. And everyone started to compliment me on my hair, so I kept growing it. I have had it cut short many times — and regretted it every time.

When I started public speaking, I had multiple copies of two identical t-shirts, a red-ish one, and a green one. I enjoyed not having to think about what I had to wear, but I never felt like my clothes complimented or supported my style or my messages.

I was in a relationship in my twenties that really shook my ability to choose clothes. My belief in myself was shaken. I was made to feel that I couldn't match clothes to save my life. Being made to feel incompetent was degrading and painful to me. I wasn't used to worrying about how to dress. I had always been content to wear clothes that looked identical, day in and day out.

When you feel trapped or like someone you're not, that's when you ask yourself, "Who do I want to be?" It might sound immature, but I felt like a rock star on stage, and that's how I wanted to dress and feel like. After the relationship, I thought: "I don't care if I make 'mistakes' with clothes or my appearance. I don't want to play it safe. I want to take some risks and dress like a rock star."

The first time I presented, dressed like a rock star was a revelation. The clothes didn't 'give me confidence'; I just felt in harmony. What I was wearing matched how I felt inside and how I expressed myself. For the first time: how I dressed supported me instead of holding me back.

When I met the two performers who I looked up to, I told them how much I admired them both. What surprised me was that they both said that they loved my image and even asked where I bought my clothes. Right then I knew that I was on the right path.

Personal Branding for Speakers

You might be thinking: "As a speaker, what's my personal brand?" Or maybe, "Do I even need one?" I have heard dozens of different opinions on what a personal brand is and how to create one. To be honest, I still have days where I find myself feeling confused about the topic because there's no standardised process to find and understand what your personal brand is and what steps you should take to implement it.

When I talk about your personal brand, I am referring to your expressions of who you are and what you believe in. Audiences enjoy your speeches not just for the content but because of you, how you speak, and how you make them feel. Even if you typed up your speech word for word and handed it to another speaker — they couldn't replicate the same experience that you would have given. Audiences will become hooked on your style and will want to experience more of it. That's when they look for you online!

We give our speeches in person, but we post them online. You probably learnt about the majority of your favourite speakers from videos. We also write about ourselves and our beliefs online. If you're doing public speaking, it makes sense to understand your 'brand' and how to keep it consistent in person and on the internet.

Have you ever heard a speech and felt so enthralled and inspired by it that you wanted to hear more? So you looked the speaker up online and found their social media accounts, their website, and their blog. I think that a lot of us have done this. But some of us would have been delighted by what we found, and the rest of us would have been turned off by what we dug up.

The use or abandonment of our personal brand has a direct effect on our audience members and will determine whether they will stick with us or find another expert to learn from. Personal branding helps to build relationships and offers a smooth ferry ride between the physical world and the online world.

From our perspective as public speakers, we can break down personal branding into two parts: How we express ourselves in person and how we express ourselves online. We are looking to express ourselves in a very similar — if not the same way online as we do offline. If you received a standing ovation for telling an audience why not to eat cheese, you don't want them to find pictures on your social media the next day of you eating cheese and biscuits. Our goal is not to have a second persona online and to act differently, but to do the same thing as in our speeches. We want to give our audiences (both online and offline) clear, applicable, and explainable messages that we believe in.

How do you express yourself in person?

When personal branding 'experts' discuss personal branding in real life, they seem to focus in on clothing and whether you smile or not. These factors are important, but I see forgetting to smile or to wear clothing that is not in keeping with your 'image' to be 'symptoms' of not being clear about who you are and what you believe in.

When you're aware of who you are and what you believe in, you will know how you want to express yourself. Wearing blazers on stage did not make me a club president. I already was the president, and I wanted to show that to guests, and so I started wearing blazers. It was because I wanted to do things differently to other presidents and saw myself as an independent thinker that I created a 'rock-star president' image, instead of the traditional suit and tie image. I believe in being positive and actively trying to uplift other people, and that's why I smile. I don't need to think about smiling, I enjoy being happy and trying to make other people happy — so it comes naturally.

The driving force behind my 'expressions' originates from my awareness of who I am and what I believe in. For me, personal branding for speakers is about discovering who you are and what experience you deliver while speaking and knowing how to deliver that through different channels.

I always struggled with the question, "Who am I?" Most people I know struggle to describe themselves. What I found easier was to compare myself to everyone else and recognise what made me different. I continue to do this as a game because it's both enlightening and fun (at least to me). If you want to try: write down a list of names; any names you like, real or fictional. Then next to each name write down one way in which you are different to them. For instance:

- Cousin Bob: I enjoy reading books more than he does.
- My friend, Joe: I love public speaking, but Joe hates it.
- My pen pal, Vladimir: I have grown up with English culture, customs, and ideas – unlike Vlad.
- Mr. Nasty Speaker: I am much kinder to my audience during speeches.
- My work colleague, Doug: I am in charge of looking after customers, Doug looks after our own staff.
- Captain Celery Face from TV: I am less impulsive and like to think about things.

When you make a habit of looking for what makes you different to other people you will see patterns begin to emerge. You will notice that there are certain qualities about you and how you identify yourself, your experiences, roles, activities, and interests you have (amongst other factors) that set you apart from others. It's tempting to obsess over who you are and why you're different, but you don't need to. Be honest with yourself and when in doubt, ask a mixture of people for feedback and ask their opinions about what they think makes you different.

As well as knowing who you are, for a strong personal brand: you must also be aware of what you believe in. As a speaker, it's essential that we know what we believe in. After all, we are sharing our beliefs with audiences.

I found that it was much easier to find my beliefs once I was better at understanding myself and knew how to describe who I was and what made me different. When you know that people are different from you, you will discover certain things that you do, or want to do that other people can benefit from. Once you find the things that can help other people, it becomes a lot easier to identify your beliefs.

What if you liked doing things quickly? One day you realised that even though you never took more than five seconds to open a can of soup, it took most people an hour. If learning this frustrated you, it could mean that you believe in:
A) Helping others to save time.
B) Helping people.
C) That time is precious and shouldn't be wasted on a trivial matter like opening a can of soup.
Or a different belief entirely. For now, let's pretend that your belief was A) Helping others save time. If that was your belief, being aware of it would have shaped your image and your interactions with others. Once you knew your belief you could have come up with the following ways to express it:

- Following a 'leaving the house' routine which is time efficient (and sharing it).
- Arriving at events early or at least on time, so you don't keep anyone waiting.
- Wearing a name badge, so people don't need to waste time asking your name.
- Using a watch or phone to keep track of time.

- Having printouts of your contact details and key-points, so people can 'grab and go'.
- Respecting people's time and being actively aware of it (and making calendar appointments).
- Completing as many tasks for events in advance as possible.
- Always speaking to time.
- Giving time-saving ideas in speeches.

Coming up with the above ideas was as simple as a snail's journey back to his house because I knew the belief. If you don't know what your beliefs are, it will take a long time to work out how to 'brand' yourself. Find out who you are and what your beliefs are first, then live your life based on these discoveries. When you do this, audiences will trust you because you're not just saying your message on stage — they can actively see that you're living your message. No one wants to learn how to release tension from a stressed-out yoga teacher or to go to a motivation coach who moans because it's Monday.

Once you acquire this awareness of who you are and what you believe in, you will find it effortless to find ways of expressing yourself and to give off the 'right impression'. From your transparency and authenticity, you will find that audience members will like your speeches and who you are. So much in fact that they will want to see and hear more from you.

The second part of personal branding is to use your awareness of who you are and what you believe in to express yourself and your ideas online.

How do you express yourself online?

There are many different places where you can express yourself online. Not only do you have your website and blog but there are several different social media platforms to choose from — with new ones being created all the time. You can use text, photos, audio, and video to express yourself and you can even mix and match.

What you need to be aware of is that each website and social app has its own culture and customs that you need to be aware of and to cater to. This does not mean compromising who you are or what you believe, it just means learning the most effective way of doing things for each site and app. Basically — don't blindly paste your content everywhere!

If you take a selfie during a speech and post it across every social media platform, it will not only be an ineffective effort, but it might also annoy people who follow you on several platforms: "How many times do I have to see this picture of her posing on stage with a teacup? It's following me everywhere!" The convention is to upload or post content that has been tailored for the site it's being sent to.

If creating all this online content and making it fit each site sounds like a lot of work, it doesn't have to be. I would suggest looking up how to repurpose content. Now you know not to paste your content everywhere we can begin taking your personal brand online.

As a public speaker, you need to think about what someone who looks you up will be seeking. An audience member will most likely be looking to learn more about your ideas, to find a piece of content so she can share your ideas with others and to be a bit nosy and find out more about you.

Learning more about your ideas

Ideally, if an audience member enjoyed your speech, he should be able to go online to find out more. The online landscape provides such an incredible opportunity for you to showcase your ideas, to expand on them, and to bring life to them using several different mediums. Your first objective is to actually have some of your ideas ready to be posted online so that your audience member can find you and learn more.

When you have ideas ready to share, you can bring your personal brand into play. What you need to remember is that your audience member didn't just like the idea in your speech, he also liked you and how you delivered it. You heard me correctly — he liked you! Therefore you want him to have a similar experience reading your blog or watching your video as he did watching your speech. I use colourful and comedic examples in my speeches, and so I use them in my online writing. I want to maintain the important parts of me and my beliefs that people enjoy experiencing in speeches — in my online content. I recommend that you do the same.

Once again, think about how you differ to other speakers and make sure that the positive differences appear in your online content. Your specific talents can also help you choose the best format for sharing your ideas. For instance, if you're known for performing the best celebrity impressions: use audio. If on the other hand, you are known for your body language: use photos, and video. Some people might call this 'playing to your strengths'. In my opinion, it's ensuring that online you hold onto the qualities that audiences love you for.

One popular question is: "Should I be serious or funny online?" The answer depends on who you are and what you believe in. If you deliver a hilarious speech, people will be confused when they go online to discover a collection of solemn videos. This sounds like common sense, but it isn't to a lot of speakers.

People seem to think that posting online is a private activity because they can do it at home. The reality is that what you post could have even more viewers than your next speech. For that reason, you need to use your awareness of who you are and what you believe in just as much online as you do when you are out in public or when giving a speech.

Being aware of who you are and what your beliefs are will set the tone for how to present your ideas. This includes how you format your ideas, what images you use, and what your 'writer's voice' sounds like.

I can tell you from experience that it's easy to obsess over what colours and music you should use. My answer for speakers struggling with formatting and design options is to think, "What would I do in a speech?" If you can't decide on your 'brand colours' consider what colours you feel best wearing while giving a speech. Or to think about what would be most pleasing to your dream audience. And if you can't find some royalty free music you like, think about what track you would feel great walking on to for your next speech — and if it would fit the tone of your speech.

When posting online, you are able to cover far more concepts and ideas than you would be able to in person. For this reason, you don't want your audience member to see your speech, feel pumped up, and then watch the exact same speech again — but this time with less awe and amazement. You want him to be able to continually re-experience the excitement, inspiration, and motivation he got from watching you speak, through new and expanded ideas online. When you get to this step, people who like you and your ideas will probably want to share them with other people.

Sharing your ideas

I love being able to share videos with friends and family. Instead of having to memorise an important idea word for word, I can send the video off for them to watch. Frequently a conversation arises, and I say: "I read a great post on that recently," or: "I saw a video yesterday on that exact topic," and of course, "look: this is what I was talking to you about!" There will be times when your subject will come up in conversation, your online ideas just need to be easy to share.

In speeches, I am relentless in telling speakers to have a clear main message. The same applies to online content. For something to be shareable, it needs to be self-explanatory. No one wants to write a few paragraphs explaining a video before sending it to their friends. It needs to have an explicit message and to either be on a specific topic or solve a problem. If my friend and I want to try out fencing I could find and share, 'An introduction to fencing' video. Or if we start fencing but struggle with how to lunge, my friend could find a, 'How to lunge in fencing' video and send it to me.

Your online content also needs to explain why the sharer likes you as a speaker. A sharer does not want to send one of your blog posts and then have to justify sending it by explaining: "She was an amazing speaker. She was so friendly in real life, on her post she's a bit cold — but she's not really like that. I also loved her idea of using sun-cream for home decorating. She briefly mentions that for two sentences somewhere. You can skip the bits where she's ranting about hating cats, as in her speech she said she loves cats..." Your posts should convey who you are, your beliefs and what your idea is — without being given a blurb by the sharer.

Your content should be easy to share. By looking at your online content a viewer should be able to find out more things about you than what they learnt in person from your speech.

Finding out more about you

Online you not only get to share more about your ideas and beliefs, but you can also further express who you are.

Expressing who you are does not necessarily mean going off topic. I cringe when someone I follow online starts streaming video games, posts Sunday morning 'dressed down' pictures, and begins talking about sports. Not to be rude but how do these things inspire me or benefit me? They just waste my time by having to scroll by them. If however, you do want to go off topic, consider if what you plan on posting will be consistent with your 'In person' personal brand. Would you make an audience member watch you play video games? No? Then don't do it online. Would you go out in public wearing your 'comfies'? No? Then don't post those kinds of pictures. Would you talk to people about sports? Yes? Okay, just don't talk to me about sports!

Off topic content can still be relevant to your online audience if it's in keeping with your personal brand. If you speak about animal rights and are known for being a fun and positive person, it's off-topic to share photos of you having fun with friends — but it will inspire people to go to new places and have fun. Or if you speak about history, but you are a huge science-fiction fan and everyone who meets you hears about it (or notices your robot t-shirts) — it's off topic, but a video of you at a comic convention would interest your online audience.

Just remember that when you go off topic, ask yourself: "Would I let people see this in real life? Or during my speech?" Remember to use your awareness of who you are and your beliefs.

If you don't want to go off topic, you don't have to. You can always express who you are while still discussing your subject of expertise. You can use personal props and backgrounds, film at one of your favourite locations, and tell more anecdotes that relate to your discussions (with photos).

In a speech, you explain how your message relates to you and your life and your online ideas are no different. For this reason, if you want to stay focused on your ideas at all times online, you can. You can also make it personal at the same time, just like in your speeches.

When your personal brand is implemented successfully, an inspired 'live' audience member should easily be ferried over to your online content and become an inspired online audience member and vice-versa. This will mean that the people that you inspire will stick with you instead of looking elsewhere for expert advice.

Having a consistent personal brand across the offline and online world will also allow you to inspire more people indirectly: Either through word of mouth or by online content sharing. Before you know it, you will have a consistent audience who have learnt from you and will support you and want you to succeed. For me at least, empowering and uplifting people and making new friends is what I love the most about public speaking.

Try not to overthink personal branding. Get started on your personal brand by looking at who you are, and what you believe in.

How Writing Can Help Your Public Speaking

I firmly believe in the benefits of writing. You do not have to write a book to reap the benefits. (But what's stopping you?) You could blog about your specialism, write notes every day, or even answer people's questions on social media. Any form of regular writing about your subject will help your public speaking.

A problem with your speaking that regular writing will highlight is whether you know as much about your specialism as you think you do. You need to enter the process of writing everything out to obtain an accurate measurement of how much you know. That way, you are not deluding yourself. If you write 20,000 words and then you say: "That's it. That's everything I know on the subject. I can't think of anything else," that's okay! It's far better for that to happen than for you to pretend that you could speak for days on your subject.

If you hit a wall where you feel that you have written everything you know about your subject, I recommend two solutions. The first is to learn. If you are passionate about something, but you know little about it: educate yourself. Learning is not limited to reading books. You can attend live events and gatherings, speak to experts and most importantly get yourself more practical experience.

One of the best ways I learnt more about public speaking was through going out and speaking, watching other speakers, and writing down what I had discovered as soon as I got in the door. This included what things I thought worked, didn't work, and what I was thinking about during the experience. I even did this after every magic show or play I saw.

When you make a commitment to writing down your thoughts and observations: you will start to develop opinions on your subject. Over time, your opinions will evolve into your own unique perspective on the industry or discipline. This kind of thinker is who people want to listen to. They don't want someone who read a book once and is good at reciting it. People want to see someone who has their own way of looking at the subject, which they learnt through experience. These people make fascinating speakers.

My second solution for when you have nothing else to write about is to set yourself more diverse questions. What if you were a speaker who spoke about canned products and you worked at a canned soup factory? With your writing, you might have simply written about how soup is canned. And then you hit the wall — there was nothing else to say about the canning process for soup. But then you started to ask more diverse questions:

- How are other products canned?
- What are the benefits of canning over other storage methods?
- How are the cans made?
- How are canned products helping people who are less fortunate?
- How has the marketing and visuals of canned goods changed over the years?
- Why should people care about cans?

If you broaden your horizons and answer questions like these, you will never run out of things to write about (and later — talk about). If ever you don't know the answer to a question, think about it, research it, and ask people for their opinions (so you can see how yours are different) and you will grow as an expert.

From broadening your horizons, you will have more chances to speak because you will be able to speak about many topics surrounding your subject. For instance, speaking about other issues and ideas surrounding canning, not just how soup is canned. If a can-convention was to contact you tomorrow and tell you that they are running a talk on the history of cans — you CAN speak for them (sorry for the pun). And if a charity asks you to speak about feeding people in crisis, can you speak for them? Too right you CAN!

Instead of giving up when you have nothing else to write about, try my two solutions: learn and at the same time ask more diverse questions about your specialism. If you become committed to your writing, it will help you become an expert speaker like no other.

Let's say you've worked hard at writing and you have now written a lot on your subject (over 50,000 words). How will what you've written help you? It will help you find your key ideas, and it will make speech preparation a lot easier.

When I wrote my first public speaking book, what I found surprising was reading it back: "I wrote that?" was something I often thought, and another was: "That's such a great idea. I can't believe I forgot that." It was not until I had 60,000 words all typed up that I was able to take a step back and understand my perspective on public speaking. Reading through, I could easily see my key themes and what parts of public speaking were most important to me. When you read your writing, you too will see key themes emerge. And nothing is stopping you from going through your writing and making a list of your favourite quotes.

You will see speakers who talk confidently about their solution, presented as a clever-sounding acronym or their 'seven rules' and you might be wondering how you can do the same. With a list of your favourite quotes, it's a simple matter to arrange them and to make an acronym so other people can remember your ideas. But in my opinion, that's a somewhat myopic goal (and having one clear main message is far more memorable).

What I would recommend would be to use your list of quotes to remind yourself of your key ideas. Then you can see how your key ideas form beliefs and you can continually discover more about them. When I think about my favourite speakers, I instantly know what they believe in, because their clear beliefs sculpt not only their speeches, but their entire way of living. Discover your key ideas and see how your beliefs will empower your speaking.

Speech preparation feels so much easier when you have your own writing to refer to. I will be honest, it feels like you're cheating on a test. When you're asked to talk about a specific topic, you simply re-read your written thoughts on the subject and, "Poof!" You know exactly what to talk about. No headaches or brain scratching required. It's like you have the test answers! Except you're not cheating, you've done the work, and now it can help you to prepare for your speech.

A lot of people like to be set a speech, write their speech out, and then memorise it. What I prefer to do is to have already written about an idea and then to bring what I've written to life. That way if I have a short amount of time to prepare for a speech — I don't need to squander the majority of it doing research or looking for a main message. I will have a main message and points to back it up ready to go so I can begin creating a speech out loud, straight away. I can then focus on presentation and how to tweak my speech, so it's effective and valuable for where I'm speaking and who I'm delivering it to. It's a stress-free way of preparing for a speech.

Another benefit of writing is that having written extensively on a subject changes your presence on stage. When you stand on stage after writing so much, you will feel like you live and breathe your subject. You will be able to answer questions from an audience so much more eloquently than your competition.

Other speakers might laugh off 'crazy' questions or struggle to answer any query that does not directly concern their specialism. You will be able to answer these kinds of questions and to not only discuss them but to also have the ability to give insightful answers that wow everybody. You will be remembered as a master of your subject.

I am the first to admit that writing extensively on a subject is a lot of work. Its work that most 'experts' aren't doing. I hear people talking a lot about not feeling qualified to talk about their subject to an audience. It's probably because they haven't put this work in. When you continue to write, you feel like you've done the homework and that you're qualified to speak about your subject.

In my humble opinion, putting the work into writing is the difference between being a casual speaker on a topic and being a subject expert. If you don't write about your specialism, I implore you to start.

Does Every Speaker Need a Book?

If you go to see a public speaker, you can usually jump online and buy their book. Very few books that I have found this way have been 'great' or life-changing — the majority were mediocre. In the past, people would speak to promote their book, that they had spent a considerable amount of time contemplating, writing, editing, investing in, and getting published. Now, a book can be produced in a few weeks, and the 'finished product' can feel like a 50-page promotion for the speaker's services. I'm going to give my perspective on this matter. Like with everything I discuss — feel free to disagree with me!

At music events, one of the most popular things to buy is a t-shirt. The t-shirt does not play music. It does not even tell the buyer what the songs sound like or what the lyrics are. It gives her an overpriced reminder that on the 31st July 2014, she saw her favourite band. When she wears it, the t-shirt tells other people that she is a 'real fan' of the band because she saw them live and bought the t-shirt.

You might think this is not the case for a public speaker and her new book: "I don't need to prove that I'm anyone's real fan, let alone for a public speaker." Firstly, if you're anything like me: if you see a speech you like and the speaker has a book for sale at a reasonable price, it's going home with me (unless their card machine is busted). Straight away that's an example of how books are sold based on an appreciation for the speaker.

Secondly, are you seriously telling me that you have never bought something so you could keep up with the crowd? "I am a huge fan of Shelly Lettuce-Typeface,"
"Oh really, do you have her latest book?"
"No I haven't," and then you think, "Hmm I want to continue saying I'm a big fan, so I better buy that book."

Also, are you expecting me to believe that you have never made a blind purchases on an item after seeing who made it? While writing this book, people I mentioned it to were always quick to say that they wanted to buy a copy. My initial thought was, "I haven't even told you what it's about yet!"

There is nothing wrong with the above book sales, providing that the book is more than a token of appreciation/fan worship and will actually help the buyer and provide good value for money. Buying a book as a token of appreciation/fan worship alone is not what a speaker's book should be for.

A speaker's book should serve as a useful guide for audience members who want to read what you talked about, and to learn more about your particular field and way of thinking.

When watching demonstrations at magic lectures and conventions, it has always been difficult to write down notes quickly enough. That's why after a magician finishes their lecture they sell lecture notes. Lecture notes are booklets that go over the tricks that were covered in the lecture and sometimes contain a few bonuses. To me, it feels like many public speakers have gone the same way by selling their writing. The difference is that instead of calling their write-up 'lecture notes', they parade it around as 'My book'!

How can you create and sell a 'book' instead of lecture notes? If someone who bought your 'book' from you at an event can read it from cover to cover on the bus ride home, and then they never need to read or think about it again: you've made a set of lecture notes. Instead if you have provided something that will require more study time (either reading time, or thinking time) and your buyer wants to hang on to it (for reference or because of its design), then you have yourself a book.

I must clarify that it's not enough to write four hours' worth of incomprehensible ramblings. The goal is to give the reader a consistent return on investment, for the time they put into reading it. My ideal is for a reader to put the book down and think: "Wow that was like a five-hour-long one-on-one session with Matt. I am buzzing with new ideas — I'm so inspired!" I only wish other speakers would have a similar ideal while they're writing.

I have to say that if you want to write a book on your subject, it's admirable. However, if you want to sell a half-baked collection of ideas and you don't want to put the hours in: be honest. Label your writing as lecture notes and not as a book. Trust me because it's for your own benefit. I have gone off of a number of speakers after exchanging my hard earned money for a 'book' that turned out to be three tips and a junkyard-full of plugs. Don't lose a friend and a supporter for life by cashing in on your reputation as a speaker to make a few extra pounds. It pays to be honest.

Now we know what a book is (according to me), how will it help you?
Having a book for sale in person or online is helpful to you and your audience because it will allow your audience to pay more attention to you when you speak. Imagine if an audience member knew that on the way home she could order your book and refresh herself on the finer details of your speech. She could put her notepad away and enjoy getting to see you 'live'. By paying more attention to you, she's more likely to remember you and to decide that she made the right decision seeing you in person. As a result, she will be more inclined to talk about you favourably and to come and see you speak again. Plus the money you made on the book will feel like receiving a tip from your audience member. Both you and your audience will benefit.

The trend of public speakers who are non-writers is to offer to send people their slides by email. Although it's a kind gesture, it's a waste of everybody's time. The speaker needs to take email addresses or pester the event organiser to agree to email everyone. Then the speaker has to remember to send the slides or ask the organiser to send them out. By this point it's too late, your audience's minds are on other things. But suddenly: "Tah-dah!" An email arrives in the audience's inboxes with the slides attached. After all of this kerfuffle, what do people find? Nearly 100 slides of meaningless photos and some out of context bullet points. As I said, it's a waste of everybody's time.

I am not saying that if you speak, you have to write a book. If you want to sell a summary of your talk, there's nothing wrong with constructing some lecture notes (just be honest). And if you feel like writing a little more, try making an eBook. On the other hand, if you don't want to write — you don't have to.

Why not make a video or audio recording of your speech? If you have a video, you can present your audience with a shortened URL to watch it when you come to the last slide in your presentation. My suggestion would be to share a 'highlights' video. If you still wanted to receive your 'speaker's tip' you can sell the full speech with bonus content as a live-audience exclusive offer. I would advise having the video/audio file ready to share before your presentation because otherwise, you will run into similar problems as you would when sharing slides. (Please note — if you have a book, but like the sound of these ideas, there's no reason why you can't use video and audio also).

The assumption so far has been that your book will be read after your speech. What if someone read your book before your speech? Having a book has benefits for you and your audience before you even set-off for the venue. As an example, if an entrepreneur (let's call her Tara) has signed up to attend an event, she will be sent a list of the people speaking. When Tara encounters a speaker she's unfamiliar with (in this case, you) she might want to research you a bit. She could look you up on a search engine and find your website, or search for videos or you. But she might just search for your book. Having a book provides another way for people to find you.

Also when people find your book, they will look at you as a more credible speaker. I personally think this idea is outdated, but a lot of people still believe that having a book gives someone's public speaking credibility. Ultimately it doesn't matter if you or I think the idea is outdated — people are still acting on it!

Let's say that Tara goes ahead and buys your book. Assuming that it's readable, she will know what to expect from you when she sees you. If Tara enjoyed the book and it resonated with her, she might begin to think-up questions to ask you (so it won't just be crickets filling the silence during your next Q and A). Or she might binge-watch/read/listen to your online content. Either way, Tara would have changed from someone who has never heard of you, to someone who knows what you believe in and who can't wait to see you speak. On the day she might even ask you to sign her book. An audience member who purchased your book before your speech has helped you both.

There are undoubtedly great reasons for having a book. It can benefit you and your audience. However, it's up to you to decide how much you want to share. If you make a book: be honest and determine whether there's enough value in what you made to warrant an audience member investing their time and money into it.

A well-written book will help both you and your audiences.

What's Your Advice?

Without trying to be profound or philosophical, have a think about what kind of advice you find yourself giving to people:

- Do you give tried and tested wisdom won from hard experience?
- Do you offer advice that you read in a book or saw in a film that inspired you?
- Do you just offer common sense?
- Or do you find that you never have any advice to give?

My perspective is that the kind of advice you give defines who you are as a person. The more you understand yourself, the easier it becomes to find what you believe in and how you want to affect people when you speak.

Whenever people have asked me for advice outside of public speaking, I have always felt flattered.

One occasion that stands out to me was when a teenager asked me for advice. This wasn't any teenager, he had done a lot with his life already in the arts. I just couldn't believe how much he had achieved. Yet he was considering giving up all of his 'hobbies' so he could study something 'serious'. I had a gut feeling that this was due to parental or peer pressure. He wanted my advice on what to do.

What would you have said?

I explained my own experience: "What you choose to do in your free time is important. So far in my life, it's always been my passions and interests that I've pursued in my own time, off my own back that have paid off." My thinking behind this is that the things I've chosen to do in my spare time because I love doing them — have stuck with me. I might sound boring or predictable, but my core interests have been rock solid for over a decade. I love public speaking, I love magic tricks, I love making people laugh, I love cooking, and I love running. The media I like to watch or listen to might fluctuate, but my core interests are simply immovable. If I'm not doing them, I'm thinking about them, talking about them, writing about them or learning — so I can get better at them!

For me, this is where common sense comes into the equation. The things you stick at are the things that you're going to improve at. So doesn't it also make sense to acknowledge how important your passions are?

It was by studying my piece of advice that I uncovered an important belief I hold. The importance of not giving up on your passions and how to use them to find new ways of analysing the world around you and expressing yourself.

Pay attention to the advice you give — you can learn a lot from it too.

Final Thought

Why There Are No Standards for Public Speaking

If we had a random roomful of people, we could easily find who is good at golf by seeing who could hit the ball into the holes with the fewest swings. If we wanted to see who in the group was good at tennis, we would see who could consistently hit and direct the ball and maintain a rally. Finding out who is a good magician is trickier to assess. If a member of the group can perform tricks without giving away the secrets, we would assume that they are a good magician. But how can we find a good public speaker? And more specifically, how should we judge a speaker?

- "We could ask the group to give us a speech in front of an audience. Those who display that they are nervous must be the non-public speakers."
  We can't say someone isn't a public speaker because they felt nervous. If we could disqualify people for feeling nervous, school exam halls would be empty.

- "We could judge their speaking based on an audience's reaction."
  This also won't work. Different speakers get different reactions based on who's watching them.

Of course, one of my goals in public speaking is to be able to inspire and delight the audience in front of me, but different audiences will be looking for different kinds of things. A wedding audience would have no interest in a technical presentation but an audience at a technology conference would. That's why it's unfair to judge a random group of people with the same audience.

- "What if we used strict criteria and marked the people on their speech structure, vocal delivery and use of movement?" If you're good at writing, hire a director, and perform a speech like a scene in a play — does that make you a public speaker? That's all that kind of marking criteria is going to capture. The main reason why we will get winners from that system is due to the judges being biased towards the speech they liked the most/thought was best or because they got the right verbal nudges to tick boxes. If that's what's happening, what makes the judges truly qualified to begin with?

When we were looking at who was good at golf, it was a simple matter. If you could hit the ball into the holes with only a few swings: you must be good at golf. If you could hit the ball but it took you forever to get it into the holes: it indicated that you could play golf but weren't necessarily 'good' at golf. With tennis, if you could consistently hit the ball over the net, in the place you intended, and maintain a rally: you must be good at tennis. If you could hit the ball, but often inaccurately and/or inconsistently: it would show that you could play tennis but weren't necessarily good at tennis. And with magic, if you could perform a fooling magic trick: you must be good at magic. But if you could perform some tricks, and they were easy to work out: you could clearly perform magic but weren't necessarily good at magic. With each of these examples there's a clear, "Yes I can" or, "No I can't" present at the very beginning:

"Can you hit a golf ball?"
"Yes!"
"Great, you're able to play golf."

"Can you hit a tennis ball?"
"Yes!"
"Fantastic, you're able to play tennis."

"Can you perform some magic tricks?"

"No!"

"No problem, that means you can't perform magic at the moment."

Either you know magic tricks or you don't. And either you can hit the ball or you can't. But when you ask someone: can you speak in front of an audience? People will say no because they haven't tried or learnt to enjoy it, but fundamentally — anyone who can communicate can do it.

The dilemma that arises from anyone being able to do public speaking is what happens when people want to know who is 'good' at public speaking. It's not a clean cut matter of having accurate swings or consistent rallies or being able to present a fooling trick. Now it's a baffling case of what are we going to judge them on?

Speakers are mainly judged on paper by perceived 'experience' and by association. If a teenager wanted to give a speech about baking, she would be ignored. A child wanting to do it would make a cute story, an adult has 'experience' to share, a teenager has neither of these perceived qualities.

If the same teenager had recently appeared on television, had a cake-book published, and was seen with a huge social media following — she would get booked. None of the factors that got her booked were due to her talent as a speaker or what her message was, it was due to 'buzz'.

You might say that in the second example she was doing more and deserved to be taken more seriously. But what if the un-buzzed version had just as much, if not more experience from her own blog, working in a cake-shop, and volunteering locally? What we define as 'experience' or what ticks our checkbox of, 'qualified to speak to us about this' is incredibly subjective.

If our baking teenager had spoken to some of the biggest companies in the world, she would be far likelier to be hired by a smaller company because of the association with the big companies. The reason for being hired has less to do with her skills as a speaker or her message and more to do with her associations and the buzz surrounding her.

At conferences and events are the speakers judged fairly? If one speaker has a littering of 'fans' in the audience who will cheer and clap at anything he says – those who aren't his fans will perceive him as 'the best' because of the buzz. What happens if some speakers are introduced more favourably than others by the host? What if the event generates a lot of 'buzz' around some speakers and gives little attention to the others? How will this have an effect on an audience's willingness to walk into the room, let alone to listen to these speakers?

What's the answer? Is there one?

That was the ending of the original essay, I left it open-ended. I liked the idea of having something for the reader to think about and it gave me something to contemplate. As you have bought this book, I would have felt disrespectful not sharing anything that could help you solve the problem.

My perspective on the matter is that I found public speaking had a lot of unspoken rules (which I covered many of in this book). One of the biggest was the idea of having a main message and knowing what you are trying to achieve with your speech. A golfer wants to knock the ball in the hole. What do you want your speech to do? How do you want to affect your audience? Once you have that goal, you can make enhancements and ask for help achieving it.

Similarly, why have you been asked to give a speech? What's the main message of the event or institution you're speaking at? This is yet another goal post for us to judge speakers on.

The problem with looking for a systematic way to rate speakers is that for me, the best speakers don't only transmit thoughts but also feelings. Feelings are much harder to rate and examine than ideas alone and yes or no procedures. Public speaking is a form of communication, but it's galvanised with self-expression. At the ripe old age of 26, I'm not afraid to admit that I don't currently have a definite, universal, unbiased answer for how to systematically tell you who is a good public speaker and who isn't. But as I have shown throughout this book, I know what I find to be important in public speaking and what I think makes a speaker unique.

When I watch a speaker, I hope to learn something that will impact me and benefit my life. I want my perspective on life to be challenged and remoulded, so it's more beneficial to me. I want to leave with a vivid memory of the speech, knowing exactly what I need to do to change for the better. I also want to be able to share the message alongside an amazing story of this life event with the people I care about.

While watching the speech: I want to like, respect, and admire the speaker and to be taken on an emotional journey. I want to sit there, relax and to think: "This makes so much sense." While I watch, I want the speaker to cater to my attention span and hook me back in when my mind wanders. I don't want to be made to feel guilty or like I'm missing out because I didn't process the odd sentence.

When I leave, I want to be buzzing with new ideas and infinite potential and to be profoundly inspired. But I also want to know in my heart that I have grown as a person and that the page has turned and the next chapter of my life has just started.

Questions and Answers

With Questions From:

Rachel Nagy, Paula Coutts, David Lark,

Tim Patmore, Henry Bowles, Don O'Neal,

Paul Ovington and Nick Dewey

1. Rachel Nagy:
"How do you find your voice?"

I think that the biggest issue with finding your voice is creating a sense of consistency. If an audience member sees you perform a speech on several occasions, as you pointed out there should be some kind of connection between the speeches. Otherwise, confusion will occur.

A speech can be seen as a chapter in your life-story. It's a snapshot into your life. If someone hears more than one chapter, they will want the chapters to be written in the same style, with the same values, and for you as a speaker to stand out in a way that only you can.

If the messages of your speeches clash and your audience comments: "That was entirely different to what I saw last time," then your 'voice' isn't consistent. Imagine the confusion if you joked around as you talked about 'Why you should always make people laugh' in your first speech and then in the second speech you droned 'Why you must always be completely serious'. This is an extreme example, but that's how much an audience can be thrown around from speech to speech without a consistent 'voice'.

I would break down your voice into four components:
1. What your beliefs and values are.
2. What experience you have.
3. How you see and express yourself.
4. How you make people feel.

If you can be mindful of these four components, you will have a consistent 'voice' across your speeches. Please note that the contents of these categories are not set in stone. There will be growth and changes over time, but as long as it's a gradual change, you will still have a consistent 'voice'.

Being aware of your beliefs and values will guide your perspective on a topic. Having an awareness of what you believe in and value will help with consistency. I believe in being optimistic, as well as uplifting and inspiring people so it would be out of character for me to approach a topic from a 'doom and gloom' perspective. That is unless I was doing it humorously.

If you're determined to give a speech in a certain way because you saw someone else do it that way, and it doesn't feel quite right, you might be trying to defy your beliefs. It's for that reason that I didn't want to be an actor, portraying sadness and anger really goes against the grain for me.
If you want to hear a negative and angry speech, I'm not the speaker for you.

Your experience will determine how you approach topics. A speaker who has been an accountant for fifty years will give a speech about numbers in a different way to a painter. So be aware of what experience you have.

Thinking about how you see and express yourself will help you to realise who you are trying to be on stage. How do you see yourself? And how are you trying to come across? When this image of yourself matches up with your experience, beliefs, and values, and what your audience sees, you will have a reliable self-image. A strong voice.

2. Rachel Nagy:
"How can you empower yourself?"

Because of my early experiences with education and learning things, I went through school doing my best to keep my ideas to myself. I was conditioned from a young age that what I said was 'wrong'. It didn't matter how hard I tried, I would always be 'wrong'. And so I kept quiet, assuming that what I had to say would probably be wrong. I'm sure there are a lot of other people who have experienced this. It wasn't until I had the good fortune of having teachers who encouraged me to share my ideas that I started to question my assumption.

One day at university I thought to myself, "*I am never wrong, but I'm not always right*," and to me, this one thought was incredibly empowering.

If I were to make a bad decision such as paying £1000 for a tissue, what I did probably wasn't 'right' but I didn't make the wrong decision. If you'd had the exact same life experience as me, the exact same body, and were in the exact same set of circumstances — you too would have spent £1000 for a tissue. This is because in that situation, that was the best answer I had based on the exact situation I was in, what I knew, and what I had available to me. The thought of: "Hey, I can get a whole box for a pound from the shop around the corner," wasn't available. It's like taking a multiple choice test where the right answer isn't featured on our paper.

I stopped worrying about whether the things I said would be 'wrong'. If it turned out that I wasn't right, I could learn from another person's perspective of the world and therefore have the correct answer available to me.

Another way that I have empowered myself can be described simply as — do what you love doing. I love being the funny guy who offers people Christmas cake during the peak of summer and spending my time making others feel great about themselves. So that's what I do.

3. Paula Coutts:
"What is the best way to adapt or overcome your personal style?"

The way that I think public speaking differs to acting is that in acting you play many different roles, each one containing part of yourself. Whereas in public speaking you play yourself, but in different situations. If you're giving an inspiring speech, a humorous speech, a toast, a business presentation, or even a eulogy — you're always doing it as yourself, just in a different situation.

The way that I think speakers can make it harder on themselves is if they try to adapt how they speak in one situation, to another: "I'm great at business presentations. Oh, I need to give a humorous speech soon, how can I adapt the way I do a business presentation, so it's funny? Maybe I could put in a few jokes or something..."

Imagine yourself with your friends and family, or when you watch a film — what things make you laugh? What do you do when you want to make someone laugh? Imagine yourself presenting in this situation, instead of during a business presentation.

A certain amount of adapting to the situation depends on your understanding of yourself and your values. Be honest — what do you love and what are you great at doing? If you love attention to detail, this will not only help a formal business presentation but a humorous speech too! Noticing small details and commenting on them is a huge part of comedy. If you're a whizz at statistics — use your skill outside of business. You could research stats that are quirky and generate a lot of laughs.

When you know what you love and what you're good at, different kinds of speaking engagements will become a lot easier.

4. David Lark:
"Can a great speech not be a personal story?"

I think that the term 'personal story' is too easy to latch onto. A lot of competition speeches feature an extended 'personal story' as their speech. What the audience don't know is that many of the details in these kinds of speeches have been made up or exaggerated. Competition speakers can even lie by saying things like: "This is my Grandfather's pocket watch from the war," when they actually got the watch for free with a magazine, and their Grandfather was never in a war. This doesn't sit right with me. I see public speaking as sharing a main message that will help and empower your audience. Your audience needs to trust you in order for that to happen, don't abuse their trust by lying to them.

Would a speech work if it was not an extended personal story? Of course. In a speech, you can discuss any topic that you care about. Your unique perspective on the issue and your way of presenting it will make your speech stand out. For instance, if you wanted to talk about the moon, you don't need to talk about, "The time I went to the moon," but you could give your opinions on the moon. You could even share some smaller anecdotes about your relationship with the moon — if they back up your main message. Your perspective and presentation style will carry the smaller stories and make them stand out.

A personal story is a useful starting point for beginners because it's up to you to put it into words and then tell it. This means that a personal story will be unique to you. Instead, if a beginner went online and read out a summary of a historical event, they would be imitating someone else. These are the two extremes, but we easily forget just how many alternatives are sandwiched between them.

If you researched a historical event and focused on researching what you found interesting, you would create a fresh perspective on the event. Instead of blandly rattling off facts about how a battle had one clear winner you could look into other things: How human the people involved were and what mistakes they made, pragmatism, humour, unsung heroes, stupidity. You can go in any direction you like. "This is what the pioneers of the 20th century ate for breakfast." Your direction will personalise a story.

Finally, your delivery can make a story feel not only more personal but also more real and relevant. When I speak about an event, I try to deliver it in a down-to-earth way. How would we have acted under those extreme circumstances? That's my starting point. When you can fully appreciate the situation that the protagonists in the story were in, with its many joys, and difficulties — you can personalise it.

Any story can be told in your own voice.

5. Tim Patmore:
"What's your most shocking piece of public speaking advice?"

In my first public speaking book, I discussed creating rebellious moments in speeches. Essentially, these were moments that defy an audience's expectations and were shocking. For instance: secretly giving an audience member a fake set of notes, before a speech. That way whenever you want to, you can run up to them and rip the notes up. Everyone would think you're outrageous for ripping up someone's notes, but the audience member will laugh because they know they're not their notes, so everyone will be surprised and will treat you as a fun kind of rebel.

I think the piece of advice that other speakers seem shocked by is when I tell new speakers to give some speeches without preparing. It's how I learnt, and I don't think you truly know how to prepare properly until you have spoken a few times without preparation. A lot of the details that new speakers (and even some experienced speakers) obsess over are shown to not matter after delivering a speech on the spot.

6. Henry Bowles:
"What guidance can you offer on the average words per minute at which a speaker should aim to speak?"

I personally find that words per minute isn't a reliable measurement: "I need to write 1500 words for my 10-minute speech because I speak at 150 words per minute." This is a good starting point, but it's only a rough guide. 20 seconds of one minute could be taken up by pauses. If you read a section of a book out loud, you will find that your pace will alter depending on the sentence construction.

My biggest problem with words per minute is that it looks at pacing from the speaker's perspective, not from the audience's. The more complicated a task is, the slower we will perform it. If you were teaching someone to make a sandwich, you could easily rush through the steps. In contrast, if you were instructing him on how to make an eight-course dinner, you would likely want to go at a slower pace and ensure you didn't forget anything and that you showed everything in the correct order.

When speaking to an audience think about how easy your content is to understand. If you are talking about a well-known subject, using simple sentences — your audience will cope with a faster pace. However, if you are delivering new ideas, utilising longer sentences and a richer vocabulary, your audience will need a lot more time to process the information.

You might feel that speaking at an average of 160 words per minute feels right to you — but what really matters is what's right for your audience. If your audience doesn't speak the same first language as you, they would likely appreciate a slower rate of delivery. When assessing our rate of delivery we are not just looking for what sounds good — but what rate is most effective for communicating to the audience in front of us.

What words per minute is good for is to get a feel for how fast you should be speaking. Essentially finding a 'baseline' for public speaking that can be adjusted depending on the content and your audience. If you can't help but speak quickly, try reading out loud at 100 words or less per minute. Then when you become comfortable speaking at this much slower pace, decreasing your typical rate of delivery will become a much easier task.

Without using a word count, my advice would be to get to used to speaking at a slower pace than you would in conversation. This can mean slowing down your rate of delivery, but it can also mean shortening your sentences when you speak and pausing more.

You might be thinking: "How many words per minute is too much?" I think that 200 words per minute is too many. Try speaking up to 170 and see how you get on. Don't be afraid of speaking too slowly. We're just trying to avoid the rapid, continuous stream of information being sent out to your audience. Take your time, pause and when you speak give each word you say some attention. Don't rush or skip over words.

Measuring your words per minute can be a useful guide to understand and adjust your rate of delivery. However, I urge you to remember that the measurement does not take into account the content and how much time an audience will need to process it. My advice is to speak slower than you would in conversation and to adjust your rate of delivery based on the audience in front of you.

7. Don O'Neal:

Don very kindly shared the results of a survey he conducted for Oxford Orators, for me to use in the Q+A. The survey asked guests about their public speaking fears and what they were looking to learn. Below are my responses to some of the survey's comments:

Fear of, "Being placed on the spot."

Talking on the spot is a bit like gambling. The perceived 'risk' of speaking on the spot is higher than giving a prepared speech, but the return on respect will be much greater. Oh and — it's all a fix, it's actually quite easy to do.

Speaking on the spot is an experience that might conjure images of you being picked on by a teacher. I always see it is an opportunity to have a small amount of time to shine. Often the times we have to talk on the spot are during someone else's event or presentation. I just think: "Wow, I get to take control for a minute or two — fantastic," and I shine as much as I can in that time.

If you suspect that you are going to be put on the spot, pay attention. Listen to what's being said and ask yourself questions. By being present and engaging with the information being shared, you will be a lot more likely to think: "I wish I could share this cool thought I just had, with everyone else!" And then hey-presto, you get asked.

"Tell me how to dress."

How you dress can depend on the venue (if it's a black tie event or a waterpark opening) but most of the time you have a lot of choice in what you wear. So many speakers wear jeans! Personally, I prefer faux-leather trousers...

From my experience, I would say to wear clothes that reflect how you want to be perceived. It's common sense. But at the same time ensure that your movement is not restricted, and you don't jingle like a bell because of your jewellery. Wear clothing that allows you to express yourself fully and that gives off the message you want.

If you're still struggling, try this: Search for pictures of people in your industry. Do your research and understand what stereotypes exist and what people expect — and then go in a different direction. Stand out instead of blending in. That's what I would do because I have a compulsion to be different. And it works.

When you look up public speaking club photos, you see a lot of pictures of people wearing a white or blue shirt, standing behind a lectern. Wear something different and express your individuality.

Your clothes are yet another form of expression.

Wanting to, "Work on time management skills."

I sincerely believe that public speaking would be better in general if more speakers paid attention to their use of time. It's a real turn off for me when I'm watching a speaker who hasn't timed her speech.

The phrase I use the most with my technology at home is: "Set a timer." Whenever I'm practising, I just set a timer without a second thought. It's incredibly helpful.

I personally think that timing your speaking helps a lot with structuring. This is because you get used to getting each section of your content into proportion. Whenever you practise: get the timer going!

8. Paul Ovington:
"My $64,000 Question: When should I script a speech and when shouldn't I?"

I interpret scripting as learning a speech word for word. This is something that I personally don't believe in because I like to keep speeches fresh and in real-time (where you can react to circumstances and what's happening in the room). I cringe when I have listened to a completely memorised monologue. A speech that's been recited word for word misses out on so much potential for spontaneous moments and to have a shared connection with your audience.

But are there ever times when something should be scripted word for word?

Very short speeches benefit from scripting. By very short, I mean a minute or two. On my blog, I offered enhancements for a one-minute speech. When you have so little time to deliver your message you need to ensure that you get the introduction, body, and conclusion in proportion to each other. You don't want to use up 20 seconds on a bad joke if it means you miss out on your entire conclusion!

You can also tightly script sections of your speech instead of the entire thing. If there are a few sentences that need to be word-perfect, it makes sense to script them. In particular your opening line and closing line.

My advice is to script with care. I can smell a heavily scripted speech from a mile away. This is mainly because the speaker loses their spontaneity and because of that, they appear less authentic.

9. Nick Dewey:
"During the last hour, how much creative input goes towards restructuring a speech."

I would like to mention that some speakers make things very hard on themselves. In the last hour before their speech, they decide to make last minute additions and changes. They then have to repeat things over and over in their mind so that they don't forget it. This makes giving a speech unnecessarily stressful.

The hour before a speech I'm having fun, making friends and generally doing things to get into a positive state of mind. I put a lot of creativity into this and the shenanigans I get up to. And truthfully it benefits my speaking.

Another benefit of making yourself feel great in your 'final hour' instead of making changes is that you will have a better rapport with your audience. When you are more in synch with your audience, you will pick up on more of their reactions and will therefore be able to adjust your speech more effectively. The changes actually come during the speech itself, instead of the hour leading up to it. The last hour is about making myself and others feel happy.

The only exception to this is when I am giving an off the cuff speech, or I'm invited to give a speech with less than an hour to prepare. For obvious reasons!

10. Nick Dewey:
"How do you manage nervousness and anxiety before a speech?"

I personally don't experience those things before a speech or performing. I'm very chilled out.

When you're not feeling too good before a speech, there are a number of things you can do. One of the major points of the book was to communicate my belief that if you see public speaking as fun, you're going to be eager to speak. I also spoke about focusing more on other people than yourself. This will prevent you from over-analysing yourself and will help you to learn about and connect with the people you are speaking to.

But what if you are feeling nervous and anxious and are about to give a speech?

Some people say that feeling nervous will improve your performance: "Because of the adrenaline," it won't. All it will do is make things harder for yourself — and it makes no sense to make things harder for yourself.

Make things easier for yourself.

Remove any pressure you have put on yourself by, 'rigging the race'. You do this by ensuring that the only possible outcomes will be positive. Take your worst case scenario and know that it's not a big deal. By simply going out there you would have achieved far more than sitting at home. And no matter what happens you will gain experience. By focusing more on victories, no matter what shape they come in than on losses you can park your nerves.

I would also like to advise you to get into the habit of saying yes. If you go to a public speaking club and are asked to do a speech or a role, just say, "Yes, I'll do it." Just saying yes will save you so much wasted time where you would have wrestled yourself over whether you were 'ready' or not. There's never a perfect time to start, life's not a fairy tale. Just start! The crazy thing is, if you plunge in and avoid all of the deliberating tactics that you use to delay yourself: you'll escape a heap of anxiety and worry.

Don't turn public speaking into a battle, make it a game.

Glossary

Conclusion

The last section of your speech — and often misunderstood. Always allow enough time for it as it can make or break your speech. My style of conclusion is composed of three parts:

1. A summary of your main message and what you most want your audience to remember from your speech.

2. A call to action where you ask your audience to act by doing something. This can be a physical act or even a mental or spiritual one.

3. A snappy one-liner that delivers the feeling that everyone will leave with and that encapsulates your speech. This is the line that your audience will likely remember the most, so make it count.

Evidence

Support for an idea you have presented. This can include personal evidence such as information about yourself, anecdotal evidence which can include your experiences presented as a story or the experiences of others, research, facts, or quotes.

Introduction

The beginning of your speech. Ensure to capitalise on people's attention with an attention-grabbing opening line. In the introduction, you introduce your main message and what structure you will be using during your speech.

Acknowledgements

I would like to thank everyone who has put up with every conversation about my book. In particular, I would like to thank my girlfriend Claire and my parents Sally and Adrian. Thank you for being so patient with me while I have been writing and editing this year. And also for letting me talk about it. Having a book in the world has been something that I have always wanted to achieve. As you know, I can't help but think about mortality and this book was a big step towards overcoming this obsession. Thank you for being unconditionally loving and understanding.

I can confidently say that without Rachel, this book would not be in your hands right now. Thank you, Rachel, for reading every essay I posted online — twice! Having someone who dived into my ideas and wanted to experiment with and discuss them inspired me so much to write and to share my thoughts.

I would like to thank everyone who took the time to proof-read the book, including Tim Patmore, Don O'Neal, Kasia Kowalska, Kathryn Wheeler and Lauren Binley.

Thank you to Oxford Speakers club and the many people I have met there over the years.

About Matt

Matt is a public speaking coach and Oxford-based speaker.

A creative, public speaking rock star whose purpose is to uplift and inspire others. He is here to help you find your main message and to empower your public speaking. When you have a speech looming and 'nothing to say', he's the one to call.

You can write to the author at: matt@jaggedmatt.com

Printed in Great
Britain
by Amazon